MUSLIM FAMILIES IN GLOBAL SENEGAL

Muslim Families *in Global Senegal*

MONEY TAKES CARE OF SHAME

Beth Buggenhagen

INDIANA UNIVERSITY PRESS
Bloomington and Indianapolis

This book is a publication of

Indiana University Press
601 North Morton Street
Bloomington, Indiana 47404-3797 USA

iupress.indiana.edu

Telephone orders 800-842-6796
Fax orders 812-855-7931

∞ The paper used in this publication meets the minimum requirements of the American National Standard for Information Sciences—Permanence of Paper for Printed Library Materials, ANSI Z39.48-1992.

Manufactured in the United States of America

LIBRARY OF CONGRESS CATALOGING-IN-PUBLICATION DATA

Buggenhagen, Beth A. (Beth Anne), [date]
Muslim families in global Senegal : money takes care of shame / Beth Buggenhagen.
p. cm.
Includes bibliographical references and index.
ISBN 978-0-253-35710-6 (cloth : alk. paper) — ISBN 978-0-253-22367-8 (pbk. : alk. paper) — ISBN 978-0-253-00535-9 (e-book) 1. Muslims—Senegal—Dakar—Social conditions. 2. Muslims—Senegal—Dakar—Economic conditions. 3. Muslim women—Senegal—Dakar—Social conditions. 4. Muslim women—Senegal—Dakar—Economic conditions. I. Title.
DT549.9.D34B85 2012
305.69709663—dc23 2011031946

1 2 3 4 5 17 16 15 14 13 12

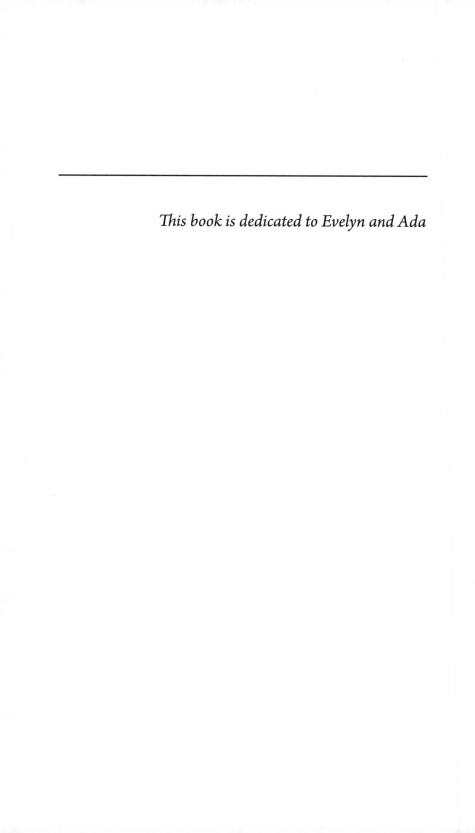

This book is dedicated to Evelyn and Ada

CONTENTS

ACKNOWLEDGMENTS

I WOULD LIKE TO acknowledge my host family in Senegal for their unending generosity and patience. I would also like to thank the women's association in Khar Yalla for teaching me about women's lives in Senegal. To protect their privacy, I have changed people's names in the text, though they did not ask me to. Unfortunately, that prevents me from naming them here, but I hope that they will accept my gratitude. Without them, there would not be a book.

Several foundations and institutions supported this work at various stages. I thank the government of Senegal for granting me permission to conduct research there. I thank Dr. Moussa Seck at ENDA SYSPRO for introducing me to the neighborhood of Grand Yoff and facilitating my studying there in 1992, and Emanuel Seyni Ndione for allowing me to work at CHODAK. I would like to acknowledge the Wenner-Gren Foundation for its support of my fieldwork in Senegal in 1999–2000; the West African Research Center and IFAN in Dakar, especially Dr. Khadim Mbacke for his invaluable assistance and Dr. Bachir Diagne for arranging research clearance; the Center for Gender Studies at the University of Chicago for support of my dissertation writing; the National Endowment for the Humanities for a summer stipend to conduct research in New York City; and the College Arts and Humanities Institute at Indiana University, Bloomington, for a one-semester teaching release to complete the manuscript.

The people who have influenced me are too numerous to list, but I want to thank those who provided me with invaluable insight, expertise, and conversation in and about Senegal: Dior Konate, Ibrahima Sene, Cheikh Anta Babou Mbacke, Cheikh Gueye, and Mansour Tall. During my fieldwork in 1999–2000, I was also grateful for the friendship and camaraderie of Erin Augis, Tim Mangin, Brett O'Bannon, and Suzanne Scheld.

My thinking about the manuscript was deepened by discussions with colleagues and students at the University of Chicago (especially the African Studies Workshop: Misty Bastian, Rob Blunt, Anne-Maria Makhulu, Adeline Masquelier, Jesse Shipley, James Smith, Brad Weiss, and Hylton

White), the University of Rochester, and Indiana University. I am especially grateful to my academic advisors, including the undergraduate professors who introduced me to anthropology and to West Africa, Gracia Clark and Maria Grosz Ngate; to Andrew Apter, Ralph Austen, and Jean and John Comaroff at the University of Chicago; and to John Hunwick at Northwestern University. I thank Katherine Buggenhagen, Dior Konate, and Ellen Sieber for deepening my knowledge of textiles and weaving. I thank Nicole Castor, Emily McEwan Fujita, and Rachel Reynolds for their insight and careful reading of this project at various stages. I also thank Stephen Jackson and Dorothea Schultz. I am grateful to my husband, family, and friends, who endured multiple fieldwork trips and the long process of writing and revising and only occasionally and with the best of intentions asked when I would finish the book.

I would like to recognize the careful work of my research assistant, Katherine Wiley, a doctoral candidate at Indiana University. I am especially grateful for the comments of the anonymous reviewers and the assistance of Dee Mortensen at Indiana University Press.

I have dedicated this book to my daughters, Evelyn and Ada, and I am also grateful to the smart and loving women who cared for them while I worked.

NAMES AND RELATIONSHIPS

ABDOUL AZIZ GÉER: second oldest son of Sokna and Demba

AMINATA (Ami): friend of Ramatoulaye

BINTU: daughter fostered to Géer family

CHEIKH CAAYA: husband of Cora

CORA: friend of Sokna

DEMBA GÉER: husband of Sokna Géer

JIGEEN GÉER: oldest daughter of Sokna and Demba

MODOU BAXA: father of Penda's child

MUSA MBACKE: Murid trader and suitor of Bintu

PENDA: daughter of Cora

RAMATOULAYE (Rama) GÉER: second oldest daughter of Sokna and Demba

SOKNA GÉER: wife of Demba Géer

MUSLIM FAMILIES IN GLOBAL SENEGAL

PROLOGUE
Welcome to Khar Yalla

THROUGHOUT THE DAY, public transport drivers who were unwilling to venture onto the unpaved streets of Khar Yalla contributed to the congestion at the roundabout. It was at one time patriotically painted red, yellow, and green by youth reclaiming and cleaning up their streets during the *set setal* (renewal) movement of the early 1990s. By 2000, it was blackened with exhaust and peeling paint. The density of the traffic in this *quartier populaire*[1] was matched by the density of its population, which led some Dakaroise to refer to this neighborhood on the periphery of the nation's capital as a *bidonville.*[2] Its early residents were evicted from the self-built structures, or shantytowns, of central Dakar. Many residents were rural exiles who had escaped declining agricultural output, and they had named their new settlement Khar Yalla, meaning "waiting for God." It was a bustling neighborhood marked by the constant movement of people striving to earn a living. There were people who were working, retired, and unemployed, and there were rural and urban exiles. Over the years, Khar Yalla has welcomed refugees from zones of conflict in West Africa, including Guinea-Bissau, the Ivory Coast, Liberia, Sierra Leone, and the drawn-out secessionist struggle in Casamance, a region in southern Senegal. It has been home to many ethnic groups from Senegal, Mali, and Mauritania, including the Wolof, Serer, Manjack, Pulaar, Diola, Brama, and Bambara.

Residents often complained about the *car rapide,* the urban van transport, which jammed the roundabout with noxious billowing exhaust. The vans' *apprenti*[3] called out the destinations of "Ndakaru, Ndakaru" or "Pikine, Pikine," coaxing aboard riders who were headed to work as traders, tailors, office workers, or teachers; to a family celebration; or to one of the major markets. If taxi drivers were not washing the dusty residue from their cars as they waited for fares, they could be found gathered under the shade of the thatched structure erected near the entrance to this urban neighborhood, where they gambled on a game called *mankala,* rolled out mats to pray, brewed *attaya* (mint tea), or ordered a sweet, milky *café Tuba* from one of the nearby rice shops, which were run by women. Overnight, many of the taxi men who inhabited Khar Yalla parked their cars at its entrance. As many residents slept, minibuses lay in wait for passengers seeking to make a nocturnal journey home to the Casamance region of southern Senegal.

Khar Yalla was one of the last neighborhoods to be settled in the larger area known as the Grand Yoff region of Dakar and came into being as a result of colonial and postcolonial attempts to control space in the capital city. As Dakar prepared to become the colonial capital in 1956, many urban residents were designated as squatters and lost their right to land. They were removed from the city center and reassigned to semi-urban locations, including Grand Yoff. The same process was repeated in the 1970s when 90,000 persons were evicted from the center of Dakar (Davis 2006:98, 102). These city improvement operations were performed under the pretense of ameliorating health and sanitation conditions that were associated with high population density and makeshift homes. These operations built upon decades of colonial urban policy (dating back to 1915) that sought to separate the African population from the French population and government workers from manual laborers, traders, and craftspeople (Sow 1983:47).

As the urban poor were removed and the temporary structures that had formed their neighborhoods were razed, they were replaced by smart modernist homes, paved streets, and sidewalks. These homes were constructed by SICAP (Société Immobilière du Cap Vert) and OHLM (Office des Habitations à Loyer Modéré) for salaried workers who, after World War II, were employed largely in the service of the colonial administration. The modern suburbs of Scandinavia inspired the French architects who designed the SICAP homes, and thus they were partially modeled on the residence patterns of Western nuclear families (Bugnicourt 1983:32). They were tidy one-story homes for the most part, fully enclosed, with indoor hallways and bathrooms, and they often lacked the open central courtyard that defines Senegalese family life. From the street one could only see the outer wall, which might have orange and pink bougainvillea spilling over it, and the garage gate.

Grand Yoff has been characterized as "an isolated and disdained suburb . . . in the process of becoming a working class neighborhood" (Ndione and Soumaré 1983:115). At the close of the 1980s, the average household in Khar Yalla consisted of twelve persons (four adults and eight children) with an average of three persons employed in some form of wage labor (Ndione 1989:3). Initially, the growth of Grand Yoff was controlled by the government and by companies that sought to provide housing for their workers. Inevitably, the area expanded beyond the control of the state through the irregular division of plots by the Lebu (the established owners of the land in the area), real estate speculation, and unauthorized occupation of land in the national domain. Some of these new residents were owners of middle-class SICAP and OHLM housing who had rented out their villas to others out of financial desperation and moved to areas like Grand Yoff (Ndione and Soumaré 1983:115). The increasing alienation of land from lineage holders through the rise of private property and the clandestine division of land without the formal transfer of deeds through the state meant that many Grand Yoff residents lacked titles, deeds, and the right to land.

Yet, the residents of Grand Yoff did not consider their condition to be unusual or clandestine. Although they may have lacked land use permits from the state, they compensated the Lebu landholders for their use of the land, creating the current contradiction between customary land tenure and the 1964 National Domain Law (Sow 1983:50).[4] Today, the Ministry of Urbanism controls the sale of land in Dakar, and although SICAP and OHLM have been privatized, the state remains the principal stakeholder. Because the land in areas like Grand Yoff was divided without the state's recording of deeds, the provision of services, such as health care, education, sanitation, electricity, and water, is based on state-recognized land ownership in the neighborhood, which does not correspond to the actual population of the area (Ndione and Soumaré 1983:115). Moreover, neighborhoods like Khar Yalla are prone to seasonal flooding because they still contain remnants of the temporary early construction, such as wooden homes constructed from reclaimed shipping crates. The state is routinely called upon to assist victims of flooding, but is hesitant to do so because that would mean recognizing the legitimacy of land claims.

In search of new forms of income, many families sought to build rental housing behind their homes or by adding additional floors. Like many other neighborhoods in Dakar, in the 1990s, Khar Yalla experienced a real estate boom financed by cash from overseas despite the withdrawal of the state from the home finance sector. Because homes were paid for with cash, they were constructed in a piecemeal fashion; owners began constructing one floor or room at a time with an indefinite date of completion. As high-rise concrete apartment buildings began to shadow the improvised dwellings, Khar Yalla increasingly became a neighborhood of absentee landlords. As in Grand Dakar, where close to 50 percent of the proprietors had migrated overseas, many of the new landlords were women (Tall 1996:2). By 2004 it was estimated that 76 percent

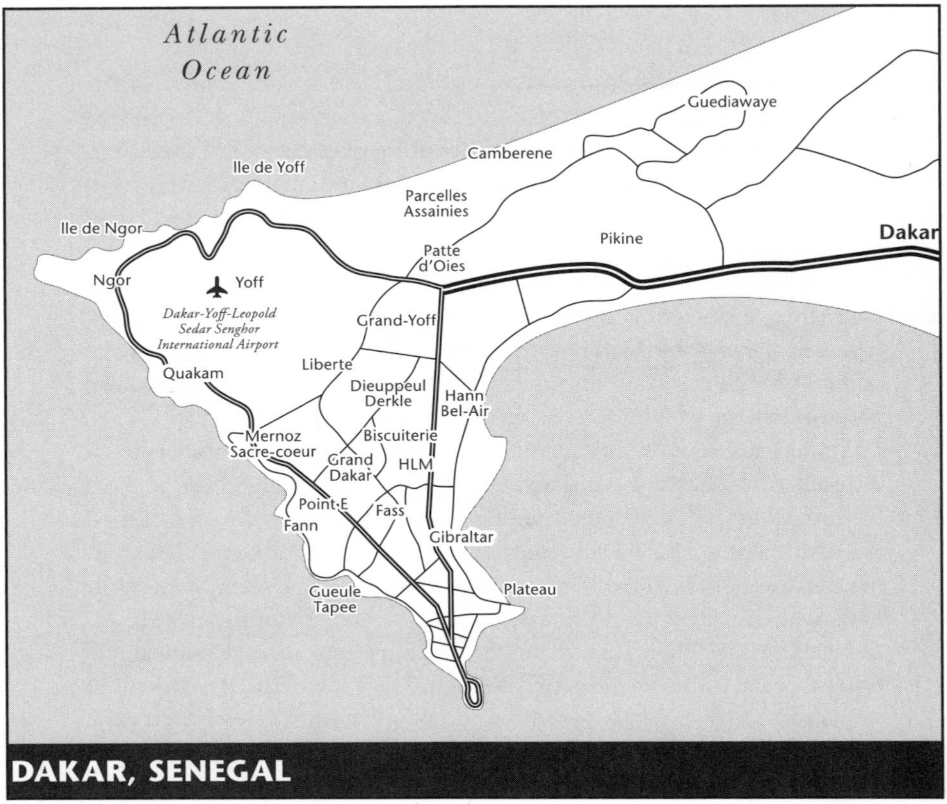

Grand Yoff, Dakar, Senegal

of households in Dakar had at least one member living abroad (Melly 2010:43).

Although many residents lack access to state services, they have crafted durable, if at times contested, social relations. Khar Yalla was not unlike other *quartiers populaires* surrounding Dakar, such as Grand Dakar and Pikine, in its struggles with land tenure and infrastructure, its high numbers of rural and transnational migrants, its absentee landlords due to international migration, and its designation as a so-called illegal or shadow city since many of its residents engaged in unofficial and extralegal economic endeavors (Sow 1983:53). Khar Yalla residents, like those in Grand Dakar and Pikine, also increasingly relied upon the intervention of religious authorities and NGOs, rather than the state, to secure social services like education, sanitation, and health care (Simone 2004).

By 2000, the era of middle-class neighborhoods financed by state capital, such as the modernist OHLM townhouses and the SICAP villas that dotted Dakar, had given way to new middle-class communities on the outskirts of the city. These developments had names like Liberté VI Extension, which distinguished the new neighborhoods from those financed by the government, such as Liberté VI, which was initially built in the 1950s to house police officers (Melly 2010). Recent migrants (both men and women) built high-rise apartments above the *quartiers populaires* and now dated-looking modernist homes built by SICAP. Features of these new multistory homes included marble-tiled facades; second-floor terraces with wrought-iron, arched balconies; awnings; tinted glass; and ceramic-tiled floors. This architecture led some to call Parcelles Assainies, an area popular among migrants, Las Palmas, after the Spanish city located in the Canary Islands. The architectural styles of these homes included decorative motifs borrowed from villas in prominent Dakar neighborhoods (Sow 1983:51). They were also inspired by styles more commonly found in Middle Eastern and North African countries. These homes stood in contrast to the more conventional cement-block, semi-urban homes, like those in Khar Yalla, with their double slope or flat slab roofs, lack of facades, and rooms that faced an inner courtyard, which served as the customary domain of female labor and as the public square of family politics (Depret 1983:65).

Support for these new styles came from both within and without Senegal: in the late 1990s, internet sites such as S.C.I. La Linguere, a joint venture between "Sénégalais résidant à Dakar et Sénégalais résidant dans la Diaspora," promoted "immobilière d'un type nouveau alliant *social* et *qualité*."[5] These villa structures were a far cry from the Senegalese homes described by the Senegalese novelist and filmmaker Sembene Ousmane in his 1965 novella *The Money-Order,* which were "nearly all identical: built of old, rotten wood, with roofs of corrugated iron, which was invariably rusty, or of old thatch that had never been renewed, or even of black oilcloth" (1972[1965]). They were also a far cry from the drab Brooklyn apartments and suburban Paris *foyers* that Senegalese workers inhabited abroad (Diop and Michalak 1996). Such dwellings were often cramped, with many men sharing a common space for sleeping and storage of their trade goods. The buildings were often in neglect, poorly maintained by their owners or the municipalities, and located outside of the city center in neighborhoods stigmatized by their multiracial and multinational populations.

MY MOTHER, THE KING

I came to know Sokna Géer in the spring of 1992 through the nongovernmental organization ENDA T.M. (Environnement et développement action du tiers monde) where I had an internship and had become interested in women's microfinance projects. I was introduced to her at the offices of the ENDA T.M. team CHODAK, which stands for *en chomage* Dakar, or unemployed Dakar, and was located adjacent to the Grand Yoff market in Cité Millionnaire. I found her stature and her presence daunting; she leaned back in her chair and said very little as she looked intently at and listened carefully to people. She often had a *sothiou*—a small wooden stick used to clean the teeth—in one hand, and she had deeply hennaed lips and gums. At some point in the conversation she would break into a smile and readjust her voluminous headscarf, and one could relax.

I barely understood Wolof at the time and felt that I was awkwardly dressed (in a knee-length flowered cotton summer dress when floor-length wrappers were the norm for young women) and too uncertain of what it was exactly that I wanted to know to approach her with my interview questions. As I sat across the table from her, a CHODAK researcher, who worked frequently with women's groups in Grand Yoff, and Madame Géer filled the awkward space with their own conversation. After several glances in my direction, I surmised that Madame Géer had invited me to live in her family home in Khar Yalla. Within the week I was delivered to the Géer home with my large black duffle bag that I could not lift, a foam rubber mattress, and a sack of rice, in a small Nissan truck driven by a researcher at ENDA T.M. I cannot imagine now what people in the neighborhood must have thought then, a young American girl arriving with no family.

My family did eventually visit. They had *boubous* made by Madame Géer's tailor, and my mother sat with the neighborhood women and learned how to make *cere,* a millet couscous. To this day, the older women in the neighborhood still talk about my parents' visit and ask after them. This was my first insight into the importance of social ties and of the relationships that make us human in other's eyes. It had a profound impact on the way I came to understand the practice of fieldwork and my particular subjectivity not as a researcher or even as a student, but as a young, unmarried woman who profoundly needed to learn how to be in a new and unfamiliar social milieu. For the next six months I would accompany Madame Géer as she attended events organized by ENDA T.M. and other development and political organizations, and family celebrations. My Wolof improved to the point where I could understand simple instructions and gain a sense of what was going to happen on any given day.

I worked under an assumption shared by many researchers at nongovernmental organizations: that microfinance projects would improve women's economic lives. Women in Senegal lacked access to formal banking structures, and the rates for loans from traders and stall owners were often usurious. Access to small loans would have an impact on the forms of discrimination that many women faced, which were based in part on gender inequities. Inequality also came from the ideas that many Senegalese held about one's occupation. Across the Sahel, one's employment is linked to membership in an occupational group, which is inherited, endogamous, and linked to a system of knowledge and power. These groups are often referred to as castes. Casted artisans, such as griots, woodworkers, and blacksmiths, as well as descendants of former slaves, were often held in lower regard than freeborn persons.

Development specialists viewed these ranked social orders as barriers to the expansion of civil society and secular democracy. Yet, as I was to discover over the years that I visited the Géer home, the women who participated in these microfinance projects often distributed their proceeds in a manner that reinscribed social rank (Ndione 1989). I watched Madame Géer use these funds to accumulate vast quantities of cloth, which she gave to her daughters, nieces, other kin, affines, dependents, and neighbors during family celebrations. Through these social gestures, Madame Géer redefined her relationship to others and aspired to repair the ruptures in social relations introduced by births, marriages, and deaths. Over time I also began to appreciate how she used these textiles to create difference by reinscribing her high status as a freeborn person through gifts to dependents, including casted artisans and former slaves, who often performed important services at her feasts, such as butchering, cooking, and praise singing.

By the time I returned for dissertation research in the late 1990s, women's microfinance programs were so strong that many had become as usurious as the stall owners. There had been significant changes in the neighborhood, a result of state projects, the remittances of migrant children, and investments by multinational companies and Gulf states. Some twenty years after residents had begun to settle in this thin stretch of Grand Yoff, the state had paved the road through Khar Yalla's small but essential market space, which was populated with hardware shops, tailors, fruit stands, dry goods stores, and a community mill. The impetus for paving the road had been the construction of a gas station owned by the French company Total, which replaced the grand tree, or *filao* (*Casuarina equisetifolia*), that marked the entrance to the neighborhood. For twenty years, people had said, "meet me in Khar Yalla *ci filao* [by the big tree]." Such remarkable trees were often the locus of political, commercial, and social activity in Senegambian towns (see, for example, Ross 1995:231). The replacement of this grand old tree by a gas station and the forms of transportation that it fed marked a further shift toward the domination of wealth from overseas over that from home.

As for the road, a lack of maintenance by the state during the late 1990s and 2000s resulted in its breaking up and sinking back into the arid, sandy soil that characterizes northern Senegal. Taxi drivers, who feared getting their cars stuck in the sand, often said "*Deedet,* I won't drive inside Khar Yalla" to Madame Géer and me. Khar Yalla lanes were also congested with foot traffic: women sold snack foods behind small benches; bands of children passed footballs; and untethered livestock allowed only one car to pass at a time. On top of all this, on any given day of the week, one could expect to find a tent erected across the streets that sheltered men, women, and sound systems from the noon sun and marked a marriage, a Muslim baby's naming-day ceremony, or a funeral.

It was not only the road and its forms of transport that the embattled residents of Khar Yalla bemoaned as they sat in white plastic lawn chairs perched precariously in the loose sand, escaping the overheated interiors of homes and boardinghouses. They complained about problems of water, electricity, and garbage that resulted, in part, from the inability of the state to resolve land tenure issues and provide access to public services. Electricity, water, and sanitation had been absent since the time when squatters who were evicted from the city center of Dakar in the 1970s first settled this area. Although by the 1990s many Khar Yalla homes had obtained electrical power, many of the neighborhood's residents still did not have access to it at all, others had makeshift connections, and all suffered the frequent brownouts that characterized the administration of President Abdoulaye Wade since 2000. These occurrences were so common that the candles that were suitable for alms giving were often used to light neighborhood homes, and irons with charcoal chambers were vastly preferred over electrical ones, since even brownouts did not provide a sufficient explanation for rumpled clothes.

The inability of the state to provide a constant supply of water was also a source of consternation. Madame Géer had the foresight to install an *ndaal,* a rotund ceramic vessel with a narrow opening that is used to store water in rural areas. This chest-high vessel was placed on the unfinished second floor of the home and a hose that was hoisted up from the single household faucet, located in the courtyard, filled it. I heard Madame Géer's adult children tease her for installing this rural vessel, but it was useful for storing water given how frequently the water company turned off its supply, though the cooling properties of ceramic made for an unpleasantly cold bath after the dawn prayer. For less fortunate residents of Grand Yoff, a morning trip to one of the forty-eight public taps for this neighborhood of 60,000 was necessary (Ndione and Soumaré 1983:115). Before even turning on the tap in the Géer home, one could tell that the water was shut off by observing the sour faces and empty buckets of women returning from the nearby public tap. There was also an issue with plumbing. CHODAK had labored to convince women not to empty their grey water into the middle of the streets where persons walked, taxis endeavored to cross, and mosquitoes bred, urging them instead to build cisterns that would be emptied periodically. Yet the high number of renters in this urban neighborhood made such improvements in infrastructure difficult to achieve.

Men's and women's grievances with the infrastructure of ad hoc semi-urban neighborhoods like Grand Yoff, Pikine, and Grand Dakar (to name just a few) were really symptoms of larger problems that had been in the making since Senegal's independence from France in 1960. Rural-urban migration, changes in land tenure, and changes in the nature of work had had serious implications for relations between men and women, young and old. Relations between husbands and wives and between fathers and sons were transformed by the decline of cash crop agriculture by the 1970s. Positions of male authority as landowners and heads of household, with the exception of titled religious leaders, largely declined as a result of land reform laws, migration, and environmental devastation. Since the 1970s, men's productive activities, once rooted in agriculture, have suffered as the state and international lenders ceased to support agricultural interventions, such as subsidies for fertilizers and seeds, and agricultural credit.

At the same time, women often have been the targets of men's laments about the loss of their own importance (see Perry 2005). Neoliberal reforms favored women's microfinance projects at the expense of agricultural development. As economic prospects for Khar Yalla families declined throughout the 1990s with the reimagining of the state and as more young men and, eventually, women migrated abroad in search of wage labor and capital, NGO funding became important to women's authority in the ritual sphere. Madame Géer drew funds from the rotating credit and savings associations to circulate cloth among women in her *mbotaye* (ritual association), *dahira* (religious association), and other associations. Although women who shared associational membership often dressed for public events in matching cloth, for which they saved collectively, to demonstrate their solidarity, they also drew upon the funds that they accumulated through their membership in these associations to dress in a manner that distinguished them from others. Cloth, the idiom and principal means by which women create the bonds of kinship, has endured as a symbol of lineage continuity and the means of creating difference and rank. Often, when Madame Géer failed to arrive at one of these meetings in a timely manner because she was arranging her dress, perfuming her boubou with incense, or searching for a particular piece of jewelry, her daughter would turn to me and joke, "Sama yaay, buur lë [My mother thinks she is a king]."

Although Madame Géer was not a king, she was a *géer* (someone who is freeborn, or highborn), and the attributes associated with her status—*rafet judo* (beautiful birth), *jom* (honor), *kersa* (restraint), and *alal* (wealth)—were passed on through her blood to her five daughters and seven sons. Her status expressed itself in her renown for increasing and distributing what were actually meager resources, rather than eating (*lekk*) them. Money that was intended to be eaten was tied up in the top corners of the cloth wrappers that were worn closest to the body. These were coins and small bills that one spent at the boutique or at roadside stands. Real wealth was meant to be redistributed and was often made visible in the large denominations of currency given publicly and the amounts of cloth worn on the body.

In the 1990s, Madame Géer's children often greeted each other with light sarcasm, saying "yangi lekk sa xaalis," meaning literally "you are eating your money" but figuratively "you are sitting there doing nothing." Madame Géer, however, rarely ate her money; although the Géers also struggled, she distributed rice on Muslim feast days to her less fortunate neighbors and gave leftover cooked meals to young boys who had been sent by their parents to apprentice with a *shaykh,* who were called *talibe* (disciples). Several times Madame Géer showed me a picture in her Wolof literacy book, which had been produced by an NGO called TOSTAN to provide women with literacy training and lessons in economic empowerment. The image demonstrated how women who *bokk ci benn loxo* (pitched in together) amassed more resources than they would have working alone. In part, this book was taken out time and again to refer to its Wolof phrases because I had disappointed the family with my recurrent grammatical errors, but it was also employed to school me in the traits of the freeborn, including openhandedness and responsibility. Indeed, women were drawn to Madame Géer largely due to her familiarity with proper comportment and, when researchers at CHODAK suggested that I meet her in 1992, she was the head of some forty organizations.

FIELDWORK AND ETHNOGRAPHY

Ethnography, as the central research method in anthropology and its principal mode of writing, does not reflect a one-way transfer of information, of asking questions and eliciting answers. Rather, ethnographic research is a process of learning how our interlocutors view their social worlds and trying to understand the questions they pose about those worlds. Ethnographic research is a mutual experience of giving and taking, an exercise in listening rather than asking. In this reciprocal process both interlocutor and researcher are transformed and come to view each other, themselves, and their worlds differently. As friendships and intimacies develop over time, research becomes even more subjective and interpersonal. I first met the Géer family as a student and over the years returned as a married woman and then with each of my daughters. The children I had met when they were five became young adults; many of the sons had traveled abroad, married, and had families of their own; and the house too had been transformed as these new families made it their home. I often had to remind the Géers and myself that I was still doing research, and these transformations interested me. Ethnography's strongest attribute is its subjectivity; we are personally connected to the lives and worlds we seek to write about.

I have privileged the problems and aspirations of women in Senegal from their perspective, rather than from the perspective of my own interests. Why was it that certain topics of conversation were thought important enough to introduce with "this is important for your research"? My attempts to address social worlds from the perspective of those whose home I came to live in raise the question of voice, which has plagued anthropology for several decades now and also affects any project of writing. In the chapters that follow I have minimized my use of the first person, because this is not a story about my own transformation, while still being explicit and transparent about the terms of my ethnographic research. Clearly, family members included me in certain events and conveyed happenings to me because I was a particular audience with my own situated perspective, which was most often sympathetic to theirs. Family members also included me in certain conversations because there was some sense that they had been misunderstood as Muslims and Africans more broadly.

Because fieldwork is a personal experience through which one learns about others by sharing aspects of the self, narrative ethnography seemed to be an appropriate way to write about people's lives in all of their intimate detail as they presented themselves to me at the time. These narratives are not works of ethnographic fiction; there are no conflated events or composite characters, though I have changed names to protect people's privacy and left unsaid many details that I thought would be damaging or hurtful. I do say in the text that a person "thought" or "believed" something when thoughts or beliefs were recounted to me as such by that person. These narratives are not meant to represent an ongoing present. The lives of the individuals in this book have changed considerably since the 2000s; they have taken directions that I could not have anticipated. In many ways their lives have improved dramatically through the hard work and sacrifice of their children, who have been immensely successful and dedicated to their families. I am optimistic about the family's future and the future of Senegal. But there has also been deep sorrow and loss. Therefore, as immediate as the narratives that follow may seem, they are only snapshots of a particular moment in this family's lifetime of experiences.

Nonetheless, the kind of immediacy and intimacy that such personalized narrative and use of dialogue bring to a text offer a kind of truth value that one cannot get through large samples from which one might generalize and predict trends. Anthropology is not a predictive discipline; it is analytic and interpretive and, some would argue, historical. In many ways, the Géer family is representative of families everywhere in their struggle to create enduring forms of value and to forge meaningful lives in difficult economic times. In other ways, they are a particular family with their own idiosyncrasies. By using ethnographic narrative, I hope that readers will appreciate how much this family is like their own, is like other Senegalese and Muslim families, and is at the same time exceptional. Ultimately, I hope that the reader will come to an appreciation of the ties between families in Senegal and elsewhere, and to a realization that decisions made in Washington by the International Monetary Fund and others have an impact on people's lives in Senegal.

I also thought it crucial to respond to the ways in which Muslim women have been stereotyped post-9/11 and to recent trends in anthropology, where it seems as though all too often people are missing from our texts. I have thus provided stories because in their uniqueness they cannot lead to generalizations about women, about Islam, or about African societies. They are told from a particular point of view, by speakers with a specific motivation; they are partial views into social worlds (Abu-Lughod 1993). These are some of the reasons that I chose to focus on the narratives, arguments, and ordinary lives of several members of a single household.[6]

I should point out that this was not a small family. At any given time, there were fifteen to twenty people in the Géer household, including the parents, their children and grandchildren, elders (some relatives, some not), children fostered to them, some country cousins, and others who were fostered to various members of the family to establish ties of reciprocity and mutual aid between families that were not necessarily blood kin. The extended family network included rural, urban, and overseas households. My research also involved tracing the Géers' relations with several hundred family members in Dakar, Tuba-Mbacke, and other rural areas surrounding Tuba, as well as in France, Italy, Spain, Saudi Arabia, and the United States. Importantly, I located myself in Tuba during the dry season and during the annual *Màggal* pilgrimage when many overseas family members returned home. I followed the circulation of members of the household and the extended family on social visits and pilgrimages, to naming ceremonies, marital feasts, and funerals.

Since in Senegal one is not limited to engaging in reciprocal relations with just family members, I also followed the extended social network of neighbors and peers through the family's interactions with ritual, religious, nongovernmental, and political organizations. In addition, I traced the relations of this family to the United States: the first son relocated there in 1992 and has been joined by his younger brother, older sister, mother's sister, and, most recently, younger sister. The narratives that comprise this book speak to the decline of big state-run development projects that largely benefited men and to the entrenchment of the polity in NGOs and their form of patronage with its new emphasis on women's microcredit projects, as well as to the rise of the Murid order and the retreat of the Senegalese state.

Rather than overspecifying the phenomena by concentrating on the Murid, Wolof, and urban aspects of the exchange circuit, I use the narratives to show how the circuit operates through particular modes of deployment, and often through gendered and generational strategies. The ethnographic material itself is the product of a plodding and constant tracking of the minutiae of everyday life, of inquiring into things as mundane as who was having their septic tank emptied and who was making do, of listening to the arguments between a mother and the girl she sent to the market over what 1,000 CFA francs would provide toward the family meal, and why it was that the kitchen equipment, especially gas tanks, were subject to thievery. I have tracked vernacular conceptions of the commoditization and monetization of everyday values, and it is precisely in these details that one can read the larger historical and economic transformations wrought by economic liberalization, migration, and global Islam.

ONE

GLOBAL SENEGAL

WOMEN'S WEALTH, ISLAM, AND GLOBAL VOLATILITY

By early 2000, it was evident that families were frustrated with more than twenty years of policies of economic and political liberalization in Senegal. These reforms aimed at economic growth, implemented under the aegis of the International Monetary Fund and the World Bank starting in the 1980s, had been accompanied by substantial unemployment, shortages of food and other necessities, rural-urban migration, an urban housing crisis, and the declining availability and affordability of health care and education. As many Senegalese men faced the declining value of the agricultural potential of their land and the inability of the state to secure their social welfare, they sought moral renewal through submission to Muslim shaykhs.

The Muslim clergy responded to this fiscal and moral uncertainty by denouncing what they deemed to be inflated bridewealth payments and costly family ceremonies, especially women's practice of exchanging locally woven and dyed cloth, a measure of women's wealth and worth, and calling for an Islamic family law through which limits would be set on these payments. Additionally, religious associations, nongovernmental organizations, and others who professed an interest in national development characterized these practices as belonging to the realm of *cosaan,*[1] Wolof for "custom" or "tradition," rather than Islam. Certainly, debates over Islam and the historical practices that predate its spread in West Africa are prevalent in the region and common elsewhere in the Muslim world as well (Cooper 1997:xxxiii). These debates have a considerable impact on women's lives. In Senegal, cloth became a contentious object of debate because—through its use in dress, display, and bestowal—it made forms of women's wealth and value visible, displaying the hidden potential of women as producers and bearers of history.

Importantly, the social criticism of women's dress and exchange practices took place in the context of protracted fiscal uncertainty. As much as women's practices were portrayed as traditional, and thus out of step with an Islamic modernity calling for moral austerity and reform, they were at

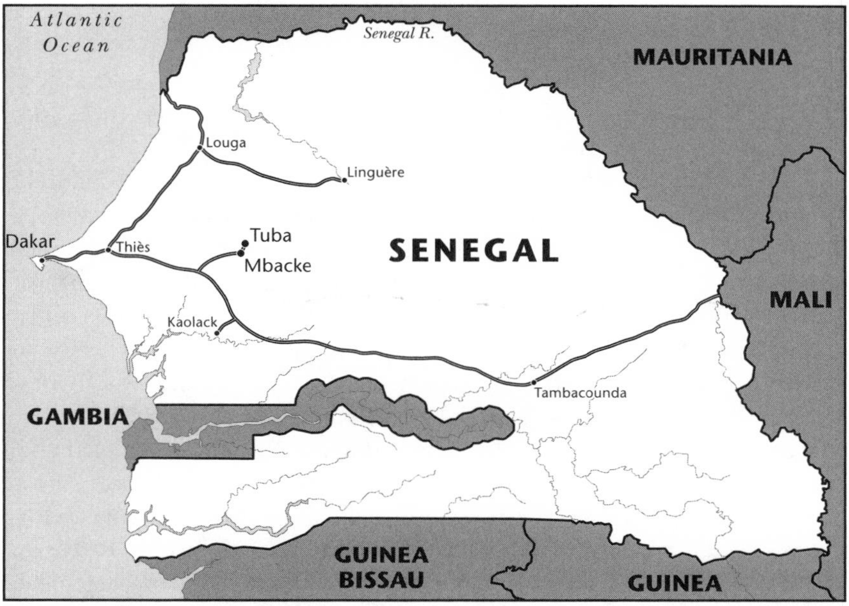

Senegal

the same time contemporaneous with economic and political shifts. Women's practices were not merely a response to or a way of making do in difficult times—what many scholars of Senegal have referred to as an economic crisis (Boone 1992; Cruise O'Brien 1988; Ebin 1992, 1993; Mbodj 1993) following the implementation of structural adjustment programs (SARS). To call these hard times a "crisis" and the varied responses "practices of making do" perhaps misses the point, for Senegalese men and women had endured some thirty years of so-called crisis by the time of this writing. To focus on the temporary nature of the notion of crisis is to overlook the unfolding practices through which men and women create new productive possibilities, of which women's dress and exchange practices are a part, even under conditions of fiscal volatility and restraint (Makhulu et al. 2010).

As African modernities across the continent have faced fundamental challenges in the wake of neoliberal restructuring and, in the case of Senegal, further entrenchment in globalized economic processes, ritual and religion have reemerged as critical junctures where men and women struggle over the terms of sociality (Comaroff and Comaroff 1993). And this is apparent in the debate over women's ritual practices and religious authority in Senegal. The moral terms in which economic realities are apprehended has been an enduring theme in the ethnography of Africa (Apter 2005; Bastian 1996; Bohannan 1959; Comaroff and Comaroff 1993, 1997; Evans-Pritchard 1940; Guyer, ed., 1995; Hutchinson 1996; Piot 1999; Shipton 1989; Weiss 1996). To understand the fiscal and moral terms in which Senegalese men and women sought social fortunes and futures, I sought to untangle the multilayered discourses of conservation and change in the Senegalese postcolony.

As I witnessed the gradual movement of most of the adult children in the Géer household and in Khar Yalla in general, who went overseas during the 1990s as students, wage laborers, and traders, I became interested in the lives of the women they left behind. How did they engage in processes of social production? How did they constitute the bonds of kith and kin and secure their future, as increasing numbers of family members left the country? It might seem that the productive activities in which many Dakaroise engaged were limited in scale—that they were merely strategies for getting by and making do in the face of inadequate economic resources. Indeed, scholars of Senegal have deftly accounted for the exceptional ways in which Senegalese *se débrouillent* (make do) (Mottin-Sylla 1987; Mustafa 1998; Ndione 1994; Roberts 1996). However, these strategies for creating vast social networks of reciprocal exchange, glossed as tradition, were not only enabling women to get by. They indexed fundamental changes in cycles of domestic production and reproduction that were under way, which were wrought in part by the vast outward migration of Senegalese men and, increasingly, women in the context of global economic volatility.

Economic hardship, not only the lack of employment but also the absence of productive possibilities, from constituting families through marriage and home building to achieving social distinction, sent many men and women abroad in search of wage labor and capital. The majority of young people who left were traders and devotees of the Muslim Sufi way, the Murid *tariqa*. Ninety percent of women and men in Senegal are Sunni Muslims, and the majority belong to one of four Sufi orders in the country—the Layanne, Tijaniyya, Qadiriyya, and Muridiyya (Villalón 2004).[2] Many claim that the Murid order is the fastest growing in part due to its economic success. More than any other Sufi order, Murids have woven cargo and currency through the official and unofficial spaces of the global economy to become an economic force in the Senegalese postcolony. Along these same routes, Murid migrants in New York City and other global cities have circulated the media of social production, including cloth, portraits and videos of family ceremonies, and religious offerings, texts, and images. Murid men and women have constructed and adorned domestic interiors and exteriors, bodies and fashions, and their sacred city of Tuba to defy the potential for loss that is inherent in the desire to circulate valued objects, to invest value in others, and to project themselves and their vision for their community into the future.

The debates over the politics of social production, women's ritual practices, and religious authority can be understood as struggles over the nature of value. These struggles over the constitution of social and moral orders took place in an era that was marked by the contradictory rise of both the market and new modes of regulation of global Muslim networks, related to the United States–led global war on terror. Yet Senegalese Muslims have created value over the *longue durée* of currency instability and global volatility through participating in what Jane Guyer (2004:128) has referred to as "repertoires" of fiscal performance, including offerings to shaykhs, operating at the interface of regulated and unregulated economies on a global scale, partaking in microfinance projects, and bestowing cloth wealth in family ceremonies.

MURID GLOBAL CIRCUITS

To be a Murid (disciple) is to be part of a *tariqa* (way or path)[3] of esoteric practice through which one seeks to achieve divine union in this life through the guidance of a spiritual master and learned scholar, who is known as a shaykh. For the 5 million adherents to the Murid tariqa, this Sufi way offers not only the promise of eternal prosperity but also access to the forms of trade and production of worldly wealth. The Murid tariqa has connected the teachings of its founding figure, the scholar Amadou Bamba Mbacke (ca. 1851–1927), concerning labor, sacrifice, prosperity, and salvation, to the struggle and strife of migrant life. At the turn of the twentieth century, men and women in northwestern Senegal who were seeking to evade French colonial rule, to acquire agricultural land for the production of peanuts as a cash crop, and, ultimately, to secure their salvation congregated around Amadou Bamba, whom they regarded as a locus of divine grace (Robinson 1991). Bamba proffered a soteriology in which agricultural labor in the service of a shaykh was an essential mode of spiritual discipline, thus enabling Sufism to become a mass movement (Babou 2007a). Murids rationalized peanut production for export and pioneered new lands in rural eastern Senegal, and thus "the old social order," wrote the political scientist Donal Cruise O'Brien, was reconstituted "on a new, religious basis" (1971b:15). Casted members of Wolof society, former slaves, and warriors found new patrons in the Murid shaykhs (Copans 1980:226; Klein 1998:199), and royal families regained their former status through marriages with the religious elite (Cruise O'Brien 1971b:35). Subsequently, those whose mothers descended from the freeborn assumed the highest positions within the Murid way (Bop 2005:1107).

In the postcolonial period, following the drop in price for peanuts (Senegal's main export) in the world market, a series of devastating droughts, locust infestations, and a massive famine that plagued the Sahel in the 1970s, rural Murid disciples, like many West Africans, migrated to urban areas to search for work and, eventually, overseas, some as university students and others to trade African art in European and North American cities (Babou 2002; Carter 1997; Cruise O'Brien 1988; A. Diop 1985; M. Diop 1981; Diouf 2000; Ebin 1993; Salem 1981; Stoller 2002). Murid disciples succeeded in transitioning to trade in the urban areas by assisting each other and seeking out new patrons in the Murid way (Babou 2002; Creevey 1970; Cruise O'Brien 1988; Diouf 2000; Ebin 1986; Irvine 1974; Mustafa 1998). These patrons offered advice, housing, credit, capital, and legal services to newly arrived urban migrants. Murid migrants continued to patronize their rural shaykhs through the formation of urban *dahira* (circle) associations and religious offerings aimed at building the great mosque in the sacred city of Tuba to fulfill the vision of Amadou Bamba.

Throughout the postcolonial period, the rural-urban migration continued and, eventually, Murid disciples extended their networks of trade overseas, first to France and then across Europe to the United States and a number of global cities. Murid traders rarely went abroad as individuals. Their sojourns were part of larger family strategies, which were frequently financed by women's participation in rotating savings and credit associations. Furthermore, women were instrumental in building the reputations of honor that underpinned the men's trade through their exchanges in family ceremonies. Trade took place often in the unregulated sectors of local, national, and global economies. Traders relied on trust, family networks, and religious solidarity to succeed in obtaining credit and capital and in building clientele.

Today, the sacred capital of Tuba is the center of an expansive import-export economy as a result of Murid industry, which is linked through the port of Dakar to an immense market. Murid merchants control the major markets in and around the capital city, including its largest cloth market, Marché HLM (named after Habitations à Loyer Modéré, the state-financed housing project for the middle class) (Mustafa 1998). Dakar does not fit conventional criteria as a global city—it is not a financial capital, nor is it a locus of technological innovation, and it has just one newly installed call center. Scheld (2003) has shown that this capital city in the global south is a hub of cultural and economic innovation, which is inscribed through the migrant bodies that filter through it and the extensive global reach of its massive import-export economy.

By the 1990s, Murid disciples had shifted their investments from agriculture to real estate, cement, and transportation. As in remittance economies elsewhere, real estate speculation and construction flourished following the decades of rural-to-urban migration. Real estate development was led in part by Murid successes abroad since overseas traders built new homes with cash, unwilling or unable to secure loans from banks in Senegal with their prohibitive interest rates. These houses were constructed in piecemeal fashion; with each trip home, additional truckloads of sand, gravel, cement, and rebar arrived on migrants' properties (Buggenhagen 2001; Melly 2010). Some of the most common stories of thievery in Dakar during my fieldwork revolved around neighbors who were accused of stealing sand from another's pile, bowl by bowl, night after night. Despite the appearance of prosperity in Dakar, promoted by real estate developers who targeted Senegalese abroad and supported by the volume of construction activity as evidenced by piles of brick, rebar, and sand throughout the city, many of these newly constructed dwellings in the city center and its outskirts were more like sandcastles: their half-built structures were worn down by the elements after years of inactivity. Some of these were like homesteads, their cement outlines on the outer reaches of Dakar preventing the land from reverting back to the government under the National Domain Law of 1964, although these homes were often razed as soon as they were discovered by the state. Among the builders were also young women who went abroad and invested their earnings in apartment complexes in the urban periphery of Dakar (Tall 1994). In addition to participating in real estate speculation, many young men also spoke of building family homes, which they constructed for potential brides, existing wives, or their parents, whom they sought to transport to the city from the countryside.

Young men and women not only invested their wealth in real estate and in building family homes in Dakar, they also endeavored to invest their earnings in the development of the spiritual metropolis of Tuba (Ross 1995) whose central mosque and the homes that radiated from this sacred center aimed to realize the prophecy of the founding figure of the Murid order, Amadou Bamba, that Tuba would be a spiritual center. In the 1990s, due to this construction, Tuba emerged as the second-largest city in Senegal and a locus of rural-rural migration (Gueye 1999). As young women gave generously to their religious associations, young men who aspired to invest in homes on the land in and around Tuba were supported by land grants awarded by shaykhs, which were employed to maintain and recruit new disciples to bolster their positions with respect to the central

Tuba mosque

hierarchy.[4] Thus, there was pressure to expand the sacred domain of Tuba beyond the boundaries initially granted to this independent administrative district by the French colonialists in exchange for the residents' cultivation of peanuts. Additionally, many sons from rural Murid villages around Tuba replaced the millet stalk homes of their fathers with cement buildings as a symbol of their success abroad. In turn, these fathers, who had once controlled the lineage through the allocation of peanut fields, lands that had long since dried up, came to rely on their sons' remittances of cash. These male elders became merely symbolic, serving as placeholders for land that would otherwise revert back to the government if it was unoccupied. Through the National Domain Law of 1964, one goal of which was to combat traditional landlordism (Irvine 1974:17), the state had nationalized 95 percent of its territory, prohibited land sales, and assumed the sole right to grant title to land (Galvan 2004:134).

Male and female disciples also gave offerings of cash, *addiya,* to shaykhs through which they entered into a circuit of *baraka* (blessings or grace); these blessings were thought to be spiritual and material at once for, through them, disciples gained access not merely to eternal prosperity but also to this-worldly wealth. Addiya initially contributed to the building of the impressive Murid mosque in Tuba and have since funded the expansion of Tuba's infrastructure as it has been transformed from a small rural village into a major residential, commercial, and spiritual center where many disciples seek to be buried to avoid intercession so that they can enter directly into heaven. For them, Tuba both ties heaven and earth together (Ross 1995) and also incorporates global locations into its center. The realization of these homes in Tuba places transnational traders at the crossroads of heaven and earth, where profits meet prophets and prayers meet prosperity.

CONCRETE WEALTH: BUILDING HOMES, BUILDING TUBA

Although many families have moved away from their reliance on the land, given the steady decline of agriculture since at least the 1960s, in the late 1990s Murid overseas traders began investing in land in Dakar and in the rural region of Tuba, the Murid heartland. Real estate speculation in the 1990s reflected the desire of Murid men and, increasingly, women to invest in and lay claim to land by home building. For young unmarried men there was a particular urgency to building a home since this was a primary means of accumulating wealth. If a young man did not build a home prior to entering into the marriage process, he could expect his kin and future affines to eat all of his accumulated assets before he could invest them in cement bricks. In the Géer family, by 2008, two older brothers who had migrated abroad to Italy and the United States had built rental units in Dakar, which included homes that their wives inhabited; a younger brother had bought land for a future project; and two daughters, one of whom had migrated to the United States, had invested in property outside of Dakar.

Whereas both men and women invested in rental real estate in Dakar and the surrounding suburbs, men in particular talked of the importance of building in Tuba. It was clear why men sought to build homes in Dakar, including, most importantly, to reap the financial rewards of owning land in Senegal's capital. Dakar was a cosmopolitan and consumer-oriented city with vast markets and shopping and nightclub districts, and it was home to the major shipping port and national airport. But how did Tuba, a three- to four-hour drive out in the country on roads whose state of repair indicated the proximity of elections, from which so many young people had fled ecological devastation in the mid-twentieth century, come to occupy migrants' imaginations abroad, especially when so many of these migrants were not originally from Tuba but rather from Dakar or other agricultural regions?

Although the Ministry of Urbanism controlled the sale of land in Dakar, in rural areas, including Tuba, the division of land was still controlled by rural notables. This was in spite of the attempts by the National

Domain Law to weaken the customary land tenure through which powerful patrilineages allocated the right to work the land (Boone 2007:561n8) by making the state the owner of all unregistered land. The architects of the law sought to spur national development by increasing access to land and thus increasing agricultural output. The attempt to reform land tenure was by its very nature political because it questioned social and political structures, the nature of state and religious authority, and the political sovereignty of persons, communal entities such as lineages and religious orders, and the state itself (559). Therefore, although the law applied nationally, it had different intentions and effects in the Senegal River valley, the Casamance region, Sine, Saloum, and the Murid-controlled areas. While the National Domain Law sought to return to an originary form of communal landownership in which all persons had access to land, in effect it continued colonial attempts to impose individual land rights and written titles, and it was largely unsuccessful in many rural areas (Cotula et al. 2004),[5] since in rural areas it was not the individual that was the legal entity but the community that determined right of access to land (Boone 2003:77). Under this law, the state would only enforce inheritable rights in disputes if the landowner were a resident of that community and had established user rights by cultivating the land for three consecutive years (562). Yet in many cases where sons sought to prove their inheritance of land that their fathers had cultivated, the powerful lineages that could prove title to the land often won (Cotula et al. 2004). Persons were reluctant to see the land as an alienable commodity, even in cases where it had been semi-alienable for some time through land pawning and other arrangements, because it was so deeply imbued with mystical significance and was connected to the integrity of lineages, particularly through the myriad forms of exchange that perpetuated these into the future.

The National Domain Law, in association with the decentralization of the state in the 1970s and in 1996, left the *communautés rurales* (rural councils) in charge of allocating rural land in their territories. In the case of Tuba, although the *communauté rurale,* the arrondissement of Ndame, controlled land and resource disputes, a lack of federal money and authority meant that the Murid clergy largely resolved these disputes. While land in Dakar was alienable and sold at market values that rose throughout the 1990s, in Tuba and its surrounding agricultural villages in the administrative region of Diourbel, shaykhs encouraged urban and eventually overseas migrants to build homes there by granting them land.

The call to build homes in Tuba began with the leadership of Abdoul Lahat Mbacke between 1968 and 1989; he instigated the creation of subdivisions around the great mosque, which he also expanded (Diouf 2000). By establishing plots on the outer perimeter of the holy city, shaykhs prevented the government from claiming the land and garnered new disciples to build their base. Homes were constructed on desiccated land that was distributed by Muslim clergy who were trying to push the outer limits of their holy terrain. In the twenty-first century, disputes over land at all levels became so intense that some posit that one of the key factors that enabled the current president, Abdoulaye Wade, to be reelected in 2007, despite declining economic conditions, was his commitment to sorting out the land claims of Murid migrants (Mbow 2008:162).[6]

Since Murid adherents began migrating to urban areas mid-century to escape declining agricultural yields, the Murid clergy has sought to draw disciples back to Tuba by reinvesting the land with sacred value. During Bamba's lifetime, Tuba first appeared to him as a vision during a *khalwa* (mystical retreat); its location was said to be revealed by the angel Jibril (Coulon 1999:199; Cruise O'Brien 1971b:41; Ross 1995:224). The name of the holy city Bamba envisioned refers to the Tree of Paradise, or Tûbâ; in Muslim thought, "this tree is the closest one can possibly approach God . . . a cosmological symbol—the *axis mundi,* transcending the earthly and heavenly spheres" (Ross 1995:223). Bamba envisioned a substantial mosque, instructed his followers to build a house and a school for Islamic learning, and designated a place for his own burial, all of which underpinned his religious authority (Babou 2005:409; Ross 1995:231). Yet Bamba actually spent very little of his life in the present-day location of Tuba. He was born in the neighboring town of Xuru Mbacke, which was founded in the late eighteenth century by his great-grandfather Mame Marame, a renowned jurist (Ross 1995:249). For a large part of his life he resided in Kajoor and Saloum with his father, Momar Anta Sali, who was a teacher and advisor to local kings (Babou 2005:408). Bamba only had the opportunity to live in Tuba briefly from 1888 to 1895, after which he retreated to Jolof because Tuba had become crowded with his followers and their families, which increased the alarm of local chiefs and colonial administrators, who subsequently exiled him to Gabon (410). Bamba never returned to Tuba as he remained either in exile or under house arrest, always under the watchful eye of the colonial administrators.

With its colonial legacy as an independent administrative district, and therefore a tax- and duty-free zone, Tuba has become the center of a global trade network (Cruise O'Brien 1971b, 2003:65; Gueye 2001:107). Tuba's population doubled between 1988 and 1998 and its developed area expanded from 575 hectares in 1970 to 3,900 hectares in 1990 to more than 12,000 hectares in 1997 (Gueye 1999:1, 2001:107). More than 300,000 Senegalese out of a national population of 9.5 million[7] inhabit or maintain a home in this rural region (Gueye 1999), which is often plagued with the weekend traffic of urban disciples seeking respite in the country, a visit with their shaykh, or a long holiday weekend and family reunion. Much of this growth was artificially sustained by the remittances of those from abroad (108). Although many overseas migrants built homes in or around Tuba, they often live elsewhere, either abroad or in Dakar, to which they were drawn by the milder temperatures, access to potable water (the water in Tuba is too salty to drink), markets, business opportunities, and leisure activities (bars, clubs, gambling) that are not sanctioned by the Tuba clergy.

The spectacular growth of Tuba, through the labor of overseas migrants and rural-rural migration at a time when most rural areas were in decline due to decreasing agricultural yields and a lack of viable employment for young men, could be understood as the product of the purposeful activity of the Murid clergy to ensure its dominance in the latter half of the twentieth century. Not merely an agricultural town, Tuba's very existence depended on its connection to globalized economic processes. This was land that had brought persons into the market economy through cash cropping under colonial rule, land that in the early part of the twentieth century offered a reprieve from filial obligations and that, by the turn of the twenty-first century, eventually became the very means of honoring those obligations despite the declining value of its agricultural potential.

CORPORAL WEALTH: CLOTH, DRESS, AND FAMILY CELEBRATIONS

In addition to the rising visibility and debate surrounding Islam in light of the mounting power of the Murid order, increasing ties with global Islam, and the growing dissatisfaction with the West and its economic agenda, by the 1990s cloth and clothing in Senegal had become symbols around which the moral discourse of the state, Islam, and the family revolved. There were debates about the veiling of Islamist women at the University Cheikh Anta Diop (Augis 2000) and about the emerging role of high-ranking women as fashion mavens in tailor shops, a sphere that had long been associated with men and casted women (Mustafa 1998).

Additionally, criticism concerning the demise of the family, amid conditions of fiscal austerity, centered upon women (91).

By 2003, the 1972 Family Code of Senegal, which legislated many aspects of domestic life, including capping payments at family ceremonies, came under scrutiny by a new organization, the Comité Islamique pour la Réforme du Code de la Famille au Senegal (Islamic Committee for the Revision of the Family Code of Senegal). This organization was composed of both Sufis and Islamists who fought to make the Family Code compatible with Islamic law (Villalón 2004:67). Muslim leaders protested the intrusion of the state into family matters such as marriage, divorce, and inheritance. Perhaps the support of the central Murid hierarchy for reform of the Family Code also pointed to their fears that large social payments at family events could erode the disciple-shaykh relationship, which was signified by the addiya and which had already been made tenuous by the vast outward migration. To counteract this, the Murid hierarchy sought to direct the profits of its overseas trade toward the sacred development of Tuba. Their projects focused on sewage and sanitation, Qur'anic education, electrification, and, especially, home building to prevent the land in and around Tuba from reverting back to the state under the National Domain Law.

Social criticism of the Family Code often focused on women's dress in fine cloth during family ceremonies as well as their practice of bestowing locally woven and dyed cloth on kin, affines, and neighbors to create social ties. Some of the most intense social criticism surrounded what was seen as women's ostentatious dress on the occasion of naming ceremonies and marriages, perhaps in part due to the connection between dress and power (Allman 2004). Senegalese women have a long history of using dress as "a visual medium of politics," including the popularity of the *robe bloc* in the mid-twentieth century in support of Lamine Guèye's party, the Bloc Africain, and women's right to vote; the earring called the *wow ou dede* (Wolof: yes or no) as a referendum on Senegalese independence from France (Johnson 1994:49); and donning commemorative cloth in support of candidates for political office, religious figures, and economic and social initiatives (Konate 2009:229).[8] Women's dress indexes negotiations, debates, and contestations over social, economic, and political boundaries and status. Debates about the politics of dress in Senegal are also about the limits of fashion and the expenditure necessary to achieve it (Grabski 2009; Heath 1992; Mustafa 2006; Scheld 2003).

Senegalese women for the most part have eschewed the somber and austere fashions donned by many women in the Muslim world. It may appear that the display of skillful and beautiful dress that Senegalese women are known for, a practice called *sañse,*[9] belies the notion of restraint (kersa) in bodily comportment that is commensurate with gender constructs in Islam. Yet in Muslim thought and practice, the properly dressed body is the beautiful body, as opposed to the nude in Western art; it cannot be distinguished from the self (Biaya 2000). For Senegalese women, the display and distribution of cloth were not directed at demonstrating individual wealth or personal vanity, but rather made visible the strength of women's social networks (Buggenhagen 2008; Cooper 1997; Schulz 2007). It was through these social ties that women made ends meet, created enduring forms of value, and engaged in critical practices in tough financial circumstances.

Women's dress practices were dynamic and combined vibrantly colored, tailored, folded, and wrapped fabrics, blurring the distinctions between cloth and clothing, past and present (Hansen 2004). Senior women often dressed in a *grand boubou, or mbubb,* for family ceremonies. A grand boubou consists of ten meters of fabric, including a piece that is minimally tailored to drape over the body with cutouts for the head and arms, a wrapper for the lower half of the body, and a folded headscarf called a *musóor.* Underneath the wrapper of a grand boubou, women might also wear one or more two-meter pieces of locally woven strip cloth called *sër-u-rabbal.* These woven textiles are wrapped around the lower half of the body, and also used to swaddle and carry infants. They are a "social skin," to use Terry Turner's term, linking the surface of the body and forms of bodily adornment, bridging the frontier between the body and society, and between the individual and the collective (Turner 1980).

First-quality cloth boubous are made from *mbaseñ riche,* a cotton damask fabric made from a fine yarn manufactured in Germany. Damask is a kind of satin weave that pushes the threads to one side or the other of the fabric, producing a tone-on-tone texture that is somewhat shiny. Poorer quality damask is available from China, among other places. The mbaseñ riche often has a surface decoration applied using resist techniques, such as starch resist, wax resist, tie-dye, hand- and machine-stitched and -folded resist, and stamping. The wax-resist cloth is not as highly valued as the hand- and machine-stitched and -folded resist cloth (Gillow 2003:19). The finished product is called *cuub.* Though dyers once used indigo and kola to color the cloth, currently most use synthetic dyes that produce a spectrum of brilliant hues. Dakar is famous for tailoring, and Bamako is famous for dyeing. Sizing such as starch or gum arabic is also applied to the cloth to produce a papery, crisp effect (Mbow 1998:146).

Sër-u-njaggo (strip weaving). *Mathers Museum, Bloomington, Indiana*

The cloth is pressed in a process called *tapp* in which it is beaten by men called *batteurs* with a wooden club on a block of wood that is flat on top. This method impregnates the fabric with the pigment, polishes it, and enhances the shine. As it is beaten, it is folded into smaller squares so that when worn the stiff folds are visible. Often, the neckline or hem of a boubou is embellished with machine embroidery.

Contemporary sër-u-rabbal are composed of six bands of woven cotton cloth, often embellished with colorful metallic thread, which are then sewn together selvage by selvage to form a wrapper. Though yarn used to be spun by Wolof women who, as patrons, then had the right to the cloth woven by their dependents, present-day threads are industrially produced. These wrappers are often made by Manjaka weavers on a narrow horizontal loom with a double-heddle shedding mechanism (Picton and Mack 1979). These wrappers are called *sër-u-njaago* after the Wolof term for Manjaka, *njaago.* Manjaka weaving has been influenced by the *pano de obra* that were woven in the Cape Verde Islands during the era of Portuguese rule. Manjaka weavers have migrated from Guinea-Bissau to Senegal where they have found wealthier patrons. The designs are often a collaboration between the artists, their patrons, and fashion demands. Though the wrappers can be woven in many colors, at present women say that they prefer a dark or black background, which brings out the vibrant hues of the synthetic yarns such as Lurex, rayon, and polyester.

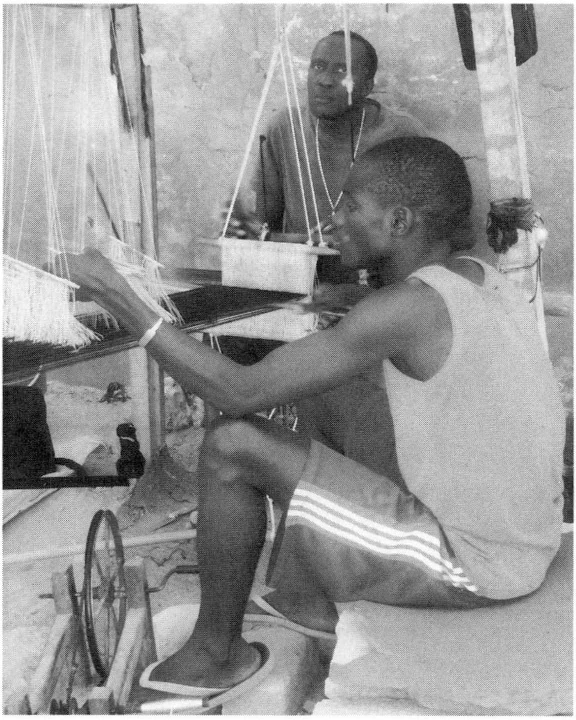

Manjaka weavers in Dakar, 2009. *Photo by Katherine Buggenhagen*

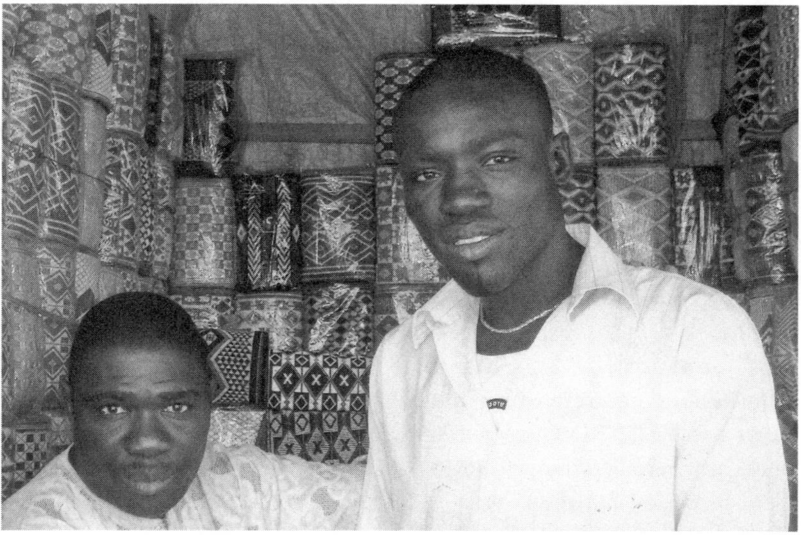

Cloth merchants in Marché HLM, Dakar, 2009. *Photo by Katherine Buggenhagen.*

Though sër-u-rabbal are used in both Wolof and Manjaka life-cycle ceremonies, their meanings and symbolic associations vary greatly. For example, the Manjaka weavers have names for and an elaborate body of spiritual knowledge underpinning the textile motifs, and they use a loom that is largely unknown to their Wolof freeborn patrons, although Wolof women often draw on textile traditions from the wider region of West Africa and farther afield. Their choice of textiles for dress and exchange reflects the ways in which the meaning of the cloth for Wolof women derives from its role in exchange and consumption (rather than its production) (Perani and Wolff 1999:14). Varieties of sër-u-rabbal were commodities in the regional trade and for a time were important forms of currency in precolonial and colonial Senegal along with guinée cloths (both locally woven and those imported from India by the French), which tied the region into the global market through their trade (Curtin 1975; Kriger 2005; Roberts 1992).

Importantly, the colors, materials, and motifs of stripweaves have changed with fashion over time, dissolving the distinction between folk dress and fashion that often predominates in discussions of non-Western dress (for comparison with South Africa, see Comaroff and Comaroff 1997). Moreover, Senegalese dress and cloth fashions belie the distinction often made between tradition and creativity (Picton 1992:43) for though the sër-u-rabbal is associated with tradition (cosaan), it is the product of artistic creativity through time. Though senior women often chose to wear the grand boubou and sër-u-rabbal to important events because of their symbolic association with women's productive and reproductive power, these were fashion-forward ensembles for which Dakar tailors remain famous. For example, surface decorations such as resist-dyed patterns have names and go in and out of style along with particular color preferences, and sër-u-rabbal have been marked by the popularity of certain motifs, colors, and yarns. Styles worn by younger women have introduced more tailoring in the top to emphasize women's waistline and bust, and they often incorporate machine-made cloth such as imported Indian silks or hand-cut voile lace fabrics (often called African voile though the fabrics are manufactured elsewhere).

Senegalese women's dress practices and their generational differences thus do not reflect a simple binary between fashion and tradition, young and old. Senegalese dress works the forces of conservation and change (Weiner 1992) that are so crucial to managing fluctuating economic conditions (Heath 1992). Where dress historians, museum curators, and art historians have focused on the clothing and textiles as their subject matter, anthropologists have focused on dress practices in the larger sociocultural context (Eicher 2000). But cloth and clothing in the context of Senegalese dress practices collapse these distinctions between cloth and dress practices, encouraging researchers to look at both the social context of dress and the materiality of cloth and clothing. In the Senegalese context, cloth and clothing offer a window onto the debate over Islam, custom, and social reproduction in contexts of fiscal volatility and of meaning, practice, and value that can only be addressed through field-based research. Cloth and clothing as material objects offer their own visual and tactile arguments to what can be gleaned from observing, talking to informants, and consulting broadcast and print media and archival sources (Allman 2004:4).

As I mentioned, men often talked about women's dress and exchange of cloth during family ceremonies as belonging to the pre-Islamic world that had been under the control of women, and as part of the system of social stratification based upon hereditary occupational orders, or castes, that the anthropologist Judith Irvine (1974) described so well, in contrast to Islam. Scholars of Islam in Senegal have often taken these male categories of custom at face value, dismissing women's gift-giving practices and objects of adornment as folk beliefs and claiming that Islam hardly touched the world of women (Cruise O'Brien 1971b; Gamble and Ames n.d.). Scholarship has relegated life-cycle rituals to the domain of the private and the profane and assumed them to be associated with pre-Islamic practices. This perspective also reflects a bias in Western thought where women's involvement in biological reproduction is often assigned a negative value (Weiner 1992:3).

When I observed that women's wealth and their circuits of ritualized exchange were under attack in public forums, I pressed my male interlocutors for an explanation for this discourse. They often responded that women's social visits, their forms of commerce, and their concomitant family ceremonies—events where women circulated cloth—were *affaire-u-jigeen* (women's business). While this phrase has often been understood to be dismissive, it became clear to me that men were not writing off the significance of women's practices; in fact, they were acknowledging their complexity, a point also made by the anthropologist Annette Weiner in relation to Trobriand exchange (1976:12).[10]

Despite a discourse of devotion to the Murid way, consisting of boasting of one's addiya to shaykhs through which one benefited from the baraka of the masters (Buggenhagen 2008; Cruise O'Brien 1975:62n8), Murid men and women kept certain wealth objects back, resisting the

pressure to give to the shaykhs. They did so by entering into a second circuit of exchange based on honor in which women gave *ndawtal* (gifts of cloth) to kith and kin during family ceremonies. Senior women bestowed new pieces of stripweave, dyed fabrics, and manufactured textiles upon women during Muslim naming ceremonies for newborns to index their honor and that of their lineage. In particular, through the circulation at life-cycle ceremonies of locally woven wrappers, which were used to swaddle newborns and to shroud the deceased, women bound the living and the dead (for a comparison with Madagascar, see Feeley Harnick 1989). As is often the case with woven textiles elsewhere in West Africa, sër-u-rabbal were handed down from mothers to daughters to create links backward and forward in time (Perani and Wolff 1999:32; Renne 1996).

Through their bestowal and receipt of cloth wealth, women were not merely creating relations of obligation based upon credit and debt, they were engaging in practices through which they made themselves known through the responses they elicited from others (Foster 1995:10). For women, exchange was not about relations between things, but rather about constructing relations between persons. They engaged in processes of social reproduction, to which naming ceremonies were central, to make visible the forms of social relationships that were vital to their definition as persons and to their social futures (cf. ibid.:12). The reproduction of social relations was not automatic; it demanded immense social labor and resources (Weiner 1992:4).

Through gifts of cloth during family ceremonies, women sought to keep lineage honor while distributing wealth objects through a strategy that is described by the anthropologist Annette Weiner (1985, 1992) as "keeping-while-giving." In addition to bestowing cloth wealth during ceremonies, women wore layers of locally woven strip-cloth wrappers and kept vast stores of heirloom-quality strip cloth, which they handed down to their daughters and nieces. By keeping some valued possessions out of circulation, women were ensuring that they themselves remained on the path of circulation. Through their hidden stores of cloth wealth, made visible through dress and bestowal at family ceremonies, women incorporated their ancestors' renown, authority, and rank into themselves; produced alternative centers of authority; and accrued religious merit. Textiles symbolized their productive and reproductive potential through their circulation and as inalienable forms of wealth due to their association with women's reproductive power, and lineage history ensured an eventual replacement that would form the basis of future wealth and lineage continuity (Weiner 1980).

It was not exclusively women who appreciated the importance of cloth wealth for creating the enduring forms of value on which social reproduction was predicated. During my fieldwork, as men spoke of their offerings to their shaykhs I came to appreciate the ways in which they discreetly drew upon their social networks to acquire cloth for wives, sisters, and mothers to be exchanged during family ceremonies. Men needed to negotiate the forms of value and wealth that were controlled by women in order to contract marriages, name their children, participate in the hajj, and die with respect, and so men distributed cloth across affinal, consanguineal, and intergenerational lines. As husbands, brothers, and fathers, men also provided livestock to be sacrificed at births, marriages, and funerals; labor, cash, cloth, and other forms of wealth for marriage payments; and clothing and cloth to pay for mundane household expenses and life-cycle events. Gifts given by men to women were often redistributed by women among kin and dependents, granting women an added measure of control over the flow of wealth and thus over persons. Grooms were expected to give prospective brides and in-laws cloth and clothing during courtship as part of a series of marriage payments that also included cash, gold, and cattle along with modern electronics, cars, and trips to Mecca. The recipients of these gifts, usually the bride's mother, redistributed them and thus constituted their status and authority, especially over the reproductive potential of their daughters, the prospective brides. Men and women were not individual agents; they achieved honor through investing in each other (Heath 1992). In distributing resources to women, men were not losing wealth; although some certainly complained that this was the case, they were, in actuality, ensuring a replacement in the future, either to themselves, through women, or to future generations (Weiner 1980).

The soft objects often circulated in relation to precious metals, coins, and other hard objects. Hard objects such as money signified submission to shaykhs, while soft objects indicated the desire to keep something back and resist the pressure to give (Weiner 1989:62). These inalienable objects were more than economic resources or affirmations of social relations; through controlling their circulation, or even by keeping them out of circulation, persons constructed their present ranks and identities in relation to others and in relation to some aspect of the past that was essential to their ongoing construction of their selves and their power over others (Weiner 1985:210).

Women's ritual practices were not relics of a pre-Islamic era, as Muslim leaders suggested. Dress and gift exchange practices were the outcomes, rather than the survivals, of processes of conversion, colonialism, capitalist accumulation, migration, wage labor, and trade. From the colonial era to the present, the forms and modalities of dress and exchange have shifted to suit the new situations of fiscal volatility that mark the region of West Africa (Guyer 2004). Nonetheless, the debates about custom and Islam were important for the way in which they brought into relief how these seemingly local practices were informed by the supralocal discourse of Islam (Bowen 1993; Soares 2000). Rather than focusing on the normative and legalistic universe of Islam, we might "treat Islam as a discursive tradition that relates to a broader scriptural tradition of Islam" (Soares 2000:281). In the debate over women's wealth, the categories of locally contextualized forms of Islam and global Islam were never fixed. The men's and women's debates over whether exchanging cloth wealth during family ceremonies was consonant with the broader scriptural tradition of Islam was itself a critical Islamic practice. In part, the dispute about women's exchange practices was also a debate about offerings to spiritual masters as the essential act of submission and as a particularly onerous obligation that was practiced primarily by disciples of the Murid tariqa. The Murid clergy cast doubt on women's practices during family ceremonies because women's control over biological and social reproduction challenged the authority of the Muslim leadership (Bop 2005; Sow 2003).

Due to changes in the nature of work, visual objects—especially cloth and its role in documenting genealogies—came to play a major role as social media in Muslim Senegal. Cloth expressed wholeness, becoming a placeholder for idealized complete families that, in reality, were sometimes only a collection of broken bonds. Cloth is an ideal medium though which to discuss the production of social futures and fortunes in contemporary Senegal, given its role as a "visual substitute for history, ancestors and the immortality of human life" (Weiner 1985); it is for this reason that it has become such a contentious subject in Senegal. The issue of visibility, unique to cloth, is also important. Not only is reciprocity as the basis for social production, for the ethnologist Marcel Mauss (1990[1950]), analyzable as a social fact *by the analyst,* but also, as Charles Piot points out for Kabre persons in Togo, it is through such ritualized moments that the nature of the social relationship is made visible *to others* as well (1999:77). In the context of an economy where many working-age men are abroad, visibility is a key unit of analysis.

Attention to the ritual and reproductive activities of women, their search for religious merit, and the efforts of the Murid hierarchy to control women's wealth and worth reveals a set of limits on the religious authority of Muslim leaders. The debate that occurred in the 1990s was about the nature of the present: the intersection of neoliberal reform, Islam, and the predicaments of social production in sobering financial times. It was a debate about Islam in Senegal, and Islam elsewhere—in history, in the global sphere, in texts, and in bodily memory and practice.

EXCHANGE AND VALUE IN GLOBAL SENEGAL

Several categories of prestations engendered endless debate during my fieldwork, including offerings to shaykhs, feasts for hajj travelers, marriage payments, and baby gifts. These larger, more complex exchanges were often mirrored in daily interactions, such as paying for another's taxi fare, exchanging bowls of food during Ramadan, and offering hospitality to visitors, especially family members returning from abroad. In addition to giving and receiving gifts of goods and cash, women in particular participated in vast volleys of borrowing. Sisters and age-mates often loaned each other clothing and accessories that in another context were also used as gifts. In one instance, when a paternal cousin of my host family demanded a gift of clothing as payment for the part she played in preparing for her uncle's hajj feast, her cousin, unable to offer a new ensemble, borrowed one from her younger sister to give to her.

Much of my fieldwork involved observing elaborate forms of hospitality with many categories of social persons. In Wolof, hospitality is often referred to as welcoming, or *teraanga,* and is intended to bestow the rights and obligations due to kin onto non-kin in order to expand one's circuit of exchange. Hospitality often consisted in the offering of tea or soda, or sugary *beignets,* fish pastries, or other snack foods to visitors, but it also included the provision of meals, especially those involving meat from animals that had been slaughtered for the occasion, and the sharing of bowls between households. Initially, I was admonished on a daily basis for not reciprocating these acts of hospitality properly, as this put my host family's honor at stake. I failed to understand at first that these exchanges of hospitality were not for me; rather, they were for those who cared for me, who wielded far more power and influence than I did. Reciprocity was part of the feasts for various events, which also bestowed on the invitee the reciprocal obligation to make a gift. Underpinning these exchanges were the various mutual aid societies in which men and women participated through religious and ritual networks, and the relationships that were forged in these contexts were also drawn upon for forms of reciprocity and loans in times of need. Finally, the most onerous forms of reciprocity, in which I could not participate due to my age and status as an unmarried woman without children but which I tracked diligently, consisted of prestations that were recorded in ledgers during family ceremonies and that were made exclusively by women at naming ceremonies.

In many instances of ritualized exchange during family ceremonies, women saw gifts not as a measure of what they had been given at that moment or in previous moments, but as a measure of how the giver valued their social relationship. Thus, as Charles Piot has argued regarding Kabre persons in Togo (1999:62–63), what is distinctive about exchange in these contexts is the emphasis on using things to construct personal relationships as the essence of gift exchange. In contrast, the political scientist and scholar of the Murid order Donal Cruise O'Brien (1975) has argued that the adherents of the Murid tariqa used their relations with shaykhs to obtain items, including agricultural materials, mutual aid, and medications; however, the ways in which people talked about their relations with religious leaders and with others belies this rationalist logic. Although people may have had a real need for certain things and this need was often expressed to various friends and family members as *dama am sokla* (I have a need), these relationships should not be characterized as utilitarian, in which elders exploit juniors (although people complained that certain expectations to gift could be oppressive). Rather, people used things to incorporate others into their social networks, and the quality of the exchange was not measured by the quantity of things exchanged but by the perceived intent of the persons involved. People often spoke of meeting someone's need as *faj*, a word used to mean both "to resolve" and "to heal." Thus it would be better to offer sodas to your in-laws when you cannot fulfill your marriage payment obligation than to avoid visiting or running into them altogether. When people talked about relationships in this context, another key word was *yaru* (respect), meaning that the exchange was marked by mutual respect. In the context of need, yaru revealed a regard for the human quality of the exchange and for the mutual promotion of dignity. I cannot think of a worse affront for many Senegalese than to strip someone of their dignity by pointing to their crass motivations.

If Senegalese Muslims, like the Kabre, focus on persons and qualities rather than on things and quantities, as Piot suggests (1999:65), they also are deeply aware of the hierarchies that are generated through exchange. Irvine's (1974) substantial body of work on Wolof caste demonstrates exactly how forms of reciprocity reinscribe forms of inequality and difference as well as mutual need and the more meaningful concepts of honor and respect.

Although I do not include here a chapter on funerary exchanges, which perhaps are less debated than other forms of gift exchange, the tensions surrounding these are stunningly told in Mariama Bâ's novel *So Long a Letter* (1981). I was reminded of this in the spring of 2005, when a close friend of my host family died at the age of forty-two from a sudden heart attack. The man who passed was an astute businessperson and a math professor at University Cheikh Anta Diop. Although his brothers and his friends in Khar Yalla were almost all international traders and lived overseas, he had chosen to marry and remain not just in Senegal, but also in the neighborhood where he grew up. He became a person of tremendous importance because he managed the financial affairs of his intimates abroad. Taking on such responsibility also entailed aiding those who remained behind by allocating money for medical bills, family ceremonies, and the like. I was told by one of the brothers in my host family that Islam requires that one's debts be reconciled upon death so that the body can rest in peace until it is resurrected on the day of judgment so, during the week following the death of this young man, people traveled long distances to acknowledge money that was owed to the deceased or money that was due to the living. However, only very large debts were acknowledged, perhaps those over 100,000 CFA francs. The brothers of the deceased repaid some persons; others, seeking baraka, forgave the deceased's debts. It is an enormous and dangerous undertaking for the person who takes on the responsibility of reconciling debts like these since, if accounts are not properly balanced, the deceased could remain in limbo indefinitely. Such an undertaking also makes visible and legible the extensive personal and financial networks of the deceased, not only through the emergence of various persons who are involved in these networks of debt, but also through the written ledgers of social and financial exchanges that one keeps for precisely this reason.

These gendered and generational projects of the here and the hereafter address a fundamental problem concerning this community, which is based in global circuits of wage labor and capital: can it reproduce itself and its forms of value? How have the material basis of social production and the ability to sustain the relations that engender wealth through social exchanges shifted in the context of structural adjustment, neoliberal reform, and the increasing surveillance of United States and European borders under the global war on terror?

I begin to answer this question in chapter 2 by analyzing shifts in social production, the constitution of households, and changing forms of value in the late nineteenth century and early twentieth, such as land, homes, and cloth. I consider the transformation of land from an inalienable possession that was held by the patrilineage in the colonial era to an alienable possession through land reform and real estate speculation in the postcolonial era. I argue that it is due, in part, to men's changing relationship to the land that their authority over processes of social production has declined since the mid-1980s. I then focus on women's changing role in the cloth production distribution system of the region in the twentieth century and how it relates to women's control of cloth in the present as a form of wealth and value. I focus on how shifts in the economy, including the emergence of peanut monoculture in the early part of the century and the role of the Murid order in this economy, affected women's control over cloth wealth. In the latter half of the century the increasing importance of an import-export trade based on moving between the official economy and its unregulated sectors also affected women's use and acquisition of cloth, especially imported and manufactured cloth.

To understand the changing relationship of men to the postcolonial state and its forms of patronage, in chapter 3 I examine the expanding Murid global networks in relation to urban migration in the postcolonial era, the reenvisioning of the state through neoliberal economic reform beginning in 1980, and the impact of twenty-first-century attempts to regulate Muslim networks globally through the United States–led war on terror. I discuss how the formation of religious associations in urban areas in Senegal and in cities abroad by both male and female disciples facilitated Murid trade as well as Murid investment in Tuba. I analyze the circulation of addiya to shaykhs to understand how Murid men and women create long-term value in the face of such economic volatility.

In chapter 4, I tell the tale of two sisters, one married several times, one not; one with a Qur'anic education, the other educated in French schools, business, and accounting; one putting her faith in Muslim diviners, the other in the market. They live in two different worlds that are marked by different ways of achieving status, and they engage in markedly different practices of Islam, one being involved in the life of the Sufi order, the other leaning toward strictly Sunni practices.

In chapter 5, I consider the case of a fraught marital alliance between an overseas Murid trader and a young woman in Senegal and the puzzle her family faced of how to return the bridewealth payments when problems arose. I analyze how generational tensions concerning ideas about love and matrimony, as well as the rights and obligations that were imposed by kin, led to the dissolution of the alliance. I also examine the discourse surrounding the inflation of bridewealth payments, the revision of the Family Code, and the attempts of Muslim leaders to regulate social payments by calling for Islamic family law. In chapters 6 and 7 I show how the movement of male traders into transnational trade networks in order to shore up a stagnant local economy and to reproduce the social and moral order has had unanticipated consequences for women's authority.

Chapter 6 tells the story of a father's hajj and the feasts that surrounded his departure for Mecca and his return one month later. Through offerings of hospitality and gifts from this holy city, Murid men and women create relations of reciprocity, extend their selves in space and time, construct their individual and collective honor in this life, and accrue religious merit that will secure their salvation in the next. Through complex modalities and contexts of exchange, families weave obligations over time to preserve their honor and circulate wealth. It is in the context of the holding of these feasts that I analyze the alterations to exchange that have been wrought by the spread of the microfinance programs that have been introduced by NGOs.

In chapter 7 I tell the story of a Muslim naming ceremony for a child who was born out of wedlock to a young woman and a Murid trader who worked overseas. I analyze the exchange of ndawtal gifts at this event in order to understand the visual and temporal dimensions of women's stores of cloth wealth—how they are hidden, circulated, and displayed on the body to create dependents, control others, and guard against loss. There is a complex politics of display, generosity, and borrowing (or replacement) of these more sensual, tactile, and visual forms of wealth, which are possessed by women. I focus on how what could be characterized as a crisis of social production—the holding of the naming ceremony before the marriage—is resolved through the symbolic means of gift giving. The circulation of commodities during the naming ceremony and talk about the imagined possibilities of gift exchange became a form of symbolic production in the face of this crisis of social production. Cloth that was circulated in this context became problematic because it went from being representative of a process of social production to being representative of processes of exchange and consumption (cf. Apter 1999:268). For women, however, this consumption was still productive of social relations. This story suggests a complicated relationship between concerns about reciprocity that are based upon the assumption of debt, and pretensions to excess that are based upon the assumption of surplus, characteristic of the neoliberal moment.

TWO

HOMES AND THEIR HISTORIES

SOKNA AND DEMBA GÉER had lived through the transition to independence in 1960, they had witnessed the decline of the peanut monoculture and the migration to the cities in search of work, and they watched their young sons go overseas to study or to earn livings as traders. The impact of these economic and political transformations on their lives could be understood from their changing relationship to their most valued possessions: land and cloth. Although land and cloth had endured as potent forms of value that conveyed individual and collective identities, men's and women's relationships to these objects had changed over the twentieth century. In postcolonial Senegal, land became an alienable commodity controlled by the state, and cloth, which at one time indexed women's production, took on added meaning as it came to signify ties to a global economy.

As declining peanut cultivation in the second half of the twentieth century eroded the base of the Senegalese economy, senior men like Demba Géer came to rely less on the land and more on remittances from their sons overseas, who were involved in networks of Sufi congregations. Senior men complained about their abandonment by the state and their loss of authority over dependents (see Perry 2005).[1] No longer able to command the work of juniors through the allocation of land and the provision of food, senior men turned to Islam in search of moral authority. They sought to achieve moral renewal through their support of Muslim shaykhs. It was not coincidental that, since the start of men's migration away from rural areas, the Murid clergy aimed to reinvest rural land that had little agricultural potential with sacred value.

Masculine virtue became increasingly linked to Muslim piety for young men as well. Many young men, who could no longer count on their fathers and other senior male kin to provide for them, sought the patronage of religious leaders. Junior men were burdened with the obligation of providing for the daily and ritual expenses of their natal and affinal households from their earnings abroad. They welcomed Muslim calls for moral austerity in dress, comportment, and, above all, ritual expenditures as a means of controlling the demands on their labor.

Although land and home building in Tuba had come to stand for one's potential for salvation, cloth, the idiom and principal means by which women created social ties and the bonds of kinship, endured as a symbol of lineage continuity and as a means of creating difference and rank. Land had once symbolized the strength of the patrilineages; cloth wealth continued to stand for the enduring relevance of matrilineal ties. Women endeavored to produce the crucial values in life through gifts of cloth even in the context of the shifting political economy over the century, from agriculture to urban and global trade. As men's lives and the fate of their families shifted over the century, women tried to secure forms of long-term value through their control of the circulation of cloth wealth.

Yet women's relationship to cloth had changed along with the shifts in agricultural production. In the late nineteenth century and early twentieth, women's identity was tied to their role in the production and circulation of cloth. Women controlled the production and circulation of cloth through their role in carding and spinning cotton into yarn. They sponsored casted weavers and descendants of former slaves, who wove for the household during the dry season and farmed during the wet season. As the cultivation of peanuts as a cash crop spread, families often abandoned crops such as millet, manioc, and cotton. As a consequence of this shift to peanut production and the introduction of industrially produced thread, many women ceased to spin their own cotton yarn.

In the latter part of the twentieth century, women's relationship to cloth production changed as Murid families shifted away from agricultural production toward trade. The introduction of industrially manufactured yarn and cloth also contributed to their changing relationship to cloth production (for similar discussions in Niger and the Ivory Coast, see Cooper 1993; Etienne 1980). As agricultural productivity declined and many left rural areas, women began to purchase yarn and cloth in the market. Cloth continued to symbolize women's productive and reproductive power, but it also linked women to local, regional, and global markets. Women continued to privilege the exchange of locally woven strip cloth, even though it was largely spun from industrially produced yarn. They also added pieces of imported manufactured cloth and cash to their gift giving.

Importantly, although they received some cloth from their husbands, women mostly purchased cloth themselves for gift exchange with funds garnered from their participation in microfinance projects. Although the state had reduced its investment in agricultural development since the implementation of neoliberal reforms in the 1980s, it had increased its investment in women's microfinance projects. Moreover, nongovernmental organizations focused increasingly on improving women's economic autonomy through sponsoring rotating savings and credit associations. As clients of local NGOs, women worked to improve their financial possibilities and to create relations of mutual obligation and aid. Through NGO microfinance programs, women were able to purchase vast quantities of cloth that they circulated in family ceremonies to create social ties.

Sokna Géer had from time to time supported weavers in her compound to produce the narrow strip-woven cotton cloth known as sër-u-rabbal for her ritual exchanges in the 1970s and 1980s. These weavers were usually Manjaka migrants from southern Senegal and Guinea-Bissau for two reasons. First, it is unclear if a strict guild of Wolof weavers persisted after the second half of the twentieth century, as they could not compete with the importation of manufactured cloth under the French (A. Diop 1981:58). Second, when women compared the weaving styles of the Wolof, Tukolor, Serer, and Manjaka, they usually said that they desired the latter, preferring the weft-faced designs of the Manjaka cloth. To produce these more intricate designs, Manjaka weavers developed a more sophisticated method. The Manjaka loom is longer and allows another weaver to operate the secondary heddles that lift the warp thread to incorporate weft floats, which results in various motifs (Dilley 1987:257). Sokna Géer's sister continued to sponsor three Manjaka weavers, paying them a small stipend and providing thread, meals, and space to weave. She then sold the cloth that her weavers created (they sewed together six bands to form a wrapper, fewer bands to form baby blankets, shoes, and purses), competing with male market traders.

Although most women purchased cloth in the market, social payments of cloth have continued to be an enduring feature of family ceremonies (Klein 1998) and remain an important means of constituting hierarchical social relations. As a gift exchanged during family ceremonies, this inalienable possession ties women to their lineages, to their ancestors, and to *sunu maam yi* (our grandparents). It represents their understanding of who they are in the present by tying them to who they were in the past.

For Sokna Géer, the exchange of cloth during family ceremonies tied her to her sisters and brothers as well as to her extended family in Mbacke Baol near Tuba. Although Demba was a devout follower of the Tijaniyya, and his family remained connected to the small Murid village near Tivouane from which he hailed, his and Sokna's children remained connected to their mother's rural relatives in the town of Mbacke. Sokna

Géer's deceased father, whose formal portrait graced the Géer family home in Khar Yalla and from whom she took her *sant* (last name), was of freeborn descent and a follower of the Murid way. Her mother was a Mbacke Mbacke, a member of the Murid elite bearing the surname of Amadou Bamba Mbacke, claiming descent from him, and hailing from the village of Mbacke, which was founded by Bamba's father. Sokna Géer's family continued to own land in Mbacke, to receive foster children from there, and to retreat there to celebrate family ceremonies and participate in religious festivals.

In Islam, which emphasizes patriarchy, one might think that matrilineal ties would be less important. For example, it is often thought that women assume the Sufi affiliations of their husbands, as they do not submit directly to shaykhs themselves (Cruise O'Brien 1971b). Moreover, because Wolof residence is patrilocal and women are considered to be *gan* (guests) in their own father's compounds, one might also think that the matrilineal ties would be less important. Sokna Géer spoke of revering both Tijani and Murid ways, rather than simply assuming the tariqa affiliation of her husband, and her children claimed membership in both congregations. Sokna often hosted the Tijani women's dahira association in the Géer home and, dressed in matching cloth with her peers and children, made the annual pilgrimage to Tivouane, the *Gamou,* in a bus that the women's group hired for the occasion. At the same time, she and her daughters honored her parents through their presence at countless family celebrations at the homes of her Murid relations, traveled regularly to the family home in Mbacke, and often attended the yearly pilgrimage, or Màggal, to Tuba. As the Géer sons formed relationships with Tijani shaykhs, they also continued to recount their elite genealogy as Mbacke Mbacke, as those who are descended from Amadou Bamba and hail from the village of Mbacke. Sokna Géer's oldest daughter, Jigeen, made her second marriage with a wealthy Murid trader, as did Sokna's youngest daughter and her foster daughter, who hailed from a Murid family in Mbacke.

The seven Géer children who had gone abroad drew on Tijani dahira networks in Italy and Sokna Géer's relations in France, in particular her Murid brother, for support. He assisted with housing, education, employment, and social payments. One reason that he did so is that when young men leave the family compound, it is usually preferable that they take up residence with their maternal uncle (Irvine 1974:245). A maternal uncle should assist his nephew with housing, work, gifts of clothing, and marriage payments (246). The mother's brother's daughter is also the preferred marriage partner. Thus, several of Sokna Géer's daughters were married to Murid traders to whom they were related on their mother's side.

CLOTH AND SOCIAL RANK AT THE TURN OF THE TWENTIETH CENTURY

The spread of cash crop agriculture between 1890 and 1914, not only on Murid communes but also broadly among small-scale farmers, had profound effects on the production and reproduction of households and social rank and on the acquisition of the forms of value that were essential to social processes, such as cloth and land. The cultivation of peanuts for export led to the wider circulation of cash in the regional economy. Earnings from cash crops satisfied new desires that men and women developed for imported commodities such as sugar, rice, and tea as well as imported cloth. More important, cash crops enabled many to escape positions of dependency. Young men acquired bridewealth, land, and livestock and were able to form new households independent of their fathers. Women purchased industrially produced thread as well as manufactured, imported, and locally woven and dyed cloth. Through the production of cash crops on Murid land, casted men and women and former slaves could also escape positions of dependency and even in some cases acquire land.

In French West Africa, women's role in cotton production, cultivation, and spinning led to their control of the circulation of cloth and their economic autonomy and political authority (Cooper 1993; Etienne 1980). Women's importance derived from their role as the provider of cloth for the family. It is difficult to know the extent to which freeborn Wolof women participated in the cultivation and spinning of cotton, if their husbands provided them with cotton for spinning, and the degree to which they in turn supplied the family with cloth and clothing. Although many households grew cotton, leading the French very early on to attempt to encourage the growing of cotton for export, present-day Senegal was never at the center of the cotton-producing region. Moreover, if cotton were grown, it was eventually replaced by peanut cultivation, which became more desirable than cotton because peanuts had a longer growing season (Johnson 1974; Roberts 1992:184).

Freeborn women's control over the circulation of cloth in colonial Senegal may have derived from their control over yarn through their spinning and their sponsorship of weavers. These weavers were often former slaves or their descendants and were household dependents who wove during the dry season when they were not working in their patron's fields in exchange for food and shelter (Searing 1988:479). Women also provided cotton yarn, either handspun or industrially produced, for village weavers to use. They were able to purchase manufactured yarn with the proceeds of their various trade activities, as sellers of cooked food and snacks, for example. With the spread of peanuts as a crop, women's access to cash increased, leading them to purchase thread for male weavers to weave into long strips that could be pieced together into wrappers and blankets. For the most part, freeborn women's economic autonomy and political authority derived from their control over the labor of these dependents—the descendants of former slaves, migrants, and casted weavers.

As the economy shifted away from local agriculture to urban and transnational trade in the latter part of the twentieth century, so too did women's relationship to cloth. Instead of sponsoring weavers in their compounds or taking yarn to village weavers, most women acquired cloth in the market. In addition to signifying women's productive and reproductive potential as controllers of the labor of dependents, cloth came to represent women's relationship to a market economy dominated by men (for a similar discussion of Niger, see Cooper 1993:52).

To begin to understand freeborn women's changing relationship to cloth and men's changing relationship to land in the late nineteenth century and early twentieth, it is important to understand the role of social rank in colonial Senegal and how that played into the importance of cloth as a social prestation. In colonial Senegal, society was divided among three endogamous groups—nobility and freeborn, casted persons, and those who had descended from slaves—despite the influence of Islam and its emphasis on equality (A. Diop 1981:27).[2] These orders were first roughly divided in terms of a binary distinction between *géer* (high rank) and *nyenyo* (low rank) (33). These ranks related in part to notions of pollution and witchcraft and to distinctions between those who performed services and asked for gifts and those who did not (Irvine 1974:118). Those of high rank included freeborn persons who were largely farmers, administrators, and titled religious leaders, and those who were at some point kin of the ruling families of the Wolof kingdoms. The quality of this kinship was reflected in the division of the freeborn into two categories: *girmi* (princes) and *dyambuur* (commoners) (Tamari 1991:224). Persons of high rank were distinguished by their control of land distribution (Tang 2007:48). Also included in this category were the *ceddo* (soldiers or police) and slaves who were connected to the crown, who largely did not have access to land.

Artisanal occupations related to the inheritance of knowledge and power; the forms of knowledge that defined each specialization were often resented by Muslim clerics who did not acknowledge these otherworldly forms of power (Dilley 2004:6). Among those categorized as nyenyo were the *wudë* (leatherworkers) and *tigg* (smiths) (whose wives were usually potters), as well as the *lawbë* (woodworkers), *gewel* (musicians, genealogists, and praise specialists, also known as griots), and *ràbb-kat* or *ràbb sër* (weavers).

Ranked below freeborn persons and artisans were the *jaam,* who bore the social stigma of being descendants of those who were slaves prior to French colonization and the banning of the slave trade (Irvine 1974:72). The legal ownership of persons was abolished by the French National Assembly in 1848, but this action merely reconfigured rather than ended entrenched local notions of social dependency. Only a third of freed slaves actually left the region and most of those who left were located largely outside of the peanut basin (Klein 1998:197). Some continued to work as *nawetaan* (seasonal laborers) and others migrated to join the Murid communes. Many former slaves had come from villages that were too distant or difficult to return to, and since they may not have known what remained of kin or had access to land to cultivate, they stayed. Others who were born into the institution of slavery continued in dependent relations with their masters since they had been too fully Wolofized to return.

The category of jaam included persons that descended from trade slaves, war captives, and domestic slaves. Domestic slaves would at some point in their service receive land and assistance with marriage payments from their patrons, while remaining dependents (Tang 2007:48). Most jaam farmed, though many also wove (Irvine 1974:66) since the production of cotton textiles was one of the most important industries in the Sudan and, although it was tied to caste, it was not restricted (Klein 1998:7). So while there persisted a specialized caste of Wolof weavers, many jaam, including war captives from other regions and ethnic groups, also wove. Wolof women carded and spun cotton fibers into thread though cotton production was not widespread in the region and was eventually replaced by peanut production (Ames 1955b:1016). With the colonial encounter came the introduction of French spinning mills, and many women turned to purchasing thread rather than spinning (Cooper 1993).

Marriages in the late nineteenth century and early twentieth took place within each occupational grouping and, in keeping with Islam, women usually did not marry below their rank (Irvine 1974:107). Each occupational specialization contained several patrilineages and these specializations defined all kinship relationships (61). Although uncommon, hypergamy between freeborn people and descendants of slaves was legitimate as long as the freeborn person was male and the slave was female and was not the first wife (93). Upon such a marriage, the slave wife did not become a freeborn person herself; she merely enjoyed the same privileges as a freeborn woman. Ames noted that such a woman would be referred to as *taara* (1956:156). Children of freeborn-slave marriages were called "child of one foot," or *doom-u-benn tàngk,* indicating that only their paternal ancestral line was freeborn. This child would be classified down, for example in circumstances involving marriages across caste, which were infrequent and disapproved of, and children of these unions did not receive their full share of inheritance (95). Amadou Bamba is often referred to as benn tàngk for being the child of an inter-caste marriage, but also for having one foot in the material world and one foot in the spiritual world.

In the late nineteenth and early twentieth centuries, the person who cleared the land controlled it. This person was called *boroom sëmiñ* (the head of the ax). More important, those who could command the collective labor of others to accomplish this difficult task administered the land. Individuals in the landowning class included chiefs, their *laman* (representatives of the chiefs), and some high-ranking freeborn farmers. Many peasant households of freeborn farmers (as opposed to craftspeople, who farmed little) acquired land from the laman, who were largely responsible for granting access to land in the chiefdoms. High-ranking freeborn farmers often paid nothing for land that they cleared themselves (by commanding the labor of others) and they acquired access to additional land through payments to the laman (Irvine 1974:189). The payment that was made in exchange for usufruct rights to the land was called *assaka,* and it consisted of either a series of small payments or a portion of the harvest (Cruise O'Brien 1971b:200). Later, claims to land and political office were also often made by placing oneself within a particular patrilineage through reciting one's paternal genealogies and asserting one's right to the holdings of the patrilineage (Irvine 1978:654). Men could make competing claims to land and political office based on rival genealogies within a lineage. Seniority could be tricky to configure since it could be argued not only on the basis of age or generation but also on the basis of the ranking of the lineage segments, which could be determined by the birth order of apical ancestors (though it is often not apparent which agnates belong in a particular segment) (ibid.).

In the households of small-scale farmers, which consisted of small patrilineal units not more than three or four generations deep (Irvine 1974:234), land was divided by the senior male household head, known as *boroom kër ga* (head of the house) or *boroom njël* (one who provides food), who determined the usufruct rights among his dependents (Perry 2005:211; Searing 2002:204). The household head managed the collective cultivation of the family's land and allocated individual parcels for cash crops to sons and to wives, who then allocated parcels to daughters.

The household head achieved honor and respect through his provision of food to dependents. This form of reciprocity was a key component in the creation of difference between those who fed and those who ate and the meaning attached to this. Value was produced in Wolof society through the provision of food, either to dependents or to strangers as hospitality (for a similar discussion in Papua New Guinea, see Munn 1992). Investing in others through the provision of food expanded one's person beyond the physical self in space and time. One's reputation and acquisition of religious merit in Islam depended on the ability to provide food for others.

To speak of women as dependents, as those who ate, is not to deny the forms of reciprocity that inhered between women and men and the ways in which male status depended on contributions by women. To begin, women did not "eat" the products of male labor. Though women received food from men in the form of grains (especially millet), women contributed to the arduous labor of planting, weeding, and processing produce, including winnowing and pounding millet, and separating the peanut shells from the plants. More important, they played a vital part in the distribution of food within the household by cooking food for others and by adding their own spice crops, such as garlic and peppers, to sauces. They created social ties among households by bestowing cooked food on strangers and distant kin through hospitality during feasts for Muslim holidays and family ceremonies. Women also farmed their own plots, in part for the economic autonomy it afforded them. They grew crops that could be marketed, such as spices and later peanuts, the proceeds of which would be transformed into objects for personal adornment (Ames 1955a:396). The household head also contributed to the home and its furnishings, as well as to women's objects of adornment. In the event of a divorce, these objects would be considered the wife's property (Camara 2007:796; Diop 1985:236). Women also had a certain measure of economic independence under Islam insofar as a daughter could expect to inherit from her father, although it would be only half of what a brother inherited and never land (Creevey 1991:363).

Through spinning cotton into thread and, later, purchasing it in the market, women likely performed the essential role of providing clothing for the family. Moreover, cloth was an essential gift that created ties among families. In colonial Senegal, cloth was important to women because through its display and exchange, they established their social rank and that of their lineage in relation to others. The lineage (either patrilineal or matrilineal) included all those who traced their descent back to a common ancestor (usually a male ancestor even when traced through the female line). Often the members of this lineage had a common surname, or *sant.* Despite the influence of Islam, which emphasized patriarchy and equality before God, matrilineal descent relations determined the social rank—as freeborn, casted, or slave—of offspring. Wolof families recognized double, or bilineal, descent (Diop 1985:15)[3] and traced genealogies through both fathers and mothers. Blood relations determined not only one's social rank but also one's social and moral qualities (Diop 1985; Irvine 1974). For example, the maximal patrilineage, called *askan,* and the patrisegment, called *genyo* (belt), transmitted the *yax* (bones), *siddit* (nerves), and *fit* (courage) (Diop 1985:17, 19–20; Irvine 1974:16–17, 19–20). The uterine lineage, or maximal matrilineage, called *xeet,* and the matrisegment, called *meen* (mother's milk), passed *derat* (blood), *soox* (flesh), *jikko* (the moral qualities of character), and *xel* (intelligence) to offspring (Irvine 1978:653). The capacity for *ndëmm* (witchcraft) and grave illnesses, such as leprosy, were also thought to pass through the maternal blood line (Diop 1985:16, 19).

In colonial Senegal, matrilineal ties were central to the recitation of genealogies. The matrilineage played a more important role with respect to hereditary occupational orders and the inheritance of *ngarmi* (noble status) (Diop 1985:21). Additionally, women were mentioned in genealogies because patrilineal segments were organized by the rank of the mothers and used to link the family to significant historical figures of other patrilineages, and because "matrilateral and affinal relationships connect a person to important living members of other lineages with whom he may wish to establish patron-client ties" (Irvine 1978:655). Through the recitation of genealogies, one could attract potential political and economic dependents and command the right to claim the labor and goods of others (654).

Social rank was ascriptive since it was determined by birth (though in practice genealogies could be manipulated). It was also ongoing since it was determined through everyday interactions (Irvine 1974:197). Thus social rank could be thought of as relational rather than absolute. Rights and duties, even one's comportment, operated in contexts involving dyads of high and low. Freeborn women expressed their social rank by displaying qualities such as courage, dignity, politeness, and humaneness (63), as well as honor, generosity, and hospitality (A. Diop 1981:61). People who had honor displayed self-control and restraint in temper, speech, and bodily comportment; showed *yaru* (respect) for themselves and others; and had a sense of *ruus* (shame). In a political sense, those in positions of authority over others were expected to have honor (123). Thus, to be freeborn was really to be recognized as such based upon one's comportment and treatment of others. This was especially the case with respect to wealth. The freeborn were generally expected to be wealthy. They were also expected to be generous in redistributing their resources (184). Wealth was closely tied to Wolof normative ideas about honor and birth, since one with a high birth would demonstrate the qualities of honor, including generosity. Because honor involved self-restraint, it was seen as essential to the freeborn person's ability to accumulate wealth and attract dependents (183). Importantly in the context of colonial Senegal, wealth consisted of the control of labor and not land tenure (187).

Freeborn women's capacity to bestow cloth was related to their ability to command the labor of dependents, such as weavers and former slaves, who produced the cloth. Although changes in cloth production and distribution in the late nineteenth century and early twentieth affected the symbolic capital that women derived from cloth, there was not a simple transformation of cloth from an inalienable possession to a commodity (for a similar discussion of cloth in Niger, see Cooper 1993).

First, cloth had moved in and out of commodity relations and served as a currency since the seventeenth century (Ames 1955b). Locally woven strip cloth, a form of cloth money, emerged in tandem with more intensive trade with European *commerçants* on the coast, where it was used as a medium of exchange, and by the seventeenth century Senegambia was already at the core of a cloth currency area (ibid.:1019; Curtin 1975:237; Johnson 1974). By the nineteenth century, cloth was widely used in this region in both ceremonial and economic exchange; it was a form of value and a unit of account (Ames 1955b:1016; Roberts 1992). Woven strip cloth was a scarce currency because it was used so prolifically in ceremonial exchanges and social payments: cloth was used between affines in marriage exchanges; it was necessary to pay the circumciser with cloth; and one gave cloth to cross-cousins at naming ceremonies and marriages as well as to members of hereditary occupational castes who contributed their labor to these events (Ames 1955b:1017–1018). Wealth at this time, therefore, consisted of cloth, livestock, grain, and slaves (Ames

1953:10); however, "the degree to which cloth was valued by the Wolof, and entered into their concepts of wealth, is indicated by the fact that the word for bridewealth, *jut,* which was stated and fulfilled in cloth, also meant 'wealth' of all kinds" (Ames 1955b:1017).

Various kinds of fabrics circulated in the region from trade with Europeans as well as from the trans-Saharan trade. Cloth from the trans-Saharan trade came to serve as a marker of social distinction since Muslim dress was associated with long-distance ties to Arab countries and to global Islam (Cooper 1993:60). Guinée cloth imported by France from its Indian colony of Pondicherry was highly desired until the mid-twentieth century because of the quality and scent of the blue dye (Kriger 2005:107; Roberts 1992). It competed in the region with locally woven indigo-dyed cloth and replaced locally woven indigo cloth in the cloth currency zone of the Senegal River (Roberts 1992:598).

Cloth, then, has been valued both as a form of personal adornment and as a multipurpose currency, despite its unwieldy form. Often, the value of objects such as cloth comes from their uniqueness and thus one might expect that objects of adornment would be unsuitable for general-purpose exchange (Graeber 1996; Munn 1992). Yet objects such as beads, precious metals, and cloth became forms of currency because they were intrinsically neither commodity nor gift, alienable or inalienable: "these terms are never fixed . . . they are always political" (Graeber 1996:12).

Second, the ways in which cloth moved in and out of commodity status related to the spread of peanut monoculture as a cash crop under French rule. One consequence of peanut monoculture was that cotton production in the Sahel region was altered, and both men and women came to purchase imported thread and, sometimes, specialty cloth of other regions or imported from abroad, which was more highly valued by some, with the proceeds from their peanut crops (Cooper 1993:55). Locally woven strip cloth was still highly valued by Wolof women for ceremonial exchange and dress, and this cloth could be purchased in the market as well. Where women had once controlled the distribution of cloth through their role as patrons, they now bought cloth or relied on brothers, sons, and husbands to buy cloth for them in the market to distribute as gifts among female kin, affines, and associates. Thus, women were thrust into acquiring cloth to distribute among their social networks through the cash economy and came to rely upon men to provide them with cloth for social exchange.

There were additional changes in the social division of labor as well. With the emergence of the Murid way, many dependents who wove left to answer the call of the shaykh, for which they were often rewarded with access to land. Many other weavers joined the ranks of the griots and butchers. This may provide an additional explanation for women's reliance on cloth bought in the market for social exchange.

Although cloth became a commodity to be acquired in the market, it still had enormous symbolic power as an inalienable possession. Occasions for the exchange of cloth, including baby-naming ceremonies, funerals, and marriage negotiations, were also opportunities for the freeborn to have griots recite their genealogy, which also assured the social and moral qualities of their offspring (Irvine 1978:653). These genealogies and their retelling were reflections of social and political relations in the present as much as they were stories about one's past (Bohannan 1959; Evans-Pritchard 1940). Persons who were reticent to recount their genealogies were scrutinized as possibly occupying low ranks and were suspected of being inclined toward witchcraft and susceptible to illnesses, all of which were held to be inherited qualities (Irvine 1978:653). To refuse or to be unable to bestow cloth during family ceremonies was therefore considered suspect.

LAND, SOCIAL RANK, AND ISLAM

Access to land, cash, and cloth changed through the spread of peanut cultivation, spurred in part by Murid efforts. These changes created tensions in the division of labor between young and old, male and female. Young men both sought to display the qualities of obedience and mutual aid toward their elders by plowing their fathers' fields and sought to achieve economic independence by cultivating their own fields, especially with the spread of cash crops. Sons and nawetaans cleared the land, planted, weeded, and harvested the crops (Klein 1998:69; Searing 2002:205), occupying the dependent position of a hired laborer, called a *surga* (Perry 2005:211). Because they did not have access to land in their own right, young men and seasonal laborers were not ordinarily in positions to contract marriages (Copans et al. 1972). Young men could only break out of the position of surga after years of building up good will through labor and then receiving land from the male elder and assistance with bridewealth payments from their mother's brother, or through migration.

Although access to land and political office was largely based on genealogical claims, status was not merely ascribed. Status could also be achieved if a young man distinguished himself by acquiring material wealth (Berry 1989:43) through migration or through warfare (Hanson 1994). A young man might also be able to earn more by working as a seasonal agricultural laborer for other households than if he stayed at home. With the spread of French colonial rule he could also trade local and imported goods or engage in wage labor. Seasonal laborers were provided with food by the family head and a plot of land to work themselves when they were not working the family plot (Klein 1998:200).

By this time, Wolof bridewealth exchanges were rapidly monetizing, although valued possessions such as cloth, slave labor (though officially illegal), gold, and livestock were still enormously important forms of exchange and could often be acquired with cash earned from peanuts

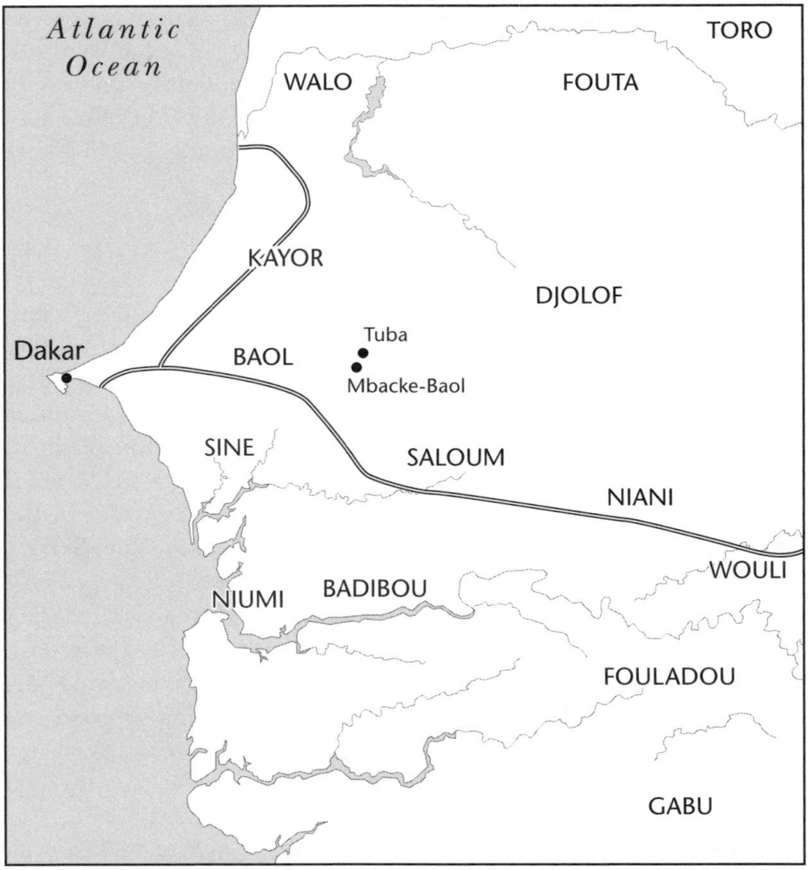

The colonial railroad; the peanut-producing regions of Kayor, Baol, and Saloum; and the Murid towns of Tuba and Mbacke Baol

if they were not forthcoming from kin. Through seasonal labor migration, young men could earn the means needed for bridewealth and subsequently marry, after which they would eventually be given their own parcel of land to work by their fathers, although they would still occupy inferior positions to them. Though their fathers could not command the labor of their daughters-in-law, these sons would be known by the diminutive *boroom kër gu ndaw* (the little household head) (Searing 2002:207). Moreover, while the oldest son of the first wife would inherit control over the family land, with his oldest sons from his first wife following him, junior members were left to seek out land on their own (Cruise O'Brien 1975:71). Nawetaans were former slaves who had escaped, bought their freedom, or been freed, or they were young unmarried men from various ethnic groups in the region, and they worked the land of others to acquire land of their own. In many cases they left their patrilineage as a result of inner feuds, which were often resolved by separating quarreling kin. Many also left because their fathers could not provide the means to contract marriages so their departure served as a way for their destitute lineages to save face.

Young male peasants were eager to answer the call of the shaykh to migrate to Murid communes in eastern Baol. They sought to escape their fathers' authority, heavy kinship obligations, or harsh economic conditions.[4] Although fathers relied on their sons' labor to cultivate fields, they would release their sons from their authority to allow them to cultivate Islam in new lands, a spiritually sanctioned calling, and hire migrant labor in their place (Copans et al. 1972; Rocheteau 1975). New adepts also sought to evade *corvée* (forced labor), the impressments into the army (especially during World War I) that accompanied colonial rule, and the head tax (Babou 2007a:105; Irvine 1974:9).

Freeborn young men in particular were attracted to Murid areas because being a disciple was preferable to being a surga (Searing 2002:249). Migrants articulated their movement in the Muslim idiom of *hijra,* referencing the flight of the Prophet Muhammad to Medina to escape oppression and to practice Islam more freely (Babou 2007a:168). Likewise, Murid migrants sought to escape the domination of the French and employed the term to describe a religiously sanctioned migration (ibid.). Aspiring devotees thought of themselves and their work differently on the Murid communes, where their labor was part of a sanctified calling to spread the Murid mission. In exchange for their labor, adepts hoped to receive religious merit, the accrual of which would secure their places in heaven, and to benefit from the grace of religious guides (Cruise

O'Brien 1971b:174). The Murid order also provided the promise of security, not merely from the French, but from the mundane mishaps that might befall a farmer in the Sahel, which was plagued by illness, disease, locusts, and poor weather (Pélissier 1966:35, cited in Boone 2003:54n15). For these reasons, farmers often turned to Murid shaykhs, and stories abound of the capacity of the shaykhs to store grain that would be distributed to disciples in times of poor yields.

Whereas peasant families paid a sum to the laman to work the land, on Murid communes disciples earned the right to work by providing religious offerings to their shaykhs, rendering the land somewhat free (Cruise O'Brien 1971b:200). New converts resided on land that Murids had cleared (often driving away the Fulbe pastoralists who had used it for grazing) or had acquired through marriage between shaykhs and local families who had the right to distribute land (199). Disciples communally cultivated land, and their collective work groups were known as *daara* (from the Arabic *daar,* meaning house). These early daara groups, which were formed before 1912, were only open to men and mainly cultivated millet for subsistence though they eventually turned to peanuts (180). Collective labor was often necessary to clear and plant fields and to provide community members with food and water. The daara system was based on slash-and-burn cultivation, which maximized peanut production but, over time, had devastating effects on the productivity of the land (Galvan 2004:67).

Murid followers cultivated their shaykhs' fields in the rainy season and when, during the dry season, the area became uninhabitable due to lack of water, they returned home, worked in the markets, or sought alms (Cruise O'Brien 1975:68). After eight to ten years of service, each adept received his own plot, and eventually daara came to form the core of some Murid villages; wells were sunk and the systems of land tenure resembled those of the Wolof villages from which the settlers came. The one significant difference was that disciples devoted a portion of their labor to the fields of the shaykhs (ibid.:71; Klein 1998:201). A lucky disciple might also receive the means for bridewealth to fund an arranged marriage (Cruise O'Brien 1971b:174). Thus women came to join the order as the daughters of titled religious families or as the wives of new converts. As the community continued to grow, new communes were established in more distant areas. The *dewrigne* (representatives of the shaykh) organized the farming, with one day a week being reserved for cultivating the shaykh's fields.

Not only did cash cropping increase the base of the peasant economy but, despite the inflation and monetization of bridewealth payments, it enabled men to marry at a younger age, and also led to migration and the establishment of more rural communes (Berry 1989:43; Searing 2002:xxxii). In fact, since it was extremely appealing for younger brothers and sons of second wives to migrate seasonally to acquire land, the power of lineage and of the laman was somewhat reduced over time by the formation of household farms (Cruise O'Brien 1971a:266). By the end of World War I, large villages had been broken up by the increased mobility of former slaves, who no longer feared raiding since slavery had been outlawed a century earlier. Large households were reduced as slaves were conscripted into the French army and migrated to newly available lands under the auspices of the Murid order and by the departure of junior kin, who earned bridewealth through the colonial urban economy or cash cropping. These events led to the erosion of the power of the "village chiefs, masters, [and] elders over the mass of dependents" (Klein 1998:219).

Although large households were broken up by the departure of young men and former slaves and many smaller household units emerged, during this period cash cropping did not significantly alter hierarchies of gender and generation within these households (Searing 2002:223). Senior men continued to farm, with significant labor inputs by wives and dependents, and women continued to grow gardens, spice, and even cash crops for themselves (with their daughters' assistance). The money garnered in the local market was used to fund their ritual expenses, such as cloth and clothing, and to augment food provided by men.[5] Daughters often received some cash from their mothers for their labor but, for the most part, they were expected to bring resources into the family through bridewealth (ibid.:205, 207). Persons continued to invest in marriage, seniority, and other forms of social status but, more important, new categories of persons were now able to participate in status-seeking activities, such as acquiring land, offices, and valuable possessions (Berry 1989:43).

In time, however, cash crop production had negative consequences for female farming when the French and later the postcolonial Senegalese state invested in new technologies that were directed at augmenting male agricultural production, for example, by providing inputs such as seeds, animal-drawn plows, fertilizer, or credit to the male head of household who, it was presumed, would distribute them among the family members. Thus women did not have immediate control or authority over the new productive tools nor were they taught the new methods of production (Callaway and Creevey 1994:25). The commercialization of agriculture also eventually diminished the large lineages, which were replaced with smaller consumption units (Cruise O'Brien 1971a:266).

Many of the new Murid adepts were young male freeborn peasants. Many also were former slaves (including men, women, and children) or members of hereditary occupational orders, in particular warriors (Klein 1998:202). These lower-status members of society did not have access to land in their own right and were drawn to Islam's message of equality. Islam provides some opportunities for manumission; the Qur'an recommends this of converts as a pious act, but it is by no means required (ibid.:12). Doctrinally, the Sufi orders do not recognize hereditary occupational orders, their forms of inequality, or their relations of knowledge and power and this, in part, explains the appeal of the Murid order to early converts (Cochrane 2009; Klein 1998:229). Furthermore, there is no formal religious superstructure in Islam that supports such distinctions since Islamic law deems that all Muslims are equal (A. Diop 1981:98; Irvine 1974:116). The Qur'an stipulates that slaves ought to be freed upon conversion to Islam, and the legal provisions for doing so include buying one's own freedom or the renouncement of the relationship by the master (Klein 1998:12).

Many former slaves came from the peanut zones of Kayor and Baol and from areas where Islam was not yet strong; "most Tijani strongholds held fast to the Tijaniyya, but their poorly educated slaves often found Amadou Bamba's version of Islam more attractive" (Klein 1998:202). Donal Cruise O'Brien points out that "slaves and castes shared a common predicament in the marginality or non-existence of their rights to land in the traditional zones of Wolof agricultural settlement. . . . Land in these areas was already overcrowded by the late nineteenth century, especially so in the region of Kayor" (1975:64–65). In Wolof society, land was the domain of the freeborn, including the farmers and the aristocracy. Those of slave origin, a category that included many young men, their wives, and unmarried girls (Cruise O'Brien 1971b:58; Klein 1998:198–99),[6] were attracted to the Murid communes because they could in effect blend in as seasonal agricultural workers.[7]

Like former slaves, warriors were also attracted to the Murid communes by the promise of land. Both social groups were affected by the social turmoil that marked the transition from an economy that had been driven by trade (especially the transatlantic slave trade), to an economy that was driven by an export cash crop, such as peanuts, and by the fall of the Wolof monarchies in the context of the encroaching French colonial presence and Muslim reform movements (Copans 1980:226).

Amadou Bamba and his successor, Mamadou Mustapha, incorporated both former slaves and warriors into systems of social and agricultural production, offering them land, security from the upheavals of the French presence, and the message of equality before God (Babou 2007a:99). While Sufism operated as a mode of resistance to colonial rule, it also operated as a mode of resistance to the system of social stratification based on birth (Babou 2007a; Searing 2002). For this reason, Bamba garnered the anger of Wolof chiefs, who eventually collaborated with the French to have him exiled (Babou 2007a:118). At the same time, the acquisition of land did not alter the low ranking of former slaves and warriors, since status in relation to hereditary occupational orders was recognized in relation to control of labor, not landownership (Irvine 1974:187).

Initially, leadership roles in the Murid community were not limited by birth (Behrman 1968:71). There was some flexibility in the social rank of the early Murid shaykhs, where honor seemed to outweigh birth. Some shaykhs of the Murid way were from Bamba's family and some came from the lower-ranking groups, although most were freeborn (Babou 2007a:118; Irvine 1974:450). However, the possibility for non-relatives and those of low status to become part of the religious elite soon ended when the shaykhs began to arrange their marriages with the royal lineages and thus to identify themselves with the nobility (Cruise O'Brien 1971b:35; A. Diop 1981:294; Irvine 1974:451–52). Thus, while in principle Murid Islam attracted members of the artisanal caste and those of slave origin through its promise of land and rhetoric of equality before God, in practice social distinctions and relations of dependence were perpetuated since those of low social status were prohibited from holding religious office and clerics continued to marry members of freeborn and noble families (Dilley 2004:200–201).

The idioms of rank and of patron-client relations continued to dominate relations between shaykhs and their followers. As was the case with patrons in general in Wolof society, shaykhs provided disciples with agricultural inputs, food in lean times, housing, cloth, and clothing as well as assistance with marriage payments (Irvine 1974:454). In some ways, the disciple-shaykh relationship was not unlike the nephew–maternal uncle or nyenyo-freeborn relationship (258). For example, in each of these relationships, the person of lesser status lived with or near the person of higher status but did not fully participate as a member of the property-holding group, received economic aid but did not inherit, and was not responsible for the perpetuation of the property-holding group. In return for their labor, dependents received land to work; gifts of cloth, food, and money during feasts and family celebrations; housing; and help with marital payments (ibid.). By the 1960s, Murid followers in the peanut basin stressed the degree to which they overcame social barriers based on caste and promulgated forms of social equality (Copans et al. 1972, quoted in Klein 1998:202); however, "within the Mourides, restrictions on marriage between géer, jam and nyenyo still prevail, and some ritual obligations persist, including symbolic payments to the master" (Klein 1998:202). These orders do not have access to land within the collective work groups organized by Murid shaykhs and their *dewrigne.*

In time, towns and villages in Murid regions began to show signs of modernity—square thatched and cement homes were laid out on a grid aligned with Mecca, and there were central mosques, wide roads, and schools (Babou 2005:405; Searing 2002:261). The villages were organized around the *penc* (public square) with the shaykh's compound and the Qur'anic school on the west side and the mosque on the east (Babou 2005:421). Adherence to the straight path created a preference for straight lines and square dwellings in the built environment, related to the centrality of the square in Islamic mysticism, which was often inscribed with numerological signification (423). Murids invested land that the French had attempted to alienate with sacred meanings by giving places Muslim and Murid names, turning the *daar al kufr* (the house of unbelief) into the *daar al Islam* (the house of Islam) (407). As Mamadou Diouf argues, "rather than adopting the technology or operational procedures of the West, Murids made a conscious effort to incorporate their unique temporality and rationality into world time by using their own vocabulary, grammar, and worldview to understand the world and operate within it" (2000:685).

By the 1930s, the French had allocated a vast territory in eastern Saloum and Tambacounda to the Murid clergy who were by that time already well established in the more densely populated Kayor and Baol (Cruise O'Brien 1971b:65–66). The shaykhs continued to grant parcels of land to their disciples in the new regions. With the help of the Murid way, French colonialists succeeded in dominating the region with the aim of establishing a peanut monoculture to satisfy the French demand for vegetable oils for light industrial applications and cosmetic products. The export of peanuts as a cash crop further tied Senegal into global processes of production and exchange, while it also produced new desires for imported commodities and manufactured goods and the need for cash to pay taxes to the colonial regime (Searing 2002:202). As cash crop agriculture reduced subsistence agriculture, people began to depend more upon goods bought in the market for the maintenance of the household and the ritual cycle. As railroad lines were extended, women began to trade along them, buying peanuts and selling imported commodities such as sugar, tea, and manufactured cloth (Cruise O'Brien 1975:47). Thus, in addition to their success in cultivating peanuts, Murids also succeeded in distributing manufactured goods in the rural regions: "they carved out, in a contradictory way, a space for themselves within the colonial system and its economy" (Diouf 2000:684).

In the postcolonial era, the Murid shaykhs became some of the largest landholders in the peanut-producing areas (Boone 1992:106). Despite colonial attempts to render land alienable, much of the land in Tuba and the surrounding agricultural regions effectively belonged to the families that cultivated it, and land was passed down from father to son (Cruise O'Brien 1971b:201). When the National Domain Law of 1964 was implemented to free peasant farmers from the burdensome payments to the laman, the Murid right of eminent domain began to be questioned, though the law changed little in and around Tuba. Since the shaykhs continued to distribute parcels of land to their disciples, who in effect over time became the land's "owners," shaykhs were constantly in need of new land to bolster their spiritual standing (212). Over the years, the postcolonial state continued to declassify forestland for Murid cultivation and Murid shaykhs continued to offer the promise of land to their devotees. In this way, the Murid shaykhs countered the commoditization of everyday lives and the alienability of land with a sanctified way of being in the world, with Tuba at its center.

THREE

THE PROMISE OF PARADISE

VISUALIZING MURID CIRCUITS

"Do you want me to plug this in? Do you want me to plug this circuit into God?" These are words that are often spoken on the radio in Senegal by a male shaykh. The "circuit" of which he speaks is the ambit of spiritual power by which baraka (blessings) radiate outward from God to those who have submitted to him through homage to Sufi shaykhs.[1] But he might as well be talking of the circuits of cash that Murid followers remit as addiya (offerings) to their shaykhs from their earnings in the Murid diaspora in Europe, North America, the Middle East, and Asia. Shaykhs' redistribution of these offerings is displayed in the videocassettes and DVDs that are produced annually to commemorate the yearly Màggal (pilgrimage) of Murid adherents to their sacred city of Tuba in the desert interior of the country. The images that circulated in the late 1990s and into the twenty-first century often exhibited the proceeds of the money that had been sent to Tuba, including several hundred head of cattle; bowls overflowing with food for pilgrims and dignitaries; the many forms of public and private transportation that brought close to 3 million disciples to the region annually; and the development of a vast infrastructure of electric service and sewage canals. These images circulated to disciples around the world who were unable to journey in person to Tuba, the center of globalized networks in which they sought fortunes no longer available due to Senegal's barren ecology and faltering economy.

Although the use of radio, the internet, cell phones, and visual media is common in religious circuits across West Africa, especially in light of the liberalization of formerly state-run media in many places (Gueye 2003; Schulz 2007; Soares 2007), it has become particularly crucial in Senegal as an increasing number of potential disciples reside abroad. The Murids also broadcast their annual pilgrimage to the sacred city of Tuba over the local television station, Radio et Television du Senegal (RTS), and unofficial copies of these productions are available in the market.

In the 1990s, the RTS productions often opened with scenes of thousands of aspirants crowding into Tuba's main streets, which radiate out from the grand mosque at the center of the town. Most of the videos included images of the rural roads jammed with buses, *car rapide* minivans, and taxis usually used for urban transport. As far as the eye could see, there would be *ndiaga ndiaye* minibuses intended for urban-rural commutes, the air-conditioned buses of the late Cheikh Mortalla Mbacke, and double-axle trucks with their trailers spilling over with disciples. The RTS productions frequently captured iconic nationalist images of the baobab tree juxtaposed with a train headed for Tuba, its boxcars overflowing with Murid adherents from the rural agricultural communes surrounding Tuba. Voiceovers often explained that these disciples came from all over Senegal—indeed, from all over the world—and that they were returning to Tuba to thank their *wali* (holy person), Amadou Bamba, the founding figure of the Murid way.

The RTS cameras would then take viewers into the mosque to witness the work of Seriñ Saliou Mbacke, the late *khalifa général* (successor or caliph) of the Murids. The most symbolic of his numerous public works projects in Tuba was the gold leaf that he added to the mausoleum of Amadou Bamba along with a crystal chandelier. Other images included disciples tossing coins, banknotes, and kola nuts over the brass railing that separated them from Bamba's tomb as they prayed for good health, employment, fertility, and the like. Between these scenes, the productions featured accomplished *rabb* (religious griots) whose wailing of Murid litanies established a historical genealogy for this media event. Between shots of political and military dignitaries from African and Middle Eastern countries and France, the viewer was instructed of the benefits that would accrue to those who follow the way of the Murid shaykhs.

To be "plugged in" to Sufi circuits was to be part of a recognized way of achieving divine union, and to be "connected" was to receive the esoteric *wird* (litanies) that would bring one closer to God. For the millions of Murid men and women at the turn of the twenty-first century, to be plugged in offered not just the promise of eternal prosperity, but also access to the forms of trade and production through which that prosperity would be crafted in the present. The high circulation of signs of wealth and well-being, including cloth, homes, cars, mosques, clinics, and schools, was remarkable in the context of a declining postcolonial state following two decades of structural adjustment programs, devaluation of the currency, failed privatization schemes of state-managed transportation and communications industries, the decline in peanut production in the 1970s on which Senegal's export-based economy depended, and the closing of the few local manufacturing plants, most notably textile plants.[2]

At the close of the 1990s, Dakar was in flux. Murid traders who had been based overseas returned home to participate in the emergent affluence of the capital city, spurred by investments of Chinese, Indian, and Gulf states in Senegal's infrastructure and natural resources extraction, which focused upon phosphates and iron ore. Grandiose homes, hotels, and casinos were under construction, walling off and privatizing previously public beachfronts. These new structures offered their residents and patrons new conveniences, including fast food restaurants featuring burgers and fried chicken and takeout markets attached to gas stations for car owners who sought imported frozen chicken parts, condiments, or French fries. Behind the tables of trade wares that congested every sidewalk, intersection, and road of the capital, chocolate boutiques and nightclubs emerged for tastes that had been cultivated overseas. Yet many Dakaroise were relegated to viewing these forms of wealth only on foot while they hawked wares, shined shoes, begged for alms, and pondered how inexplicable and unreachable the new affluence of Dakar had become. It was these forms of wealth, rather than rising poverty and fiscal austerity, that drove so many young men and a few women to endure a transatlantic voyage in wooden fishing vessels to the Canary Islands to participate in Barcelona's burgeoning construction industry between 2006 and 2008.

Against the backdrop of a history of value extraction which has shifted from peanut production to transnational trade in consumer goods such as cosmetics, cloth, and electronics, the Murids have restructured both domestic and productive processes and offered adherents new forms of community and prosperity. Whether through local and overseas trade, employment in the rural agricultural communes, or participation in Hizbut Tarqiyya (the university's dahira association), answering the call of the shaykh has continued to provide young Senegalese men and women with a morally sanctioned interstitial space between youth and adulthood. The Murid way resonates with a growing consensus shared by a generation of youth that they have been disconnected from productive activities in Senegal. In the late 1990s, a university degree could no longer guarantee employment in the public or business sector, marriages were delayed as it became more difficult to accumulate the means to constitute them, and elders no longer were able to provide financial assistance to juniors. Through the affective, intellectual, spiritual, and commercial community of the Murid way, many young Senegalese made a world for themselves in a time and a place where the benefits of wealth seemed beyond their reach.

The financial institutions and practices that Murids have devised, including rotating credit unions, principles of Islamic finance, and the logic of reciprocity, are not just traditional financial institutions or indigenous modes of financial management that can be understood outside of modern capitalism. Murids have made "marginal gains" (Guyer 2004) by working across different economies; for example, they often work both in the unregulated and in the regulated sectors of the global economy. They also participate in other kinds of financial institutions beyond the formal banking sector, but to understand them, we need to see how they operate in relation to each other. Murids employ a variety of money management strategies to create long-term value in the face of volatility and turbulence. Murid economic practices have been forged over the *longue durée* to cope with conditions of volatility.

Murid faithful circulate capital, create productive possibilities, mediate accumulation, and invest in forms of inheritable value such as cloth, homes, and land that endure under volatile conditions and ensure the future of the community. They do so largely by moving goods and creating value at the intersection of the so-called formal and informal economies and by investing in social relations that are generated in the context of the Sufi tariqa and rituals of reproduction. How are these marginal gains garnered through unequal relations and often turbulent times and invested in enduring forms of value that may offer the possibility of taking actors beyond the sort of short-term and make-do scenarios that are often emphasized in studies on African crises?

To answer this question, one must look at the multilayered connections between prophets and profits that underpin Murid global circuits of wage labor and capital, focusing on two particular moments of this circulation through which cash offerings constitute new social relations and possibilities. The first is the circuit of baraka into which disciples enter through their relations with shaykhs; these blessings are at once spiritual and material, since through them disciples gain access not merely to eternal prosperity but also to worldly wealth. The second is the circuit of sacred development by which shaykhs convert their disciples' cash offerings into the material forms of the spiritual metropolis of Tuba, a feat of architectural and economic development that aims to realize the vision of the order's founding saint, which came to him during his exile under French colonial rule. Through these financial practices and their moral dimensions, disciples enclose wealth within Murid sacred circuits to create forms of value that are not determined by the market. They do so through producing talk about different registers of value and modes of transaction; through the use of video, radio, and TV; and through sermons during meetings of religious associations, religious conferences, and pilgrimages.

RURAL EXODUS AND THE ROOTS OF A GLOBAL TRADE

Murid peasant families were among the hardest hit by the declining price for peanuts in the world market in the 1960s due, in part, to the European Community's ending of preferential prices for Senegalese peanut and oil producers in 1968 (Babou 2007b:202). Murid peasants were further devastated when, in the 1970s, due to a prolonged period of monocropping, poor environmental management, severe drought, and a series of locust plagues, the country experienced a destructive famine. During this period, agricultural exports from Senegal declined in general due to price controls, centralized marketing boards, overregulation, and the importation of inexpensive broken rice from Southeast Asia (Creevey et al. 1995:674).

To escape rural devastation and mounting debt, many disciples migrated to the urban centers of Thies and, eventually, Dakar from the central agricultural regions of the country. This was not the first instance of rural-urban migration; migration from the countryside also took place between the world wars and shortly after the Second World War when Murid merchants traveled to the colonial port of Dakar to benefit from the postwar economic boom (Diouf 2000:691). In Dakar, Murids populated the city with self-built dwellings (Creevey 1985:715; Diouf 2000:691) and became employed in the burgeoning unregulated sectors of the urban economy (Cruise O'Brien 1988; M. Diop 1981; Roberts 1996:87). At first, Murid agricultural migrants foraged in the urban areas of Thies and Dakar, recycling cleaned-up bits of string, bottles, and cans for sale in the market at the *ndiggel* (command) of Seriñ Abdoul Lahat Mbacke, the third oldest son of Bamba, who inherited the spiritual leadership of the Murid way. Over time, Murids transformed the strategy of trading in the dry season to make ends meet during lean agricultural cycles into full-time urban settlement (Cruise O'Brien 1988; M. Diop 1981; Roberts 1996:87). Many migrants lived in unofficial settlements surrounding Dakar, and those who had made their homes in the city center were eventually pushed out to the periphery through urban improvement campaigns (Sow 1981).

Although the Murid way was initially an agricultural movement, Muslims have long been associated with trade in West Africa (see, for example, Amselle 1971; Cohen 1971; Curtin 1975; Hopkins 1973; Stoller 2002). For many Muslims, including the Murids, trade has a "historical precedent and [is a] Prophetic practice; it is inherent in the words of the sacred scripture of Islam, the Qur'an, and thus has, for Muslims, the stamp of divine authority" (Hunwick 1999:72). The Qur'anic language of salvation is replete with economic metaphors, for example, worship and giving alms are referred to as "profitable commerce (tijara)" (ibid.).

Though it might have seemed that urban disciples had moved beyond the rural grasp of their religious guides and that they were in the process of becoming further entrenched in the world market through their trade, "they made a conscious effort to incorporate their unique temporality and rationality into world time by using their own vocabulary, grammar and worldview to understand the world and operate within it" (Diouf 2000:685). Urban male and female disciples congregated once a week in religious associations, dahira, during which they recited the litanies of the order, gave cash offerings to the religious hierarchy, and invested in social projects. These religious associations were not unique to Murid followers; Tijaniyya and Qadiriyya also congregated in dahira associations to express their devotion. However, the principles underlying the formation of the Murid dahira associations derived from the *daara* (agricultural communes founded by Bamba's early disciples). Rather than rote memorization of the Qur'an, Babou (2002) argues, Bamba's teachings stressed science and action as expressed through his idea of the *daara-tarbiyya,* which emphasized sacrifice for one's shaykh. Bamba's teachings encompassed work, prayer, and instruction and conveyed virtues such as patience, humility, endurance, and sharing.

Today, Murid families send young girls and boys to daara schools, some of which are day schools where children receive a moral education while ultimately remaining within the sphere of parental authority. More controversially, other children, usually boys, are sent away to live in the shaykh's compound where they beg for alms among the community and receive an education and discipline from the shaykh. The agricultural communes of adult workers, which are also called daara, continue to operate in rural areas and attract Murid youth, mainly unmarried men but also some women who are seeking employment and deferring family obligations. These daara are considered to be a noble source of employment and spiritual training for youth who would otherwise be idle.

The dahira structure, which emerged in urban areas soon after World War II, spurred urbanization and the economic transformation of the Murids from farming to trading (Babou 2002:154). When Murid farmers and craftspeople migrated to the cities, they were often associated with "fanaticism, ignorance and vagrancy" (156). The dahira associations assisted rural exiles who sought to settle in the urban areas, providing forums for participating in the litanies of the order and for receiving the shaykh's directions (M. Diop 1981). The dahira provided not only refuge, but also practical training, such as business skills, for those lacking a French education. Virtues learned from the daara, including solidarity and discipline, translated into practices of mutual assistance in trade, dealing in secondhand goods, and porterage. The dahira also provided important business connections; they could be a means of finding a business partner or securing the patronage of a more successful *commerçant* who would help with housing, official papers, or capital. An established large trader with access to international markets could advance credit and merchandise, and enable compatriots to avoid the formal banking sector. In the formal sector one encountered financial and transaction costs (Thioub et al. 1998:79) and favoritism toward owners, managers, and large depositors (Stiansen and Guyer 1999:5). Being able to rely on the social relations that were forged in religious associations for lodging, food, and protection from police was crucial for traders who often worked outside of the official economy, beyond the parameters of state regulation, or across state boundaries. Though successful and powerful businesspeople were an asset to the rural clergy who benefited from their religious offerings, they have not always been in alliance; at times, business interests have been hampered by the authority of the clergy in Tuba and their converging interests with the state (Cruise O'Brien 1988:143).

The patronage of a senior member of the dahira could enable one to engage in financial transactions within the sphere of that which is morally sanctioned in Islam, thus avoiding *riba* (interest or increase), which is associated with formal economic transactions. The Qur'an also advises adepts not to sacrifice religious practice for commercial gain in trade, that wealth should be used in the service of God, and that capital obtained through wrongdoing to others is to be avoided (Hunwick 1999:73–74). Moreover, adepts should not participate in gambling or speculation (82). In the capitalist economy, such activities were difficult to avoid; participation in Murid circuits of exchange contributed to the strategies that good Muslims could employ in seeking a living within their moral aspirations and the financial constraints of their time.

Over time, the urban dahira associations consolidated the authority of the rural-based religious clergy and the centrality of Tuba to urban residents. In addition to chanting the litanies of the order, dahira associations began to collect offerings to gain audiences with rural shaykhs. At first, the offerings were motivated by the desire to improve the mosque in Tuba, to transport deceased members to Tuba for burial, and to stand in for the disciples' voluntary Wednesday labor in the fields that were cultivated for their shaykhs in the rural areas (Cruise O'Brien 1971b:252–53). In the 1950s, dahira associations began to organize offerings to support the annual Màggal pilgrimage to Tuba. Since then, they have become active in providing social services of all kinds, to make an impression on the local residents and the spiritual leaders.

Although initially dahira associations were composed of men and women who mainly devoted themselves to the support of a particular shaykh, they came to be organized according to neighborhoods and professions, and men and women convened separately. Shaykhs understood that these associations placed them at the center of well-organized networks that were becoming a crucial means of financial and political mobilization and that attested to their status as scholars and bearers of baraka. To the consternation of shaykhs who recognized the benefits of these associations operating on their behalf in their quest for spiritual recognition, the khalifa général began to organize these associations directly under his authority, in effect transforming the outward movement of disciples away from Tuba back toward the centralization of the hierarchy (Cruise O'Brien 1971b:253–54).

Murid migrants to the city often became involved in the so-called informal sector (Stiansen and Guyer 1999) because the formal sector was controlled by private French capital and state enterprise while transportation and real estate were controlled by Lebanese businesspeople (Thioub et al. 1998:67). Those who did engage in the formal sector found that they could "work optimally when they had recourse to both kinds of systems, and therefore [they had] a real interest in the maintenance of what the 'modern sector' may consider to be a 'traditional' form of moral authority and financial power" (Stiansen and Guyer 1999:5).

In the rural areas, a lively cross-border trade with Gambia in peanuts and contraband commodities emerged as peanut producers sought to escape the control of official marketing boards; much of this trade revolved around Tuba, which had maintained the status granted by the colonial administration as an independent administrative district. This status was further instantiated in 1976, when Tuba was designated an "autonomous rural community" and thus became one of the only village-level administrative districts to have investments in infrastructure made in it by the state without the burden of taxes and customs duties (Cruise

O'Brien 2003:66). The absence of taxes and customs duties in turn facilitated its status as a center of contraband trade. As a result, the informal sector and parallel trade circuits began to expand in the postcolonial period, and in the 1970s and 1980s the state made little effort to regulate these networks.

One important reason for this expansion was that these circuits provided citizens with forms of employment and access to inexpensive consumer goods during the inflation and global economic recession of the 1970s (Thioub et al. 1998:70). Between 1970 and 1981 the cost of living tripled, urban unemployment affected more than 70 percent of the population, and inflation was at 30 percent (Mbodj 1991:124). Men and women sought employment in the informal sector where traders avoided payment of the "value added tax, merchants' registration fees, commercial profits tax, payroll tax and wage laws, customs duties and tariffs, and social security charges" (Thioub et al. 1998:70). Murids succeeded in shifting from agriculture in the colonial period to trade in the second half of the twentieth century. They became "part of the informal state structure (or more accurately, of the ensemble formed by the formal state and its informal shadow) via a web of informal concessions, carefully negotiated privileges—notably including impunity for economic offenses—and personal and political relationships" (Hibou 1999:89). As a consequence, traders operating in the thriving Marché Sandaga, the central market in Dakar, showed support for the ruling Partie Socialiste in the postcolonial period, contributing to its control of the presidency from independence until 2000.

GLOBAL CIRCUITS OF WAGE LABOR AND CAPITAL

By the 1970s, many Murid families that had been engaged in farming in the peanut basin had left for the city, or at least sent a son to labor there on their behalf, and others went abroad. The Murids were not the first to engage in long-distance migration. Soninke from the Senegal River valley preceded them (Adams and So 1996; Manchuelle 1997), as did conscripts into the world wars and pilgrims embarking on the hajj. A labor shortage in postwar France drew many former colonial subjects there to work on the docks, in maritime shipping, and in factories (Bowen 2004:44). As former colonies gained independence, an agreement between France and Senegal allowed Senegalese to move without restriction (Diop and Michalak 1996:77). Although Murid adherents emigrated to France in search of university degrees and wage labor, many more became involved in the international trade in African art, perhaps inspired by the opportunities offered by the 1966 Paris Exposition de l'Art Nègre (Cruise O'Brien 1988:139). Murid followers had migrated to French cities such as Strasbourg, Marseille, and Paris where they sold to German, Italian, and French tourists (Salem 1981).

The French government suspended immigration in 1974 when its economy suffered from the worldwide recession and the demand for industrial labor declined in the context of the global oil crisis (Diop and Michalak 1996:78). Many in France viewed immigrants as competitors for low-skill, low-paying jobs (Bowen 2004:44). The 1974 Family Reunification Act restricted emigration to family members only. Though this act did permit many more family members to migrate to France, it did not lessen ties to kin and community at home, especially religious ties (Kane 2002:246). Attitudes toward immigration worsened when French right-wing political parties spoke to insecurity and racism beginning in the 1970s, and by the 1980s conflict grew out of perceived cultural and racial differences between Muslim migrants from the former colonies and French citizens (Bowen 2004:44).

In 1993, France passed its most restrictive immigration measure, the Pasqua Law. This law was intended to stem the previously legal flow of immigrants by prohibiting non-French graduates from accepting job offers by French employers, increasing the waiting period for family reunification from one to two years, and denying residency permits to spouses who had been illegally in the country prior to marrying. French fears of violence in the suburbs, where immigrant workers' housing had been built, and of international terrorism following the hijacking of several international airliners made life in France difficult for many Senegalese.

Many Murids turned to the United States, and by the 1980s Murid communities had grown in New York, Belgium, and Italy (Diouf 2000). The U.S. amnesty law passed in 1986 facilitated a greater circular migration of these traders and disciples as their status was regularized, and the numbers of Murid in the United States grew steadily (Babou 2002:160). The 1990 Immigration Act, which introduced the Diversity Immigrant Visa Program that provided permanent resident visas to citizens of countries with low immigration rates to the United States, also contributed to the rising number of Senegalese there (Beck 2008:200). In North American cities, many Murid migrants described their predicament of being moved out of urban centers in Senegal and then Paris as partaking in the spiritual quest of Amadou Bamba, exiled several times by the French who feared he would foment an uprising against the colonial power. Based on the example of Bamba, who used his exile as an opportunity to engage more deeply in his spiritual quest, they described their travel both as a way of generating forms of knowledge and as participating in the hijra, the Prophet's migration from Mecca to Medina.

The overseas migration of Murids took place in the context of a declining Senegalese economy in the postcolonial period in which economic anxieties translated into concerns about social reproduction. By creating further distance between production and consumption, overseas trade exaggerated shifts in the relationship between labor and capital that were already taking place in the postcolony. Migration abroad accelerated in the 1980s and 1990s with the implementation of economic and political reforms in Senegal that were aimed at the "laws of the market" rather than "public decision making" (Diouf 2000:692).

Economic recession took hold in Senegal due to the decline of agriculture and manufacturing as well as the state's inability to derive revenue from the thriving import trade in contraband (Thioub et al. 1998:71). The state implemented a series of reforms mandated by the International Monetary Fund in exchange for loans from the World Bank. The first of these reforms, or structural adjustment programs (SAPs), ran from 1985 to 1992 and was followed by a new program in 1995 that sought to address the stagnant economy and increasing external debt. The SAPs privatized state assets, removed trade barriers and constraints on financial flows, introduced fiscal discipline, reduced state involvement in the economy, ended agricultural subsidies, and led to the devaluation of the Senegalese currency, the CFA franc, in 1994 (Diouf 2004:270; Hesse 2004:4; Perry 1997:233). Further steps were taken by the government to reduce public expenditures, lower barriers on imports, and privatize state enterprises such as peanut processing, water, electricity, and communications (Hesse 2004:4). The local impact of these reforms included an inflationary spiral—especially in the prices of tools, electricity, fuel, and imported rice and wheat, which were staples of the urban diet of rice, fish, and baguettes—that led to public protests and greater social and economic instability for Senegalese families (Creevey et al. 1995:669).

These new forms of impoverishment were matched by new forms of wealth as the gap between the rich and the poor increased over the decades as a consequence of economic liberalization (Creevey et al. 1995:671). The rich were largely the political and economic figures who worked at the interstices of the formal and informal economies; as the prospects of the state declined, they benefited as international financial institutions sought to increase transparency and reduce graft by decreasing the amounts of development aid and loans that filtered through the state. Murid traders who operated abroad became the wealthy class and government bureaucrats came to depend largely on them to survive.

Although initially Murids succeeded economically as a major agricultural force through investments that were made by the neo-patrimonial state, Murids gradually reinvested those proceeds outside of the state apparatus via translocal circuits. The decision by the Senegalese state in 1986 to rescind its policy of protecting Senegalese manufactured goods contributed to the emergence of the import-export and service sectors and to the expansion of Marché Sandaga, which came to be dominated by the Murid faithful (M. Diop 1981; Diouf 2000:692). In the 1990s, the business sector received a temporary reprieve from the ensuing economic hardship imposed by the structural adjustment programs when Abdou Diouf succeeded Léopold Senghor to the presidency and rescinded a number of socialist policies, beginning a program of aggressive economic liberalization (Babou 2007a:205). Although trade liberalization in 1997 was designed to squeeze out parallel markets (where Murids, among others, thrived), liberalization in Senegal had the opposite effect, instead reinforcing the extralegal and unofficial economy (Hibou 1999:80). Part of the explanation for this lies in the way in which Murids successfully shifted between the formal and informal economies and in the intertwining of personal and commercial networks. Murid economic networks drew on dahira membership, allegiance to shaykhs, lineages, villages of origin, caste membership, membership in neighborhood ritual associations, and the like.

More important, the Murid economy became rooted in a version of millennial capitalism, "a capitalism that presents itself as a gospel of salvation; a capitalism that, if rightly harnessed, is invested with the capacity wholly to transform that universe of the marginalized and disempowered" (Comaroff and Comaroff 2000:292). Murids worked between the secular and Muslim temporal realms (Diouf 2000). Murid adherents and traders were both the motivation and the outcome of the blurring of the sacred and the secular, where work or, more accurately, *naq* (sweat) formed an important part of the Murid soteriology, or doctrine of salvation. Disciples made offerings of cash and consumer goods to their shaykhs not merely to gain an audience or to "count on their *marabouts* [shaykhs] to act as intermediaries with the Ministry of Finance or with customs authorities" (Bop 2005:1106). They also gave to their shaykhs to secure their commercial success, which was seen to be a result of not only the commercial networks that membership in the dahira opened up to them, but also of the mystical power of the shaykhs themselves. Addiya collected by local prayer circles provided assurances of salvation—of ultimately being in God's presence—in an uncertain moral and fiscal terrain. One might think of the kinds of informality employed by Murid traders less in terms of absence from the formal sector and more in terms of how "informality uses a proficiency in emergent formal institutions to elaborate new spaces of operation" (Simone 2004:24). While the forms of work in which Murids engaged became less visible as they began trading and moved abroad, the products of their labor in what they could build or buy became central to their moral standing at home.

Tuba emerged as one of the fastest growing cities in Senegal, despite the absence of the usual apparatus of the state including administrative buildings and schools, and yet still retained its status as a village (Cruise O'Brien 2003:67). As the state became extraneous to Murid economic projects that were enveloped in translocal circuits of trade, many Murid followers saw the intertwining of religion and translocal trade as the only possible means of shoring up the nation-state (Diouf 2000:691n33). It is often argued that practices unregulated by the state, which often take place in the margins, contribute to "a weakening or shrinking of the forms of regulation and belonging that supposedly constitute the modern nation-state" (Das and Poole 2004:3). The very categories of official and unofficial and the assumption that official could be equated with legal and unofficial with illegal did not seem to apply to Senegal, as "illegal practices are also performed in the formal sector, while so-called informal economic networks operate with well-established hierarchies and are fully integrated into social life" (Bop 2005:1106). In fact, rather than undermining the state form, transnational citizens often challenge, renegotiate, and reconfigure their fiscal and political relations in light of their relationship to global capital (Ong 1999:214–15; Roitman 2005). As Janet Roitman suggests, the "problem of legitimacy can only be addressed if the economy is apprehended as a political terrain" (2005:6). Certainly this has been the case with the relationship between traders of the Murid order and the state.

The international migration of Murid disciples has been facilitated by the Senegalese state in the twenty-first century. The current president, Abdoulaye Wade, a Murid follower himself, was elected as an opposition candidate in 2000 after twenty years of rule by the Partie Socialiste, in part because of the organizational success of Senegalese abroad, many of whom were Murids living in New York City. Wade pursued the Senegalese business class as well as the many shop owners on 116th Street in

Harlem by speaking to their predicaments in Senegal and in New York City as Senegalese overseas voted in the presidential election (Salzbrunn 2004:471). In 2007, despite widespread dissatisfaction with the declining economic conditions and political repression of the media in Senegal, Wade was elected to a second term. His success had much to do with his courting of the Murid way through the granting of diplomatic visas and hajj trips to the clergy and through resolving migrants' land disputes (Mbow 2008:162). Wade had noted the importance of migration and remittances to Senegal as the "true motor of Senegal's economy" (161).

It is in this context that young persons sought to emigrate in search of productive activity. Among the Murid immigrants to the United States were those on student, business, and tourist visas. A number who intended to return to businesses in Senegal found the economic opportunities of unofficial markets in the United States to be lucrative and stayed on (Beck 2008:200). Many of the Murid migrants who arrived in New York City had already been trading in cities in Senegal, West Africa, and Europe, and others came from the depressed agricultural regions in west-central Senegal (Babou 2002:159). Many young male Senegalese began by migrating from the countryside to urban areas in their own country, often staying with relatives and selling small, inexpensive items that they could carry in a box to peddle on busy auto routes and on market streets. With such low overhead, these young men hoped to quickly trade up—earning a job in a shop or perhaps acquiring a space on the sidewalk. The Senegalese police force monitored such ad hoc growth carefully, razing market spaces and mandating taxes and permits for vending. Many vendors hoped to obtain a *carte de commerçant* from the Ministry of Commerce, which would legitimize their trade in Dakar and which they could parlay into a multiple-entry business visa to the U.S. Though antiquities and objets d'art were a Senegalese niche, developments in the world economy made it profitable for Senegalese to sell an array of manufactured items, such as umbrellas, T-shirts, socks, and purses, which they obtained from Korean, Indian, and Pakistani wholesalers in New York City. They also developed a special niche in the marketing of designer knockoffs. As in Senegal, overseas migrants relied on a rotating savings and credit system to finance larger endeavors (Babou 2002:160). In the twenty-first century, Murid businesses have developed shipping, travel, communications, and money transfer operations to facilitate their business ventures. As was the case with rural migrants who arrived in Senegalese cities, transatlantic migrants organized themselves in dahira associations through which they hoped to receive assistance with airfare and visa arrangements; new members were also hosted and socialized by those who were already in the United States.

Though early traders and migrants were largely male, as early as the 1980s, female traders began to visit festivals in the summer months; by the 1990s, through marriage with international traders and as recipients of the U.S. Diversity Immigrant Visa Program, the number of women migrants to the United States was growing (Babou 2002:162; Diouf 2004:276). In the twenty-first century, increasing numbers of divorced women and women seeking divorce have chosen migration as a means of achieving autonomy. In New York City, women's financial success as professionals, business owners, and hair braiders can often surpass their male counterparts' (Babou 2008). Since women conventionally keep their own earnings and draw on their spouse's earnings to cover household expenses (Babou 2002:163; Diouf 2004:276–77), their financial transactions have been the subject of some interest to their male counterparts. Women who migrated to the U.S. and elsewhere invested their earnings in real estate in Dakar (Tall 1994), made offerings to shaykhs in Tuba during the annual Màggal pilgrimage (Rosander 2004), and were watched keenly by the Murid clergy.

By the 1990s, with the aid of remittances from the Murid faithful abroad, the Murid holy city of Tuba had become the second largest city in Senegal, with a population of 300,000 (Gueye 2001:107). Some have even gone so far as to suggest that Dakar had become merely the earthly shadow of the otherworldly aspirations of Tuba (Bayart et al. 1999:20). In addition to dominating the import trade in Dakar, Murids invested heavily in transportation, real estate, and cement in this city (Gueye 2001:109). The proceeds of those activities were also invested in Tuba, which is the hub of an expansive economy in which male and female traders import electronics, cars, durable goods, prescription medications, cosmetics, and cloth. The center of this activity is Marché Ocass, which is located on the perimeter of the holy city. Only about one-third of Tuba households engage in agricultural production; the vast majority of men and women now engage in trade (Freund 2007:174).

Although the Murid clergy has replaced the state as the major agent of development, the claim by disciples that the clergy provides their followers with free electricity and water while not charging state taxes is a bit more complicated. Tuba has seen occasional state intervention in telephone lines, water supply, and road construction (Freund 2007:176), often as a means to seek Murid votes (Gueye 2001:107). Importantly, the state (in the form of police, the national constabulary, and customs officers) is found not in the city center, but rather at its fringes, a tacit recognition of Tuba's colonial inheritance as an independent administrative district. Similarly, though by 1997 the value added tax was extended to Tuba traders, it seems to be minimally enforced by state officials (Cruise O'Brien 2003:65).

Tuba is linked to a vast market in imported goods through the port of Dakar, where most merchandise arrives via maritime shipping facilitated by advances in containerization. By the late 1990s in Dakar, Murid merchants controlled the major markets, including the largest cloth market, Marché HLM (Mustafa 1998), and Marché Sandaga, the largest urban market in Senegal, which also serves as a gateway to hundreds of smaller markets throughout the city and its periphery (Diouf 2000:692). Forming the skeleton of the market area are hundreds of cinder-block shops with tin roofs, which are owned and often operated by Lebanese and Murid merchants. These merchants specialize in high-end imported goods, damask cloth, luggage, and housewares. Sandaga also offers an impressive selection of electronic equipment imported from Jeddah and Hong Kong (Diouf 2000:692; Ebin 1992:86). Spilling over the sidewalks in front of the shops are tables and tarps where Senegalese men and women sell tablecloths and napkins, bras and slips, and imported and locally manufactured cloth. Meanwhile, numerous vendors walk the streets with their wares, including tissues, toothpicks, and umbrellas, while young men lead tourists and others to the shops of their employers.

In the 1990s, Sandaga was host to numerous market associations organized by female traders of local produce, including tomatoes, millet, peanuts, and *bissap* (hibiscus juice), and some medicinal substances and local beauty products, such as sea sponges, henna, and handmade soap. It was also home to numerous tailors, who were located near cloth stalls; and a large Murid dahira, which was dominated by merchants and tailors, met in the mustard-colored, orientalist-inspired central market structure that bore a large billboard for Maggi seasoning. Market women, tailors, and traders all belonged to numerous credit associations, which were also situated in the market, many of them organized along lines of Murid affiliation.

Located in the heart of Sandaga market was Kara International Exchange, a money transfer business and import-export firm which was organized according to the principles of *hawala* (Tall 1996). Hawala literally means "transfer" and is a system that enables merchants to engage in credit-based transactions, which are prohibited in the Qur'an, over long distances without actually exchanging goods or currency (Hunwick

1999:84). Kara International allowed a trader to deposit a given sum plus a modest commission with a branch in New York City, which then sent a message via email or fax to a branch in Dakar indicating the amount to be distributed in CFA currency to waiting family members and business associates. The Dakar agent recuperated his or her funds through trade; when the Dakar agent arrived in New York City to purchase merchandise, he or she would use the cash that had been deposited with the agent there. The trader then would purchase merchandise to import to Dakar, which, once sold, would become the "bank" for the remittance operation in Dakar. Accordingly, agents would never transport money across state lines themselves.

Although money transfer, currency exchange, and short-term loans belonged to the domain of unofficial financial transactions, Kara International also acted in the formal sector. Kara was an import-export operator, facilitating the security, storage, and shipping of consumer goods between New York City and Dakar (Tall 2002:36). For small traders, Kara shipped goods inexpensively by dividing the space that it rented inside a shipping container into ever-smaller portions commensurate with each trader's stock and means. Unlike the *modou modou,* the traders who moved their merchandise in large blue and red plastic woven bags and who carried numerous shrink-wrapped suitcases through airports, Kara International's *commerçants* behaved like modern businesspeople. Carrying neither large sums of cash nor baggage, they moved unencumbered through international airports.

GLOBAL CIRCUITS OF OFFERINGS AND THE PRODUCTION OF VALUE

Returning to the RTS broadcasts of the pilgrimage to Tuba mentioned earlier, the videos often included an interview with the custodian of the Murid archive and library at Tuba. The custodian would take the viewer on a tour of the library and the video would focus on the stacks full of the numerous volumes of writings by key Muslim figures in Arabic and French. The custodian would then discuss the corpus of writing produced by Bamba himself, show the viewer a number of display cases containing personal items that belonged to Bamba, including his bed and his suitcase, and describe the *jikko ju baax* (pious comportment) of a good Murid and a good Muslim. Finally, the custodian would discuss the subject of offerings to signify submission to the path in the hope of achieving salvation, noting that the aspirant should make offerings to the shaykh because when a person holds money in his or her hand, it has *amul njariñ* (no value). However, once given to the shaykh, the money acquires value and, in return, the disciple benefits from the shaykh's baraka.

The videos then often displayed images of the offerings of prominent prayer circles that are devoted to the shaykhs. In Senegal there are many dahira associations that are composed of professionals, bureaucrats, and students; however, it is the contributions of the overseas disciples who sell their wares on the streets of major Western cities that are the focus of these productions. These translocal organizations send yearly offerings to the Murid clergy from places such as Milan, Paris, New York, Chicago, and Washington, D.C. Not only do they send cash, but they also send crates of bleach, ammonia, and toilet paper. The camera records hospitals, sewage systems, and rural electrification projects made possible by the *liggéey* (work) of disciples abroad. The broadcasts all shifted back and forth between scenes of the prayerful masses filling the streets, to images of the myriad ways in which they have contributed to developing the sacred city, to views of long lines of dignitaries greeting the shaykhs. Condensed in the forms of wealth that circulate on the days of pilgrimage—food, money, and transport—is the work of the disciples and the magnitude of the shaykh's blessings, all of which are made possible by the grace of God. The offerings that circulate in the broadcasts, videocassettes, and DVDs are recognized as being not only signs of the baraka of the Murid shaykhs, but also as containing the elements that produce the social system, that is, the Murid way itself. The Màggal is not only a display of all that the disciples have sacrificed for the development of the way, nor is it only a representation of all that the shaykhs have returned to their faithful with interest; it is also an index of the baraka that is Bamba's legacy.

Given the series of so-called crises that wracked the Senegalese economy since independence, including the agricultural crisis, the urban crisis, the post–structural adjustment crisis, and the crisis that was induced by neoliberal reform on the heels of a worldwide economic meltdown related to the failed mortgage lending market in the United States, how have Murid adepts been able to produce their community as one with a future and to secure processes of social production? Murids talk of the economy in sacred idioms and of the sacred in terms of the economy—which points to anxieties about the vectors of value in a rapidly changing and deteriorating social and physical landscape and to counterefforts by Murid followers to contain the movement of wealth within sacred circuits of development. Nowhere is this more apparent than in the overseas dahira associations. Dahira associations have provided disciples with spiritual sanctuary, camaraderie, business liaisons, and legal assistance, and they have served as a means of connecting with the spiritual hierarchy of the Murid way either through sponsoring visits of the clergy or by collecting offerings to be contributed during the annual Màggal celebration in Tuba.

As the images from the videos attest, numerous dahira associations have emerged in most major North American cities. Many of these associations are named by hyphenating the Western city and Tuba, much as Murid towns in colonial Senegal were given Muslim names to establish them as Muslim spaces (Babou 2007a). The overseas dahira associations function informally as community associations; they are places where younger disciples seek advice from older members on a wide range of issues from problems with the police to advice on a pending marriage or visa. They are places were all members can exchange the latest news from Senegal or discuss sales trends in the market. These associations also sanction marriages, organize naming ceremonies, and arrange for the burial of their deceased in Tuba.

Many of the North American dahira associations congregate annually in New York City for Cheikh Amadou Bamba Day, which is usually held in late summer. The weeklong events that lead up to this celebration include hosting a member of the religious clergy from Senegal, interfaith conferences, a major parade, and a talk at the United Nations headquarters on Bamba as a person of peace. This event begins the visit of a shaykh to major North American cities each year to provide assistance to Muslims living in a non-Muslim land. Members of overseas dahira associations pay particular homage to the late Cheikh Mortalla Mbacke, who was the last living son of Bamba. Cheikh Mortalla was particularly popular in the United States due to his efforts to provide for the communities' spiritual needs directly; he visited each American dahira once a year during the summer months. His movements overseas point to the growing significance of these communities for the Tuba-based hierarchy.

Seriñ Moustapha Mbacké Gaindé Fatma, a great-grandson of Amadou Bamba, founded the first North American dahira in New York City in 1986.[3] Today, there are about thirty dahira associations in New York City (Babou 2002:165) and, since dahira usually meet in gender-restricted groups, there are a number of strictly female dahira. One of the most prominent women's dahira to emerge in New York City is Maam Jaara Boussou, which has taken a leading part in organizing the annual observation of Cheikh Amadou Bamba Day (Babou 2002:155; Salzbrunn

Cheikh Amadou Bamba Day Parade, New York City, 2005

Cheikh Amadou Bamba Day Parade, New York City, 2005

Cheikh Amadou Bamba Day Parade, New York City, 2005

2004:484). The dahira has not only assisted in financing the event, but has also provided copious amounts of cooked food; likewise, their large presence in the mediated public gatherings has helped display the strength of the Murid presence in New York City to other city dwellers and to their compatriots in Senegal.

As in men's dahira associations, women's dahira associations give regular contributions of cash as offerings to a shaykh and also use their collections to fund pilgrimages, all-night prayer sessions, and group visits to tombs of Sufi figures. During dahira meetings, women not only collect contributions and lay plans, but they also share food, admire each other's adornment, and promote their wares since many members are often engaged in some form of trade. The organizational structure of the dahira has been vital to women's work in Senegal: promoting local leaders and national political parties; advancing their interests in areas such as education, health care, and urban development; and helping to finance their businesses.

Although African Muslims comprise only 7 percent of the 6 million Muslims in the United States (Diouf 2004:268) and the Murid community estimates its numbers at about 1,000–2,000 members (Salzbrunn 2004:479), Murids have become visible in the Harlem neighborhood of New York City. In addition to the many shops and restaurants on 116th Street, Murids also hold religious services in the Malcolm Shabazz

Murid-owned business in Harlem, 2005

mosque, an important architectural landmark on the same street. In 2001, they built an Islamic center, which includes a mosque and school at 137th Street and Edgecombe Avenue. The Murid Islamic Center becomes the center of activity during the annual commemoration of Amadou Bamba and receives annual visits from dignitaries associated with the celebration.

In the 1990s, many of the members of the New York dahira, who were also traders, moved to Chicago and other North American cities to seek new opportunities, claiming that the market in New York City had become too saturated to be profitable. Three Murid men who had arrived in Chicago in 1972 founded the dahira Tuba-Chicago in 1992. Initially, the dahira meetings were held in disciples' apartments, as they would have been in Senegal. The impetus to secure a permanent location came when a member of the Mbacke clan traveled to Chicago and decided to settle in the city. The disciples rented a basement apartment in the Rogers Park neighborhood of Chicago, a diverse area encompassing Loyola University (a private Catholic university) as well as an Arab and Indian business district. The disciples moved the dahira because they were concerned that their recitation of the order's *khassaid* (litanies) was so loud that it would disturb the neighbors, causing visits from the Chicago police department. The number of cars parked outside the building at night did draw the attention of the police, who feared that Senegalese gatherings might signal drug commerce, which was thought to be present in the Nigerian community in the late 1990s.

The disciples transformed the Chicago apartment into a Murid dahira and thus rendered Chicago an extension of Tuba. The institutionalization of the apartment through the incorporation of the dahira in the city turned this space of domestic reproduction outward. Tuba encroached on Chicago through the disciples' collective thorough cleaning of the unit, their coat of pale green paint on the walls, and the placement of a selection of new prayer rugs depicting Islamic themes. A disciple painted "Thank you, Cheikh Amadou Bamba" in Wolof using the Wolof Arabic script called Wolofal on the north wall. Both the north and east walls commemorated Bamba and his lineage with framed photographs of him and his sons and posters of Tuba and Mecca hanging side by side. The frames encompassing Bamba's photos were crafted in Senegal and depicted images of Bamba, miraculous episodes in his life, and the words of God in Arabic.

Religious Texts

When I first attended the dahira Tuba-Chicago in the late 1990s, there were few women present and no separate women's dahira had been formed. The recitation of khassaid penned by Bamba occupied a central portion of the meeting, but women do not recite the khassaid, although they may sometimes pay young men or casted men to do so for them. Through the recitation of *dhikr* (litanies),[4] disciples embodied the remembrance of their saintly leader in the Sufi tradition. Bamba's poetry expresses three major themes: his love for God and his messenger the Prophet Muhammad, the ascetic quality of labor in a calling, and his exile by French colonizers. During exile, Bamba experienced *karamat,*[5] which disciples narrate to attest to his saintly status. Karamat, unlike *mu'jizat* (miracles), which only the Prophet Muhammad can perform, are the workings of God through holy men that attest to the existence of God: "The apostle establishes his prophecy by establishing the reality of evidentiary miracles, while the saint, by the miracles which he performs, establishes both the prophecy of the apostle and his own saintship" (Al-Hujwiri 1911:220). The Chicago disciples regarded Bamba's texts as a moral itinerary for action in the world, especially concerning their ideas of travel as a form of knowledge. Remembrance played an important role during the dahira meetings as disciples recited the khassaid and contemplated its themes and the commentary that accompanies this body of poetry; however, as they applied this commentary to their daily experiences, they added yet another layer to its meaning that was not cumulative but transformative.

By reciting the karamat of Bamba, Murid adepts seemed to live in a world of memory and yet their transnational communities were a "generative locus" of cultural practices (Fischer and Abedi 1990). Daily events, processes, and relations in the present were consistently interpreted and acted upon by evoking the collective past as a charter (Malkki 1995:53). Although the purpose of telling these karamat was to give coherence to an unruly past, these tales also served as a moral guide for structuring the present in that they proscribed and made sense of certain actions. Murids recast the past in fundamentally moral terms and their karamat classified the world according to Murid principles, thereby simultaneously creating the world. These karamat made history meaningful not because they explained the past in more palatable terms, but rather because they spoke to the pragmatics of getting through everyday life.

During the dahira meetings, the disciples chanted the most popular khassaid, the Mawahib an-Nabi, which praises Muhammad (Monteil 1969:95). Reciting the khassaid was the primary means of concentrating on God and the essence of the Sufi spiritual path. In West Africa, in particular, even Sufis who know very little Arabic practice recitation in the form of a remembrance, or dhikr, of Allah: "And if it be objected that such a reading can have only a fragmentary effect upon the soul inasmuch as the minds of the readers will be excluded from participation, the answer is that their minds are penetrated by the consciousness that they are partaking of the Divine Word" (Lings 1993:25). In effect, the recitation becomes a long, drawn-out invocation of the name of God. Like the Qur'an, which is a "flow and ebb—that it flows to them from God and that its verses are miraculous signs [*ayat*] which will take them back to God" (ibid.:26), so too is the recitation of the khassaid a way of returning to Bamba, and that is precisely why Murid adherents read it.

The weekly practice of the khassaid was an embodied narrative of travel that enabled participation in the divine word as well as a means of connecting with their wali. When reciting the khassaid, Sufis use outward gestures—swaying in a circular motion—to achieve inward concentration (Lings 1993:60). Unlike most Muslims, who strive to achieve a state of blessedness following death by carrying out prescribed works to achieve indirect and symbolic "participation in Divine truths" (Burckhardt 1995:15), Sufis believe that it is possible to achieve direct knowledge of the divine in this life; this is to be achieved by spiritual travel, where one will meet with revelation at each progression. One "travels" by deep study of the Qur'an and recitation of Sufi litanies.

Religious Offerings

In addition to the recitation of liturgical texts, disciples collected addiya during the dahira meetings. Disciples of the dahira Tuba-Chicago explained the practice of making offerings to shaykhs by citing the well-known story that Bamba professed such great moral disdain for accumulation that his boubou was sewn without pockets and he refused to touch money. They told of how followers would gather around Bamba to receive his blessings, often leaving offerings in various forms, and that Bamba would instruct them to place their offerings in a bowl next to his person from which he would instruct destitute disciples to take what they needed. Addiya like these are part of the Murid soteriology, or doctrine of salvation. Although the offerings are given to shaykhs to redistribute, they are ultimately offerings to God; the shaykh is a mere intercessor who mediates between supplicants and God.

Sufism posits that salvation is also achieved through asceticism, usually in the form of prayer, and Bamba proclaimed a doctrine whereby labor in a calling—as a form of ascetic practice equal to prayer—would also bring salvation. Consequently, disciples who resided on the early Murid communes often worked the communal fields of the order or, after they had received their own plot of land, reserved one day a week to work in the shaykh's fields or donated a portion of their harvest as an offering. Today, cash offerings represent the work of disciples, traders, and wage laborers.

Although many West African Muslim societies practiced giving offerings to religious masters (often in exchange for Qur'an lessons), some argue that cash offerings did not become institutionalized among Murids until 1957, when they were collected to complete the great mosque that was begun in 1927 following Bamba's death (K. M'Backe, personal communication). The collection of addiya in the form of cash in the 1950s also coincided both with the movement of Murid followers away from their agricultural bases to towns and with the founding of the early dahira associations. Murids maintain that the practice of addiya was sanctioned in the Qur'an, and further commentary on this practice was given in verse 40 of Masalik-al-jinan, a well-known khassaid written by Bamba. Offerings to shaykhs are different than *sadaqa* (alms of sugar, candles, rice, or sour milk that are given to the poor) or *zakat,* the practice of setting aside

10 percent of one's income for charity as one of the five pillars of Islam (A. Diop 1981:300). Although all three practices of divesting oneself of wealth bring merit, the addiya alone signifies voluntary submission to the Sufi path. This kind of offering is first made at the time of the *njebbel* and is thereafter given on a regular basis (Cruise O'Brien 1971b:92). In my field-based research, disciples often insisted that their contributions were voluntary, were given without thought of a return in this world or the next, and that offerings made in this manner by a willing donor resulted in religious merit, the accrual of which would secure one's place in heaven (see Parry 1989:66). Few distinguished between offerings made in cash or in kind, and many expressed pride at being able to make such offerings as individuals and as part of a dahira association. If the addiya was given in the presence of a shaykh, disciples might also benefit from the transfer of baraka by being in the presence of a bearer of grace and receiving words of benediction from him. Women tended to give addiya through their dahira associations, which organized collective contributions of cash and cooked food that usually supported pilgrimages and shaykhs' visits to disciples in the diaspora (Rosander 1998:152).

Disciples at the Chicago dahira insisted that their financial success was a result not only of the commercial networks that membership in the dahira opened up to them, but also of the mystical power of the shaykhs. The shaykhs enabled the disciples to think of money as a vehicle for salvation and to resist the demands of kin, especially with respect to expenditures that were viewed as forms of immediate consumption rather than long-term value. Moreover, the offerings were a way to collectively protect wealth outside of what was often a volatile market (Guyer 1999:237; Zelizer 1989). Disciples earmarked these transactions through terminological designations, such as addiya. The desire for such wealth protection is often the result of a "supernatural sanction and emotive power associated with certain objects and transactions" (Guyer 1999:238).

When disciples gave offerings to shaykhs, their money garnered meaning through its circulation and produced long-term value (Akin and Robbins 1999). These meanings were produced in part through talk about the significance of the offering, thus setting it aside from the mundane world of work. The collection of addiya during the dahira Tuba-Chicago meetings was a highly ritualized activity involving talk, persuasion, and drama. The contributions were not gained easily. Long pleadings and much discursive work appealing to the principles of the Murid way were necessary to sway the generosity of the members. At every meeting, after a discussion of salient business, one member circled the room collecting wadded

$5 bills for addiya. As he snapped his fingers, he snatched contributions, unrolling the bills and praising the principles of the Murid way. The person who was charged with eliciting offerings would often say things like, "Bamba worshiped labor. In the Qur'an it says 'may you eat on the sweat of the forehead: labor, pain, and sweat,'" or "The three most important things in Muridism are work, worship of God, and addiya. Working is worshiping God too. Muridism is the five pillars of Islam plus addiya. The principle of addiya is very important in Muridism; it is a very important act. Murids have been praying to Seriñ Tuba [Bamba] to give them money and power, so giving addiya is just giving some back." Through debate, negotiation, and lecture, the dahira secured an acceptable amount of contributions at every meeting, but only after the collection of offerings continued for about three rounds. The total sum each week was then recorded in a book and deposited in the dahira's bank account.

The offerings of Murid followers to their shaykhs have long been scrutinized by scholars of Islam in the region who have sought to resolve what seemed like a contradiction in the disciples' claims that they followed the Sufi path voluntarily, while at the same time they displayed submission and self-denial to achieve salvation. The colonial Arabist Paul Marty (1917) characterized the Murid order as a reinstitution of the practice of slavery based on his view of the offerings that disciples gave to their guides. Indeed, while descendants of slaves often made assaka payments to landowners and masters and continued these symbolic payments long after slavery had been formally abolished by the French, the Murid order in no way practiced the legal ownership of persons.

In Donal Cruise O'Brien's foundational work on the Murid order (1975), he refuted the idea that Murid guides exploited their followers by arguing that disciples were motivated to make offerings to their masters by the "material services" that the shaykhs offered in return (61). He argued that earlier analysts had taken disciples at their word as they claimed that they divested themselves of their wealth "for paradise alone" (62). Cruise O'Brien argued that in a disciple's "own devotional language, he is in fact boasting. . . . there is real reservation beneath the ostentatious subjection" (62–63). How to understand the adherents' reservation, their desire to keep something for themselves against the pressure to give, is a point to which I will return. For now, the important aspect of Cruise O'Brien's argument is not that the disciples were saying one thing and doing another, that they were merely boasting about their offerings to shaykhs, but rather he is pointing out the social labor, the talk that went into the moral framing of the offering. To frame the transaction of offerings as "interested reciprocity" neglects the degree to which disciples sought to transform their moral personas, in part by benefiting from baraka, but also through moral renewal, by discursively marking the offering and setting it outside the temporal world of market transactions (Werbner 2003:102–103).

There are many examples in African ethnography of the moral valuation of money and the ways in which African men and women distinguish different registers of value, including Parker Shipton's (1989) discussion of bitter money in Kenya and Sharon Hutchinson's (1996) discussion of the relationship between cattle and money among the Nuer. In Senegal, Murid disciples put a significant amount of social labor into the moral framing of their exchanges through the language of salvation. Thus, their practices of supplication, symbolized by the offering, constructed a spatial and temporal domain apart from the mundane. As I mentioned, the addiya is central to Murid soteriology that links the submission to a religious guide to salvation. Murid men and women engaged in performances of devotion, often through talk about offerings to shaykhs, as part of a repertoire of possible economic practices that secured their vision of an Islamic modernity. They did so because money is an object and, like any other object, it is susceptible to different readings. The money form in particular can be characterized by its indeterminacy and openness (Maurer 2006:17). Thus the representational quality of money is often fixed through talk: "objects require the reflexive capacity of language if they are to serve as fully efficacious media of social relations" (Keane 2001:74). When cash is given to a shaykh through the institution of addiya, it is no longer an alienable commodity, a standard of value, or a symbol of the state; instead, it signifies both submission in this world and the next to the path to divine union, and also the recognition of the shaykh as a worthy guide.

For example, Murids never say that they *jend* (buy) inalienable items, including sacred texts such as the khassaid or images of Bamba, even though these are monetized transactions that literally take place in the market. Rather, they bargain for these sacred objects by employing a language of *wecc* (exchange), asking the vendor something like "For what will you exchange that object?" Murid adherents label currency in its commodity form by using the term *xaalis* (silver) to distinguish it from currency used in social transactions, including offerings and *dimbali* (mutual aid). Importantly, what marks these transactions as alienable or inalienable is the talk surrounding them and the social labor that goes into maintaining these distinctions (Keane 2001:70).

Both disciple and shaykh work to extend influence over each other through the exchange of offerings, the promise of salvation, and the redistribution of these gifts (Munn 1992). A willing disciple first initiates a relationship with a shaykh by presenting an offering that is merely meant to demonstrate teraanga (hospitality); it is only with time that the offering comes to signify njebbel and that the aspirant is awarded with knowledge of the wird. Though the addiya itself is given without thought of a return, in other transactions the aspirant's aim is to move the shaykh to reciprocate in material and spiritual terms, perhaps at a later date, perhaps with interest. In the process, the disciple creates his or her identity as a good Muslim which is, in turn, recognized by the religious guide, hence the claim by Cruise O'Brien that disciples boasted of their capacity to sacrifice to their shaykhs (1975:63). Therefore, being a good Muslim is, in essence, constructing oneself as a candidate for salvation, which translates into prosperity in this life. In giving wealth to one's religious guide beyond the symbolic addiya, something that a successful businessperson might do, one would not only receive material rewards or political intervention in return, as Cruise O'Brien argues. Such transactions do not merely represent the exchange of one commodity or service for another; rather, one would also ensure the sacred legitimation or "authentication" of one's property and business, burial rights, and salvation, all of which would lead to the affirming of one's social rank and status by religious figures whose authority was uncontested (Weiner 1992:34). Not only would the donor benefit from this relationship, but it would also be transferred to his or her heirs, further ensuring the continuity of rank and difference.

It is only with the advent of the long-distance dahira that money became the direct object of Murid labor and the principal means of signifying submission, rather than the acquisition and recitation of the litanies and regular transmission of the sacred aspects of the order. This is not, however, to say that this social relationship has been undone. Disciples attain salvation not through accumulated wealth, but by constantly divesting themselves of money. Consequently, Murids say that the disciples who hold money in their hands have no *njariñ* (value). However, once given to the shaykh, money brings the disciple baraka. Thus, in many ways, the shaykh is the adherents' lifeline. Through offerings to shaykhs, disciples access paradise. Like the words of the khassaid, the cash offering is a miraculous sign that will take a Murid back to Bamba. Disciples believe that their offerings will return to them with interest in the future. Thus the addiya is a means of participating in the order's spiritual path.

A dahira from Spain waits for an audience with Seriñ Saliou Mbacke, Tuba, 2000

Only through the cash offering is the distance between the shaykh and his follower diminished. Practices of supplication and travel construct a spatial and temporal domain in which both the shaykh and the overseas disciple can dwell. Thus, the exchange of money constitutes a set of social relations.

In receiving the money, the shaykh is constructed by the disciple as a spiritual master of sufficient baraka, one who can deliver the benefits of salvation in this world and in the next. The shaykh establishes his or her status through accruing a following, which constitutes his or her authority by attesting to it. Wealth, for the religious class, is defined in part by the number of their disciples, whose allegiance must be cultivated through regular and visible redistributions of wealth (Guyer 2004:70). The shaykh is expected to redistribute the offerings to the poor, sick, or disabled members of the congregation, to put them toward the development of Tuba, or to store them away as a form of social security for the community (Cruise O'Brien 1971b:96). For example, the shaykh is among the few who can afford to stockpile grain for the lean season. Shaykhs are also expected to contribute offerings or to call their followers to provide labor for projects of those occupying the highest positions within the Murid order, and their capacity to do so is a measure of their status (Babou 2007a:94). A shaykh's ability to move money through the congregation attests to his or her baraka since, after all, this wealth is a sign of divine providence. However, to generate value, wealth must not stagnate in the hands of the shaykhs; it must circulate, as Comaroff and Comaroff argue was also the case for Methodists in southern Africa: "there was only one way to avoid its [money's] corrupting qualities: to let it go. If it was to generate virtue, it had to circulate visibly and constantly" (1997:172). In this context, then, money and accumulated wealth in the hands of the shaykhs was not a sign of the exploitation of disciples, nor of the rational give and take of economic life; rather, "money was a medium for a relational life, rather than a goal as a store of wealth" (Guyer 2004:70).

The cash offerings of the disciples and the social relations they contract are not made, however, without moral danger. Offerings that underpin processes of reproduction can at the same time threaten the reproduction of existing social orders (Akin and Robbins 1999:22). This sense of danger is apparent in the proliferation of stories and cartoons in the popular media about "maraboutage," or the practices of Muslim religious leaders which often involve sacrifices, the making and wearing of amulets and talismans, numerology, astrology, and divination based on Islamic occult sciences (Dilley 2004:12). In the protracted period of financial austerity that characterized the turn of the twenty-first century, stories abounded of wealthy or successful businesspeople and politicians who had been tricked by their religious guides into giving away the bulk of their assets. Part of the problem lies in the ease with which money offerings could be diverted and turned toward other purposes. Moreover, the acceptance of offerings is also a dangerous business since, once the shaykh receives addiya, she or he accepts moral responsibility for the salvation of that disciple. On the one hand, shaykhs are the perfect vehicle for salvation because they are able to transcend this world, guaranteeing the efficacy of the offering. On the other hand, their transcendence of this world is jeopardized as they are dragged down by the bond that the offering creates between themselves and their disciples (Parry 1989:74). Consequently, accepting addiya opens shaykhs to the possibility of charges that an offering was unreciprocated because their immersion in this world prevents them from delivering the full benefits of salvation to their disciples (67–68).

This is a central tension between a Murid soteriology "which denies reciprocity and a social order which is premised on it" (Parry 1989:77). In principle, shaykhs are not tainted with the money they receive because they are expected to return it all (with interest) as a sign of their baraka. The idea that exchange adds value to each transaction is crucial to ideas about the potency of money and to beliefs about the mystical power of the shaykhs; however, it is quite impossible for shaykhs to maintain their authority by exemplifying wealth in the form of multiple wives, many offspring, cars, and general largesse and also to redistribute all that they accept from their followers. Shaykhs' houses are never empty, and the bowls of rice and fish flow endlessly as they receive disciples daily who, out of poverty or piety, turn to their shaykhs for nourishment. The development of the community is also measured by the development of Tuba as an objectification of this entire process of circulation, especially the redistributive aspects.

Thus far I have analyzed the circulation of earnings from Murid merchants and wage laborers overseas and their investment into a sacred economy and its various forms of value through which disciples create individual and collective identities, secure processes of social production, and create social futures. The value that is produced through these transactions and conversions is neither of the market nor of tradition. Contrary to Bohannan's (1959) formulation of spheres of exchange in the Tiv economy in central Nigeria, the incorporation of money into African spheres of exchange did not diminish the ability of men and women to distinguish among different kinds of value (Guyer 2004:13). It was not things in themselves, such as brass rods or cattle, that separated different spheres of exchange. Rather, it was the "social relations through which they flow[ed] [that] differentiate[d] spheres of exchange" (Hutchinson 1996:90; see also Piot 1991). Furthermore, rather than think of Murid transactions from money to commodity to offering as conversions, one might think of these as part of a repertoire of possible practices that Murid adepts have honed over time to confront the volatile conditions of West African economies, situated as they have been at the cusp of local, regional, and world markets. That repertoire includes the intertwining of formal and informal economy transactions, the economic and the spiritual, various currencies and trade goods, and different scales of value, including the market, the social, and the spiritual. At any given time, a disciple and his or her shaykh are engaged in multiple registers of exchange of often incommensurate values, including buying, selling, borrowing, lending, and offering mutual aid, gifts, and sacrifices. Thus the modality of exchanges, the differentiating of transactions, and the temporal aspect of exchanges are largely missing from Bohannan's work, while they are central to understanding Murid value transformation (Akin and Robbins 1999:9).

It should be clear by now that, though Murids have been involved in the money economy through cash cropping and participating in urban economies and global trade networks since the inception of the order, market value has not replaced other values (cf. Carrier 1991; Miller 1994; Zelizer 1994). The use of money is not inimical to the production of social and sacred value (Akin and Robbins 1999; Keane 2001). The distinction that Marcel Mauss (1990[1950]) made between gifts and commodities, indeed between nonmarket and market societies, never truly held for African economies (Guyer 2004). Murids were always part of the capitalist economy. So it should not be surprising that Murid adepts distinguished the exchange of alienable objects from that of inalienable objects, often through talk, whether or not those transactions involved the exchange of money: "the capacity of objects to serve semiotically as representations and economically as representatives of persons is unstable and requires constant effort to sustain" (Keane 2001:74). Thus, when Cruise O'Brien suggests that offerings exemplify the same kinds of rationality as market exchange, he is undervaluing the statements of his informants, who insisted that offerings are made without thought of return as a way of discursively distinguishing the exchange of inalienable objects (which in this case could be money) from that of alienable objects. The disciples were expressing the problem inherent in exchanging objects as representations of themselves in that they must be detached from these representations in order for the objects to circulate and create value. Yet what disciples fear most is the risk of the loss of value and thus the loss of self in giving offerings to shaykhs, should the guide not prove to be worthy of the gift.

Disciples were motivated in their commercial activity by these forms of consciousness and value. For Murids, the spiritual community of Tuba as symbolized by its central mosque, clinics, and schools was a form of social value that was achieved through their offerings. Tuba was "the place where the Murid memory and imaginaire [*sic*] were elaborated, the place where their economic, social, architectural, and cultural successes were inscribed" (Diouf 2000:688). While they voluntarily submitted to Sufi shaykhs through their talk of offerings (the very products of their worldly success), they achieved moral renewal, transformed their moral personas, and transcended this world by confronting the turbulent times that characterized the Senegalese postcolony.

FOUR

A TALE OF TWO SISTERS

"I WANT TO HELP PAY for the new tile floor in the courtyard for Bintu's wedding, but I cannot," said Jigeen, her eyes fixed on the stained concrete floor. "I have to pay my daughters' school fees because their fathers are not here."

"Jigeen," her sister Rama said in a low voice, "we are all doing our share. Abdoul Aziz has already given money and so have our brothers in France and the U.S. We are all adults now and we must support our parents." She then turned to one of her younger sisters and snapped, "*Yalla,* bring me some sugar, this coffee is too bitter." She smiled weakly in my direction and gestured with her glass.

Abdoul Aziz jumped in, raising his voice, "You returned to this house thanks to us. *We* pay the electricity, the water, and provide sacks of rice every month. *You* are not doing anything."

Jigeen leaned back in her chair, facing the street, looking away from her family, and said, "I don't need anything except what God gives me, only what God gives me. I don't ask for anything more. I don't need anything more. I am fine. I am fine. I don't need you to do anything for me or for my daughters. If you don't think I should be here, then I will leave."

Her mother, Sokna Géer, cut in, "*Baay ko, baay ko rekk.* Leave her alone."

Sokna Géer had arranged several marriages for Jigeen and had accepted that her daughter had returned to her natal home in the end, divorced with three daughters in tow. She had watched the gowns and gifts of cloth, gold jewelry, enameled bowls, and glassware as they were packed into Jigeen's wedding trousseau each time and later unpacked when she divorced and returned to the family home. With pity, she had noticed that each time fewer and fewer items came back with Jigeen. A marriage was supposed to enrich a woman's worth in life, not impoverish her. She thought of her granddaughters and imagined their marriages and their meager trousseaus, which would reflect Jigeen's inability to build herself up through exchanges with other women. Jigeen's precarious financial state reflected her limited education, her tendency to indebt herself to too many women (thus endangering her reputation), and her unfortunate marriages.

In contrast, Sokna Géer's second oldest daughter, Rama, had steadfastly refused her mother's attempts to arrange her marriage. Rama was now entering her early thirties, and it was becoming clear that she had misgivings about the merits of marriage and its accompanying exchanges meant to demonstrate women's economic and social strength. The two sisters, like many women of their generation, expressed uncertainty about the intrinsic worth of gift giving and the relationships it created, which demanded constant regeneration. The demands of social life were unending, they often said, and sometimes fickle. As alike as they were in their concerns about their mother's generation and the ways in which older women sought meaning and value, I always noticed how different Jigeen and Rama were. They were striking—tall with high cheekbones and exceedingly well dressed. They both wore Wolof clothing well and more often than not chose clothing in this style: long flowing gowns, expensive fabrics, and high heels. Yet one was married several times over, one not; one had a Qur'anic education, the other a French education; one placed her faith in Muslim diviners, the other in the market. Jigeen and Rama lived in two seemingly different worlds that were marked by different forms of achieving status within their families and communities. Equally, they had different religious sensibilities, with Jigeen being much more involved in Murid life and Rama eschewing any strict allegiance to a single Sufi congregation. They represented two different ways of being in the world and of creating meaningful lives in uncertain times.

AT HOME IN DAKAR

One late summer afternoon in 2006, I watched Rama count out a stack of banknotes and lay them, one by one, on top of a pile of gowns sewn by her tailors. She gave the money and the prêt-à-porter garments to her long-time friend Ami, who was headed to Bamako, Mali. Bamako women admired Dakar couture and as Rama explained, "These khaftans will earn a nice profit, which is what I want." Rama explained to Ami, "This client requested a lime-green-dyed *mbaseñ riche* cloth; this one would like plum; and this one the color of jade. I am writing it all down for you on this envelope and after you sell these dresses you are to buy these pieces of cloth." Then she said to me, "All Dakar women desire mbaseñ riche from Mali. You can't get the same colors in Dakar and the designs are unique."

As I watched Rama slip her hand under each satiny gown and then count out each smooth banknote, layering these two items one upon the other, I thought of how I often had seen women lay large bills on top of rolls of locally woven strip cloth, which were exchanged publicly during family ceremonies. I thought of how women often hid smaller denominations that were used for daily expenses by tying them in the corners of these same cloths, worn as wrappers concealing the lower body. I thought of the many ways in which women had described these textiles to me, giving tactile and sensual descriptions of their forms of wealth and how they were made visible through dress, portraiture, and gift exchange. I had seen cloths stacked in armoires, the same way they were stacked in market stalls, as part of women's inalienable stores of cloth wealth. I had been shown heirloom pieces handed down from mothers and grandmothers during weddings and naming ceremonies, pieces used as baby blankets and coverings for cold nights, and newer pieces that they had received from friends and female relatives at family ceremonies. Rama's expertise in textiles and clothing trends stemmed from her appreciation of their capacity to index women's prosperity and value. Her sartorial astuteness also derived from her determination to defer marriage and to acquire cloth wealth through other means.

I became friends with Rama and Ami, following them to women's parties called *tuur* and to nightclubs, and I often shared a room with Rama during my research trips to Senegal. They were becoming part of what I saw as an emerging circle of women entrepreneurs: cosmopolitan women who traveled abroad, trucked in beauty supplies, opened tailor shops, and attracted clients and dependents.[1] Unlike many women in their natal neighborhood, both Rama and Ami remained unmarried well into their late thirties. Marrying later, or not at all, was a trend among Dakar women, as growing numbers of men have moved abroad since the 1990s. The women left at home were often unemployed and thought to be poor marriage partners as a result. Some women, like Rama, were able to remain unmarried through the support of their brothers abroad who sent them trade goods, which they sold locally, although Rama confessed to me, "You have to have a very good strategy to refuse marriage partners offered by the family." Although her mother had presented her with many cousins, Rama rejected each in turn, acquiring a reputation as *naxari* (inflexible).

Rama and Ami's successful trading had enabled Ami to leave her family home. She rented a modest room in Parcelles Assainies, a newly built beachside neighborhood that was characterized by glaring white stucco villas in neat rows along increasingly congested roads that were bordered by shops offering tidy displays of bathroom fixtures. Overseas traders desired this neighborhood because of its proximity to the airport. That Ami had moved out of the neighborhood of her youth was striking, considering that many young people remained in their parents' homes well into their thirties. Many women only had the opportunity to leave their natal homes upon marriage, when they moved into the home of their affines until their husbands were able to build or rent a room of their own. Ami eventually left for Paris from where she continued to work with Rama, selling her garments to a West African clientele abroad.

When I asked Rama if she thought of going abroad, she shook her head vehemently and said, "*Deedet* [No]."

I persisted, "But how can you earn a living in Dakar, especially if you don't have a husband to help you out?"

"This is my country. This is where I want to live." She continued, "I am responsible for taking care of my brothers' affairs since they are abroad and they cannot follow up on all of their investments and projects." One of Rama's brothers had financed her business degree from one of the many private universities that had sprung up in Dakar after several years of student strikes at the national university, Université Cheikh Anta Diop. Since the early 1990s, she had explored various entrepreneurial projects including her latest, opening a tailor shop to build upon her successful cloth trade with Ami. Finally, she garnered esteem among friends and even older women as someone who knew how to create innovative fashions. They would say, "Rama knows cloth." Rama employed three male tailors and created truly cutting-edge ensemble garments using a wide variety of fabric from strip cloth to saris to linen to batik. She often incorporated costly heirloom fabrics into her gowns. Her fashions pointed to women's traditional forms of wealth and at the same time reflected a new select class of urbanite women, who acquired these textiles through means other than marriage.

Rama acquired distinctive fabrics that set her creations apart from anything seen in Dakar. For example, she would use narrow strip cloth from Benin, which young women may have normally dismissed given this fabric's association with senior women, its extraordinary expense, and the way its heavy folds eclipsed the feminine form. Rather than sewing the strips into wrappers of the sort that were exchanged during family ceremonies, Rama used them to trim linen and mbaseñ riche khaftans that emphasized a woman's silhouette. Rama created her garments on command and rented a separate boutique that she used as a showroom for her creations. She supplied her Senegalese girlfriends in France with outfits, which they then sold to Senegalese and other West African women who lived abroad. Women migrants frequently sought out the latest in Dakar fashions for their social visits, religious events, and family ceremonies. Thus, while Rama's designs depended on access to regional and long-distance markets, her clients abroad sought access to fashions from home, which reflected their continued ties to West Africa.

Rama was not the only woman I knew who was reluctant to marry. Throughout the 1990s, many urban and rural women commented on how fragile marriages had become, especially with many husbands migrating abroad. During my fieldwork, I heard numerous stories of young brides whose husbands had consigned them to the supervision of their affines while they traveled abroad. Brothers-in-law monitored the comings and goings of these young women and cautioned them to tread carefully where honor and restraint were concerned. Their mothers-in-law and senior co-wives assigned them their tasks, including assembling the numerous children in the household for breakfast, cleaning small stones from rice for the midday meal, and bringing cold drinks to visitors to the home. Occasions for visits from the new wife's family could be rare since she was considered to be *gan* (a stranger or guest) and therefore would not be in a position to provide hospitality for her visiting kith and kin.

As I visited with Rama and Ami in Ami's new room, I thought back to a similar visit in 2000 in the same seaside community, where I had interviewed the wife of an overseas trader. I thought that the visit was off to a good start. The young woman sat opposite me on the couch with her brother-in-law's wife by her side. Both women responded thoughtfully to my prepared questions while their mother-in-law sat quietly in the corner with one of her grandsons. Soon, however, the room was populated with neighboring women as the lights were dimmed and the television turned up for *Le cercle de feu*. This particular episode of the Brazilian soap opera from the late 1980s showed an older wealthy woman cutting up the credit cards she had given to her young lover after learning of his infidelity. It triggered a rousing debate among the women, some of whom envied the power her wealth brought her in the face of her lover's betrayal. After the soap opera, the young woman I had come to interview said, "You must walk with me near the beach."

"But isn't it dusk, isn't this called *timis* [the witching hour] when most people seek shelter indoors?"

She laughed at me, grabbed my hand, and led me outside. During our walk, she confided, "I lived in Italy with my husband. He worked in a glass factory. Italy isn't good, I didn't like it. I sat in my apartment alone and no one ever came to visit me. Life over there is too lonely." As we passed several homes and heard the evening call to prayer, she continued, "When I came back, I thought that my husband would return for the Màggal, but he couldn't afford it this year."

I responded sympathetically, "I can't imagine how that must have felt. Is this common?"

"There are so many women," she said, "who wait for their husbands and they never return." She recounted stories of women in Tuba and its neighboring village, Mbacke, who had extramarital relations, of children who were not their husbands', and of the rising divorce rate. She spoke of wives who were outright abandoned and who never received remittances, and of others who were denied a separation by strict parents and in-laws. More commonly, she warned, "The remittances that women receive are not enough to allow women to get by." She also said, "I wouldn't be surprised to learn that men do things in Italy they would never do in Senegal." We then talked about a recent radio broadcast on the network Walf Fadjri in which male migration was linked to rising HIV rates in Senegal. The program had discussed the predicament of some men who were driven to participate in the extralegal economy, including drug trafficking and prostitution, so that they could send money back to Senegal. She then stopped, faced me, took my forearms, and said, "Many of the men neglect to send their wives even housekeeping money during their sojourns, and then they return home and invest all of their earnings in constructing villas so that other people can witness their success abroad."

In Ami's seaside room, with the money and the dresses still between us on the bed, I listened as Ami and Rama discussed Ami's new quarters; though it barely allowed for the substantial bed and armoire, the confined space was improved by the freedom it represented; it was at once a sanctuary and an escape. I also thought of Rama's divorced and destitute older sister, Jigeen, who could not find refuge even in her own room. Ami turned to me and teasingly asked, "*Eh,* why haven't you found me a good husband? I am so desperate that I would even accept a *tubab* [white person]." At this, she and Rama doubled over in laughter. Rama then returned to her piles of textiles and continued counting, first the cash, and then the khaftans. She encouraged Ami as she slipped on a yellow-gold chiffon khaftan with copper-colored embroidery and a neckline mimicking that of male garments: "*Yangi sañse,* you are dressed for a feast."[2] Ami then removed the gown and started folding the garments.

"Are these going to fit in my suitcase?" she asked Rama, who was flipping a packet of portraits of women that Ami had brought back from a naming ceremony during her last trip to Bamako some months earlier. Ami then left with the dresses to see if they would fit into her suitcase, which was laid out on a neighbor's living room floor down the hall. Rama quickly slipped one of the pictures into her purse, a portrait of a radiant, middle-aged woman wearing a peach-dyed brocade boubou with an expansive neckline and minimalist embroidery framing her face. She looked at me and explained, "*Beggnaa jell photo bi ndaxte moom dafe rafet* [I want to take this photo because she is so beautiful]."

Rama and I had frequent visitors in the small airy room that we rented together in a four-story boardinghouse across the dusty lane from her hectic family home in Khar Yalla. Visitors to our room often complimented our tidy and stylish decor, particularly the freshly painted rose-colored walls, the ample floor-to-ceiling curtains, the lime satin coverlet, and the black armoire, which covered an entire wall and in which we stored our belongings. We had ottomans for our guests to sit on, and Rama's bureau, which was littered with beauty products, had a large mirror that the other women in our building often used. Our visitors would often say, "Here, there is privacy." They would talk about our ability to close the door and create a privileged space in which we could negotiate our most personal, intimate matters. Such privacy afforded a refuge from the gossip that flowed in the busy homes, whose bedrooms were shared with children, siblings, rural kin, and frequent visitors. In this heavily populated neighborhood, houses shared walls, and courtyard spaces could be easily viewed from the second floor of neighbors' homes. Our room, rented away from the prying eyes of her siblings, social seniors, and neighbors, enabled Rama's movement across the social landscape. Here, she held private meetings in which she brokered love affairs and business arrangements, kept her reading materials such as romance novels and magazines, stored notebooks in which she tracked social payments related to life-cycle rituals and mutual aid associations, and made loans and gifts to those in need. Here, in her locked armoire, she hid her own savings and stores of cloth wealth as well as the pots of numerous rotating savings and credit associations in which she and her mother participated. By concealing and enclosing her affairs in the material boundaries of our room, Rama constructed her social persona as someone with *fit ak fayda* (courage and importance). By making her wealth visible and putting it into circulation by displaying a certain sartorial acumen and bestowing hospitality, aid, gifts, and credit to kith and kin, she crafted a reputation for movement and mobility that attracted others to her.

Our room was in a cement-block dwelling typical of Khar Yalla, which had been built for rental income and was occupied by families, single mothers, teachers, and male immigrant casual laborers who most often came from Guinea-Bissau and Mali. Our monthly rent of 30,000 CFA francs[3] was average for the neighborhood, an area in which one found many multifamily dwellings along with the remnants of self-built housing from when the neighborhood was first settled by refugees from city improvement campaigns in the 1970s. The rooms were organized around an open-air, communal hallway that contained shared cooking space, a Turkish toilet and shower stall where one could bathe with a pail of water, and an open central courtyard on the first floor. Water was available in the courtyard for 10 CFA francs a bucket, although I could not seem to keep much of it in the bucket as I climbed the stairs to our second-floor room, and I wondered how others fared. The second-floor balcony gave us a clear view into Rama's family home across the way with its open central courtyard. From here, Rama could call down to her younger sisters and command any number of services, such as buying baguettes and packets of powdered Nescafé from the corner store, removing her laundry from the line on the top floor of the family home, or bringing buckets of water and rags to wipe down the vinyl floor, a daily ritual of keeping the sand at bay in windy, coastal Dakar.

Though Rama and I shared the same bed, our room did not feel crowded to me; four of Rama's teenage sisters shared a room with a queen-sized bed in the family home, and her older sister, Jigeen, slept in the same bed with her three children. I was often traveling with other women in the family to Mbacke, the natal village of Rama's maternal grandmother, to take part in religious observances, naming ceremonies, weddings, and funerals or simply to visit maternal kin. Rama rarely traveled with us to the countryside. She vastly preferred the freedom of the city—its markets, shops, and soirees and her coterie of well-traveled, single, female friends.

Rama's family said that she was a daughter who had kersa (respect) and fayda (determination and importance). However, at times they also said she could be naxari (inflexible), and perhaps it was this combination that led to her success in business, real estate, and interpersonal matters. In the summer of 1998, attracted by its balcony, she had rented our room in preparation for my arrival to do research. She was an unmarried woman, so it is doubtful that her father would have allowed her to live outside of the family home, but she earned his approval by discursively constructing the room as a form of hospitality toward me. I quickly realized that the room was also an important means for her to assert her fiscal and moral autonomy; she kept it for several years, holding it for me each time that I returned for fieldwork and visits.

It was through her residence there that she gained entrée into the rapidly growing real estate market in Dakar. She befriended the owner of our building, a gentle older man, whom she called Pa, who lived in a government-financed (and now semi-privately financed) SICAP villa, and they became confidants. She was skillful in extracting rents from the inhabitants of our building and in resolving the tensions and quarrels that inevitably arose with so many different families and individuals sharing space. Her accounting skills—perhaps seen as some kind of complex numerology, but also as the result of her training in business—earned her the trust of Pa, and she was eventually put in charge of managing the rental of the rooms. The residents recognized her growing stature in the community and her affectionate demeanor toward the elderly man who owned the building, and they often acquiesced to her demands when confronted with her commanding figure robed in novel and expensive tailored pantsuits with the long, flowing jackets that are popular in northern Muslim countries. During her tenure as manager of the building, she cautiously deflected an offer of marriage from Pa who, as it turned out, had four wives already. But his fondness for her and her family's respect for him, which was displayed by their bowed heads each time he descended from his pale blue, early model Mercedes in his old-fashioned, starchy, blue boubous of ample cloth and pointed, yellow *baboush* shoes, ensured that she was well cared for.

Rama's success surpassed that of most of her Dakar relatives. She was often dressed in a new outfit and was always talking about the enterprises that she planned to undertake through the generosity of her brothers, who sent money or goods from their overseas trade. Rama's carefully culled income, which was small but regular, and the way in which she wedged herself into a profitable situation in the apartment building earned the praise of her mother, Sokna Géer. She had excellent credit among her peers, and the various market vendors and shop owners would willingly extend her favors. I was part of the reason for her good credit: how could she default on any loans with a tubab in her room? She was also the reason that others hesitated to ask me for money; they recognized that Rama already had a claim to my resources. With the assistance of another brother, she had wisely finished her program at a private business school and deflected several offers of marriage arranged by her father, thus managing to remain within the sphere of her brothers' responsibility. They were liberal with their gifts, for how would she attract a suitable marriage partner without the latest imported fashions? In the meantime, her older brothers came to rely on her to manage their affairs at home because she was not only capable, she was discreet.

Rama carefully and quietly invested her earnings in a rotating savings and credit association that was organized by a local NGO with the aim of building a home on a piece of land that she had bought in a seaside town a bit outside of Dakar. During this time, she held several unpaid internships—one at the airport and another for a Danish shipping company that specialized in container vessels—but neither resulted in lasting employment, as was the case for most college graduates in Dakar. Though Rama obtained the use of a taxi and hired a driver who was recommended by her father to work for her, one could always hear her complaining, "*Taxi du dox.*" To say that something does not *dox* is to say literally that it does not walk or move; the word is commonly used to indicate that business is either doing well (*dafay dox*) or not doing well (*du dox*).[4] Whether or not she actually owned the car remained ambiguous. Rama insisted that she did not, for reasons that were never made clear except perhaps to discourage others from thinking that she was accumulating wealth or perhaps because it was an uncommon business for a woman.

Though Rama possessed business acumen, she had the unfortunate habit of falling in love with *doxkat* (literally, "those who walk"), which is to say that they were men who had numerous lovers. Once, she fell for a broad-shouldered Catholic Guinean who had just returned from Portugal. He was fond of sport coats and cravats and avoided speaking the Wolof slang that he had grown up with in favor of French. Their families inhabited opposite corners of the same intersection and their mothers shared membership in a rotating savings and credit association. Rama joked that she ought to return with him to Portugal to avail herself of the business opportunities there, but she knew that he was a bit of a heartbreaker. Moreover, her fear of offending her father by marrying a non-Muslim kept her from accepting his advances.

In line with her fiercely independent demeanor, Rama was not a devout follower of any particular Sufi congregation; she did not, for the most part, participate in visits to shaykhs, offerings, or pilgrimages, and she showed a clear disdain for practices of Muslim divination and healing. She spoke out against the mendacity of politicians who sought shaykhs' support through gifts and favors and was a fierce defender of the secular state. She understood that creating a pious persona was relevant to her success in business but didn't rely on the invocations of masters or their potions to thrive. Rama did, however, occasionally participate in the annual Tijani pilgrimage to Tivouane with her father and attended conferences led by Muslim intellectuals that provided instructions on the straight path and moral righteousness. My favorite picture of her was taken at a Qadiriyya religious conference that she attended, and it sat prominently on her bureau: she wore a crisp white boubou trimmed with a thick, white lace border and a voluminous white scarf wrapped around her head to frame her face. Rama's understanding of the relationship between the sacred and the secular aspects of her persona could be gleaned from the portraits that she displayed on her bureau. She placed photos taken at Islamic conferences next to those taken at conferences on development initiatives at the local nongovernmental organization and portraits of herself at family ceremonies. This coupling of the religious and secular realms of social experience exemplified her understanding of the flow of baraka as grace, prosperity, and potentiality. For the most part, she focused on achieving religious merit through adhering to an upright life in which she disdained gossip, refused debt, was fastidious in her dress and beautification practices, and comported herself with the restraint, respect, and discretion that are becoming to a Muslim woman.

ANYWHERE BUT HERE

When I returned for fieldwork in 1999, I was shocked to learn how much Jigeen's life had changed since I first met her in 1992. I had not seen her much in the intervening years as she had married a couple of times and lived elsewhere.

In the early 1980s, Jigeen had migrated with her first husband, a trader, to the Ivory Coast. Her first two daughters were from this marriage. From the Ivory Coast, her husband traveled to Italy and occasionally sent back gold jewelry and other things for her to sell in Abidjan. To supplement her income, Jigeen rented rooms in her house to two men, one a trader from Senegal and the other a trader from Gabon. By the early 1990s, it became clear to Jigeen that her husband had abandoned her. Though she had succeeded as a trader and had built up a substantial network of clients, she chose to return to Senegal, seeking a divorce. Those who might have turned their backs on her when she returned from her ten-year stay in the Ivory Coast celebrated her return to Dakar when she arrived with two armoires, one for her mother and one for her father. She said that it was this trading capital that she had amassed in the Ivory Coast that ensured her continued respect in the community.

Soon after she returned to Dakar, Jigeen entered into another marriage, which also failed. She then met up with a prominent trader who was related to the Mbacke family, the direct descendants of the founding figure of the Murid order. Her new husband dealt in auto parts and she could not help but hope that she was going somewhere with him. But this marriage also ended badly. Jigeen clashed with her co-wives and, as Sokna Géer explained with regard to Jigeen's husband, "*Ah, moom, baax-ul. Lekk naa xaalis am.* [He was a bad husband. He ate her money]."

When I returned in 1999, Jigeen often said to me, "My *warsek* [luck] is in Abidjan." Raising her eyebrows and puckering her lips, she would add for emphasis, "Dakar, here, there is no luck." It was at this time that I first learned that Jigeen and Rama were *jubbo-uno,* which meant that they had ceased speaking to each other. Rama said that Jigeen was too quarrelsome, "She has no patience and restraint [*muñ ak kersa*]." Jigeen said that Rama was too independent and didn't respect her seniority as her older sister.

Jigeen had run into trouble with her other siblings as well, especially in relation to providing for her parents. She had given up her room in the boardinghouse and moved back into her parents' house. "It isn't normal," Jigeen would say. "A middle-aged woman should not live under her parent's roof." She would continue, "I'm tired, and every time the phone rings it is another naming ceremony and another feast, every week." The subject of money, especially debt, seemed to consume Jigeen, to constrain her every move, and it dominated most of our conversations.

Because Jigeen could not manage money, she was often reticent to participate in family ceremonies, which would incur more debt. Sokna Géer would say to her accusingly when Jigeen refused to represent her at an event, "*Yow, begg-uloo sa famille* [You don't want your family]." And sometimes I heard her say as she pointed her finger in Jigeen's direction for emphasis, "*Yow, doom-u-xaram nge* [You are an unwanted child]."

Jigeen often complained to me that she lacked the money for the gifts and that *gacce* (shame) kept her at home. Although each of the daughters could expect to receive remarks like this from time to time, Jigeen was often stung by the insult. Jigeen would explain, "People will not respect you if you do not have money. When it is time for family decisions to be made, they don't ask me, even though I am the one who was taken out of school to raise them. They should respect me."

Jigeen often talked about leaving Senegal and traveling abroad. This desire was tied to her realization that she rarely had the means to sustain, let alone initiate, relations of reciprocal gift exchange with women in her family and community. Jigeen saw travel as a means of extracting herself from social obligations. For older divorced women and women who remained single well into middle age, migration and trade provided an escape from societal pressures and new options for autonomy and control over their assets (see, for example, Reynolds 2006). For Jigeen, as for many Senegalese men and women, engaging in trade seemed like the only way to earn a living and become respected in Senegal. Jigeen desired her own apartment and often said that, if she could, she would travel to Dubai or Hong Kong and import cloth and cosmetics to sell in her own stall in Marché HLM, the cloth market in a suburb of Dakar. She said that she would take part in family ceremonies, help out people in need, and contribute to the household expenses so that she would be respected.

In 2000, I heard that each of the Géer sons had contributed to completing the second floor of the family house. When Jigeen and I talked about this development, she made me conscious of the merits of having a room of one's own. Jigeen had heard Rama complain that I liked to take notes late at night, an activity that Jigeen seemed to appreciate, and she said to me, "You are just like the Murid mystics in that *jinn* [invisible beings that can be either harmful or helpful] visit you in the night with revelations, a reward for working hard when others are sleeping." After careful consideration and much discussion with Sokna Géer, I decided to help the family build one of the rooms on the second floor, where I would stay for the duration of my fieldwork. I had hoped that I would be able to leave my room for Jigeen when I left and that would take some pressure off her. The room gave form to Jigeen's imagined possibilities as she pointed out the parallels that it had with the activities of returning overseas traders. Like them, I had built the room with money that I had garnered overseas and, once I had done so, people in the neighborhood regarded me differently, coming to my room to describe their problems and seek my opinion. As Jigeen had observed, my room served as a refuge where persons caught in the middle of conflicts sought to have their side affirmed. We could shut the door and talk without our words traveling down the stairs. This was significant in a neighborhood where most women did not have private rooms.

In the late spring of 2000, I approached Jigeen about the upcoming Màggal pilgrimage. I wanted to interview her Murid contacts from Abidjan who would be making the pilgrimage. I asked if she would accompany me to Tuba. Jigeen accepted my invitation since she would amplify her prosperity by making offerings at the tombs of the deceased saints of the Murid order. She would also earn the respect of her family and peers for fulfilling her religious obligations and from their recognition of the potential for garnering religious merit that a pilgrimage offers. Sacrifices like the expensive transportation and the sundry gifts that were required to be purchased to undertake such a journey were known to contain future rewards. I was able to arrange and pay for our transportation and Jigeen worked quickly to arrange our lodging with a family in Tuba that she had known in the Ivory Coast.

For several months, Jigeen plotted and planned; she visited friends and distant acquaintances and assiduously paid off her debts, quietly, one by one. She began to spend even more generously on Muslim diviners. Jigeen saw her financial problems in relation to her luck. Jigeen was a devout adherent to the Murid way, and her devotional practices included frequent alms giving, supplications to religious guides, and visiting Muslim healers and diviners. Although Jigeen never sought gnosis, the Murid way nevertheless provided the moral framework for her experiences. Jigeen embodied a common Murid disposition toward accepting suffering and seeking out travel to acquire knowledge and to achieve moral renewal. Like many Sufis, her personal spiritual journey involved renouncing her immoral self—the part of her that acquired debts, gossiped viciously, and was unable to sustain proper relations with others. This personal journey was bound up with that of others, including the exile of Amadou Bamba at the hands of the French colonizers, the journeys of adepts who embarked upon the sacred hajj pilgrimage, and even the travel of disciples abroad in search of a livelihood.

Jigeen accumulated personal favors and sought out Muslim diviners and healers who offered her medications and made *gris-gris* (amulets) for her to repair and regenerate her relations with others. Visits to these specialists could be quite expensive. At the very highest end, one diviner said that he received 300,000–600,000 CFA francs for his work from important figures like ministers of state and, at the low end, Jigeen said that she often paid 10,000–20,000 CFA francs for these services. In one case she was asked to pay for a number of items that would enable the diviner to perform his work efficaciously over the course of a week, which included sacrificing a guinea hen, procuring the hair from the back of a hyena's neck, purchasing paper, and locating a white cow. For her part, in addition to the payment of cash for his services (the amount of which he never specified, only saying to her, "Ah, you know how deep your pocket is"), she was to bathe for seven nights with a text that he prepared for her, which she was to soak in water first until it disintegrated, and she was to give alms of sugar at the mosque.

Rather than articulating her lack of economic and social opportunities—such as her lack of education, employment, and housing—as a failure of the Senegalese state, Jigeen spoke of her difficult position as a personal and spiritual failure. This was one of the fundamental features of economic and social reform as informed by neoliberal international and state policies, which emphasized individual responsibility. Her narrative of her experience was a story of struggle, which paralleled the experience of Amadou Bamba and his exile by the French colonialists. For Jigeen, this struggle related to the process of self-knowledge and knowledge of the divine for which she would ultimately be rewarded with either salvation or worldly wealth. Jigeen, like many Murid adepts, described travel, whether on pilgrimage or in search of a living, as deeply transformative. Pilgrimages offer the possibility of transforming the self. One embarks on these journeys by symbolically shedding the mundane self by distributing alms to the needy, and one returns with symbolic objects, cloth, religious paraphernalia, and special foods that are imbued with the baraka of the wali (Werbner 2003:101). Since moral renewal is an achieved state that calls for recognition by one's social circle, one revitalizes these relations by bestowing on others the sacred objects that were obtained on pilgrimage. Thus pilgrimages are central to women's moral reputation and respectability (Rosander 2004:70).

For Sufis, travel is rife with sacred meanings since it is the principal metaphor used to describe the experience of revelation. Likewise, the categories that Murids construct as historically salient, such as travel and self-discipline, point to the karamat (events that attest to the presence of the divine) of Bamba. Jigeen, like many Murid adepts, framed her opinions by reciting these. When she asked her mother or her grandmother for assistance, she would quickly follow their refusals with, "What God gives me alone is enough, I don't need any thing else." She later referred to karamat that tell of how Bamba survived exile in Gabon on an island full of snakes and devils, or how he was placed in a cage with a hungry lion, saying that she could withstand any difficult situation except being motionless. Jigeen understood the social friction she encountered and her financial failings as manifestations of her luck. These shortcomings could only be addressed through social, spiritual, and geographical mobility. This was why she devoted a large portion of her meager income to countering affliction with visits to Muslim diviners in search of *gris-gris* and medications that would activate her relationships with others and attract money to her so that she could ultimately journey abroad.

For Jigeen, the period leading up to the annual pilgrimage to Tuba, the Màggal, in 2000 was filled with frequent trips to various diviners, distributing alms, and making *sarax* (sacrifices). Such sacrifices, she explained, would "*ubbi sama warsek* [open my luck]" and amplify her prosperity; only by giving money could she attract money. Jigeen spoke of the Màggal as the "*sarax bu mag* [big sacrifice]," the moment when one's offerings would be bound up with those made by disciples from "the four corners of the world." The event was, after all, the most *mag* (important) annual celebration for the Murid faithful (Coulon 1999:196) and was a particularly potent time to make demands since adepts struggled to find ways to magnify their sacrifices by serving others. Jigeen, for example, would frequently say that she would not have any luck if she did not give alms and that it was her fate to give alms often. At least once a week, she pounded uncooked rice with sugar and water and distributed these sweets to children or offered them millet porridge with sour milk; she often gave candles to passing strangers; and she distributed chickens at the neighborhood mosque to the men who prayed there.

Jigeen's debts had made her the victim of vicious gossip by her female kin. They lashed out at her for spending considerable amounts of money on diviners, their *gris-gris,* and their medications, rather than repaying her debts to friends and family. I recall several occasions in the spring of 2000 when we would visit two to four diviners a day as Jigeen pleaded with them to let her have this or that medication, usually herbal drinks, despite her lack of payment. Her Gabonese friend from the Ivory Coast, Demba Ba, sent her money to cover her debt. He had become a successful entrepreneur of bootleg videos and DVDs in Brooklyn, New York. Yet even he feared that she would squander the money on her cadre of diviners, so he sent a Western Union money order directly to her younger brother, who called her creditors to the house and paid them back on Jigeen's behalf to save the family honor.

Jigeen was in dire financial straits indeed. She had gone to Gambia in December with money that had been given to her by another trading partner from the Ivory Coast, al Hajji Ndiaye, who was now living in Tuba. Ndiaye's young son had succumbed to the deadly combination of yellow fever and malaria that had devastated Tuba during the rainy season. When Jigeen attended the funeral, Ndiaye heard of her divorce, which had taken place a year earlier, and grasped her hand, flattened it, and placed a roll of banknotes into it, gently folding her fingers back over the bulk, perhaps to honor an old obligation or perhaps to turn away his ill fortune through generosity. With this money Jigeen traveled by bus to

Gambia, a frequent way in which women trade, benefiting from trade liberalization following the reforms undertaken by Senegal in the late 1990s in the midst of the World Bank's structural adjustment programs. She brought back bolts of cloth and sold them on installment to her female kin but, by the time the Màggal rolled around in May, most had failed to pay her due to her own long history of debt and lack of repayment, which spurred no one to repay her quickly.

With this Màggal to Tuba, Jigeen was planning to change her fortune. She hoped that her last ex-husband, the *mbacke mbacke* auto parts dealer with whom she had strived to stay on good terms, would press banknotes into her hand as he had on so many other occasions when she had been to visit him. She also intended to call on some wealthy Murid traders whom she had known through her second husband in Abidjan. At first I thought she was seeking to reestablish her trading networks, to see if she could convince her former partners to advance her the capital necessary to trade. I was to learn that she had something else in mind.

Leading up to the Màggal, regular television programming was often interrupted with announcements from a military commander who stood in front of a series of maps, diagramming traffic patterns and water allocation during the pilgrimage week. These public service announcements would often prompt Jigeen to reexamine her wardrobe for the four-day trip. She would review which ensembles she would wear and which she would give away to the women who would host her in Tuba. Her activity prompted her mother to pull from under her bed a suitcase, which was full of scarves, some white, others striped or polka-dotted, others made of white organza embroidered with white floral patterns studded with crystals. These scarves had been sent by Sokna's younger sister Maam Dara, who had migrated to Jeddah. Not only had she sent back cloth, she had also begun construction on the second floor of the family home by sending remittances of cash to her household, which consisted of her mother, another sister, and her sister's husband. She had initially gone to Jeddah for the *umra* (the smaller hajj) and to purchase trade goods, and had stayed since she had met a man.

Jigeen admired her aunt Maam Dara. She envied her freedom to come and go, a freedom rarely available to women in Senegal, who were carefully watched by in-laws, brothers, and other prying family members. I thought that Maam Dara's freedom to travel had also cost her no small amount of heartache. Before she left for Jeddah, I had been helping Maam Dara write letters in English to an estranged lover whom she had met in France. He was an American airline pilot and at one point they were engaged to be married. However, he abruptly left France and returned to the U.S. with little explanation after being mugged by an African man. Before he left, she heard, he had come to see her at the short-term occupancy hotel where she was staying. The deskman told him that she was not in, suspicious that she was using her room as a base of prostitution. Her pilot got the wrong idea and, coupled with his anxiety after his recent mugging, fled without a word. Maam Dara waited for him in France until her family eventually brought her back to Senegal.

Unfortunately, Jigeen Géer did not begin her Màggal on an auspicious note. Less than an hour outside Dakar, in the village of Bargny, a middle-aged man, dressed decorously in a brown grand boubou, desperately pounded on the door of our taxi as it slowed to a stop in traffic. Opening the door, he said, "I pray you, my whole family was on that train." We made room for him, and as he wedged himself sideways into the rear passenger seat, the events of the recent train wreck unfolded. Spinning in and out of the sandy ruts between the train tracks, the taxi driver maneuvered past hundreds of cars, buses, and passenger minivans whose occupants sprawled out onto the road. We saw that several packed passenger cars of the train had recently overturned, crushing those who rode for free on the roofs, a practice that was normally prohibited but was allowed during the pilgrimage season since it was considered part of the collective spirit and fervor of being a young Murid follower. President Abdoulaye Wade's special Màggal 2000 helicopter had been hovering over the scene at the time of the accident, reporting on the pilgrimage, the special trains that the government had commissioned for the event, and the trucks, buses, and other forms of urban transport that were all heading toward Tuba from the "four corners of the world."

Trapped in the stalled traffic, the three- to four-hour trip soon turned into five to six hours. As we passed the time, Jigeen and I turned to talking about our stay in Tuba. She advised me that she planned to pay a visit to several traders she had known in Abidjan in the 1980s, including al Hajji Ndiaye. Ndiaye's home, like many others in Tuba, fulfilled the ndiggel (command) of Seriñ Abdoul Lahat Mbacke that disciples who migrated abroad should build a home in Tuba where they could retire and eventually be buried.

When we finally arrived in Tuba after the hot and dusty ride, we bathed at the Ndiaye compound. The Ndiaye home was an impressive two-story, white cement villa with expansive archways and pillars on the second-floor terraces. Within the compound, a number of cars were parked on a cement lot that also boasted a well and a courtyard space set off for outdoor cooking. A short wall covered with a broken-tile mosaic separated this area, which contained a shelter and two storerooms. It seemed to me that the architect of the villa had ambitious intentions for the house, which looked like it was still under construction. And yet inside it was clear that this home was not built recently. The furnishings, once-grand velvet and carved wood, now slouched under their dusty covers, showing their age. Other aspects of the house were unfinished—wires still hung where outlets and switches were planned but had not been executed and, although the bathrooms had been built in the European style with standing sinks, bathtubs, and toilet fixtures, the plumbing had never been installed so water had to be carried to them from the outside well.

Al Hajji Ndiaye's wives had plenty of help drawing water from the well in the courtyard and bringing it up to their respective rooms. They seemed to be in an ideal situation, as Jigeen described it to me. Not only could they draw on the help of two daughters-in-law, they also each received from al Hajji Ndiaye the generous sum of 5,000 CFA francs a day for housekeeping expenses and daily meals. He also kept his storehouses stocked with coffee, milk, and sugar, which were luxuries outside of Dakar. Each of his wives had a suite of rooms, including a bedroom, a bathroom, and a living room, which opened into the hallway of the enclosed villa structure. The wives also sold merchandise in Tuba's Marché Ocass and thus had accumulated their own wealth as well.

Ndiaye swelled with pride as he waxed on about the changes he had seen in Tuba since disciples began leaving for Dakar or abroad in large numbers following the famines that struck the area in the 1970s. He talked about the new villas and neighborhoods that were springing up outside Tuba on land that had been devastated by the peanut crops, but that was now fertile ground for Murid families. He told us that one of his sons had been employed at a shipping company in the United States for seven years and had just returned to Senegal to open a stall in Dakar's Marché Sandaga. In addition to importing merchandise from North America, he also planned to import goods from Dubai. Once we had bathed, rested, and visited with the Ndiaye family, Jigeen announced, "It is four o'clock and the heat has dissipated somewhat; now, we should visit the tomb of Amadou Bamba."

After crossing the enormous courtyard that surrounded the mosque, where vendors sold herbal medications and Muslim texts, we crowded into line with hundreds of women in the hot sun, our heads and arms covered by voluminous scarves, and entered through one door while men entered through another. In the mausoleum we moved through the crush of supplicants prostrated in silent veneration at the tomb of

Women on the Màggal, 2000

the wali and those who tossed offerings through the brass railings that enclosed the tomb. To touch anything that has come into contact with a wali is to benefit from his or her divine sanctity and to receive his or her baraka, and it is for this reason that visiting the tomb is a central rite. This central component of the Màggal is called *ziyara,* and adepts approach the visit to Bamba's tomb with an emotional intensity that is remarkable. This moment best exemplifies the altruistic and humanist orientation of Sufism (Werbner 2003:103). It is in the presence of the tomb that supplicants speak their innermost desires for family peace, fertility, well-being, and salvation, since Bamba plays an intercessory role, mediating between aspirants and the divine. Once we completed our time at Bamba's mausoleum, we moved on to visit the mausoleums of other significant religious figures of the order. Many disciples also visited the Well of Mercy where one could fill a bottle with its healing waters, the Murid library that houses Bamba's writings and that of other important scholars of Islam, and the university under construction.

As a ritual practice, ziyara involves the recognition of and respect toward living religious figures, the descendants of Bamba to whom pilgrims offer greetings, hospitality, prayers, supplication, and offerings. Visits to pay homage to family elders, who may or may not be religious figures, are also called ziyara and may take place during the Màggal if the family hails from Tuba or the surrounding region. Ziyara, then, and the practices associated with it give form to relations between men and women, old and young. As a ritual moment, it holds both the potential to reinforce hierarchies of age and gender and the possibility to alter those hierarchies.[5] Though the rites surrounding the pilgrimage to Tuba in many ways define what it is to be a Murid, these practices are in no way commensurate with the esoteric aspects of Sufism, such as extended study and retreat from the world (Coulon 1999:196).

The Màggal is a spiritual pilgrimage to the tombs of Murid shaykhs. It is also the moment when disciples and overseas Murid dahira associations give cash offerings to the religious hierarchy to constitute new social relations and possibilities. The annual pilgrimage offers a moment when the relationship of disciple and shaykh is reestablished, as are the myriad social relations that emanate from ideas about greetings, hospitality, prayers, and supplications. In addition to offerings and sacrifices, the Màggal is also the time of requests and entreaties. Like the experiences of the impoverished in Aminata Sow Fall's *The Beggars' Strike* (1986), the Màggal offers an opportunity for those at the bottom of social hierarchies to enter into patron-client relations because, in order for disciples to practice qualities of generosity and munificence (the qualities of those who are destined for salvation), they must find recipients for their actions.

The spiritual framework of ziyara, the practice of respect for and recognition of living or deceased persons' potency, also extends to visits to social superiors, including patrons and elders. Thus, the Màggal provided a meaningful context in which Jigeen could visit the homes of her associates from the Ivory Coast. Over the long, hot afternoons when life seemed to stop in the midst of the Màggal frenzy, we shared mint tea and cold beverages with her hosts, with whom she engaged in lively conversation. At each house we were offered elaborate displays of dates, kola, fruit, and meat since each Tuba household had slaughtered a cow and distributed its parts to guests, for which the household was rewarded with religious merit.

I soon discovered the true motivation behind Jigeen's pilgrimage. She sought the contacts and resources that were necessary to apply for a multiple-entry U.S. visa as the spouse of a trader. This was not the first time she had called on these connections; some years earlier, one of these contacts had been particularly generous in helping her younger brother apply for a student visa for the United States by providing a bank statement and a letter of affiliation or support. This time Jigeen flaunted her single status, coquettishly announcing her interest in resuming trading, spoke of her various friends and relations abroad, and recalled with sincerity how she had aided these traders when they were young and struggling to enter the Ivorian trade networks, reminding them of the meals and kind company she had provided them in Abidjan. She spoke of her connection with Demba Ba, a successful wholesaler of bootleg films in New York, whom she had hosted in Abidjan. She hoped that when she made it to New York she would be able to call on him and that he would help her to get settled as he had done with her brother.

Jigeen talked about the Murid trade networks in sacred idioms, constantly trying to locate her luck along the circuits of wage labor and capital and framing her experience as one of trial and self-knowledge, drawn from her knowledge of the karamat of Bamba. How she incorporated herself into these circuits, however, involved a high degree of pragmatism and scheming. Jigeen not only called in favors and old debts during the Màggal, a potent time of sacrifice and display of Murid solidarity. She also deployed the art of *mokk pooj* to influence her trading contacts. Displaying the qualities of mokk pooj involves being considerate, foreseeing the needs and desires of male companions, and being docile and obliging. Although it is said that men are boroom kër ga (heads of household), women are *boroom neeg* (heads of the bedroom), which is to say that they influence men's decision making in matters private and public in the intimacy of their bedrooms. These bedroom secrets enable each party to save face in public by relegating contentious issues to private conjugal space. Senegalese women deploy this kind of feminine mystique by lighting incense, preparing delicious meals, and wearing *bin bin* (waist beads) to bed. By preparing for the conjugal visit in this way, women wield their power of influence so that their spouses will be more willing to consider their requests for everything from an addition to the house to an increase in the housekeeping budget. In general, the person who is mokk pooj is a *mokk* (expert) in managing the social dance, or *pooj*, which literally translates as "thighs" (Underwood 1988:50).

Women also perform as mokk pooj in less intimate settings, as Jigeen did with her former husband's business partners to garner their assistance with her immigration visa. Her coquettish demeanor showed respect for hierarchies of age and gender as she sorted through personal favors, debts, and obligations, which are meted out in various formal and informal ways. Most important, since she had approached these traders in this fashion, they could trust that she would keep their dealings confidential. Thus, Jigeen was able to take advantage of the Màggal as a ritual moment to extract commitments from both her former trading partners and those of her ex-husband because their prospects for prosperity were tied to their generosity during the Màggal season. She was also able to amplify her prospects of receiving aid through her religious visits and supplication to the tombs of Bamba and his descendants.

FIVE

A LAMB SLAUGHTERED

"BUT I DON'T LOVE Musa Mbacke," Bintu whispered, eyes downcast and legs folded under her slender body as her maternal kin—aunt, great-aunt, uncle, and mother—pressed her to explain her refusal to enter into the marriage that they had arranged. "I love Abdoul Aziz," she said, her voice faltering slightly when she looked toward Sokna Géer, who was seated on the bed. "*Eskeiye!*" Sokna gasped, placing her hand over her mouth when she heard her son's name. The elders all looked away, and weighty silence fell in the tightly packed room in the rural village of Mbacke.

A few days later, Bintu's kin dispersed to their homes in the urban capital of Dakar and discussed how to untangle the web of obligations that had been woven by the series of marriage payments that Musa Mbacke had sent over the previous year. Sokna Géer said that she wanted to bring the marriage process to its completion. She said that it would be difficult to return the marriage payments that had already been made. She also pointed out that Ramadan would be starting in two months, which would mean that the ritual life of the community would be put on hold for the strict observance of the month-long Muslim fast. There would be no wedding celebrations or festivities during this month. Moreover, Ramadan imposed certain financial obligations. Sokna needed to set aside money to purchase meat for special dishes that would be shared with her extended family during Ramadan and to purchase rice to distribute to dependents. She also needed to save money for the Korite feast at the end of the month when her family would want to slaughter a lamb and wear new, formal clothing.

During these discussions, the women in the family said many times, "*Xam lépp, wax lépp baaxul* [It is not good to know all and to say all]." They said that Bintu could have chosen a number of discreet, prudent, and acceptable ways of backing out of the arranged marriage without mentioning her feelings for Abdoul Aziz. These feelings were problematic because the two had been raised in the same household and thus were, in a sense, brother and sister. Her maternal kin might have helped her to settle the matter privately to protect the family's reputation. The women said that Bintu recklessly threatened the family's *daraja* (dignity, respectability) by refusing the union after some of the marriage payments had been accepted. She also had opened the family to suggestions of incest by speaking of her relationship with Abdoul Aziz. When Bintu declared that she loved Abdoul Aziz, she cast doubt upon her own virtue as well as that of Sokna Géer. Sokna refused to back down because Bintu was to be a *wurusu jabar* (wife of gold), which signified her position as the *doom-u-nijaay* (daughter of the groom's mother's brother) and thus as the first choice for a marriage partner. Musa and Bintu came from Wolof families where the preferred mode of marriage was *ngën ci jabar* (cross-cousin marriage) (Ames 1953:45; Diop 1985:81–82), a union that was generally considered more durable than other matches since interventions by kin to resolve conflicts often result in fewer divorces (Ames 1953:45–47).

Sokna respected Musa, who was the son of one of Bintu's paternal aunts and thus considered *xaalisu jëkër* (husband of silver),[1] signifying the extensive marriage payments that he would make to the bride's family. A husband of silver was a husband of money, which had taken on new meaning; as a successful overseas trader who spent portions of the year in Milan, in Dakar, and in the Murid heartland, Musa Mbacke was considered to be quite a catch. He was not a solitary trader, but rather a devout member of the Murid way and, despite a faltering national economy, his submission to the Murid way offered him the potential to garner the resources, networks, and spiritual backing to succeed financially, socially, and morally. Marriage is an expensive undertaking, and Musa would have to rely on a large network of kin and associates to successfully carry out the process.

Despite Bintu's objections, Musa and Bintu were united in the preferred mode of Wolof marriage. Yet, their relationship as cross-cousins introduced its own set of tensions and conflicts. They were related on both the maternal and the paternal sides[2] and thus had multiple ties of kinship—ties that were reconfigured depending upon the politics of what was at stake at any given point in time.[3] In this case, through the receipt of social payments like bridewealth, family members gained status, prestige, and authority within the lineage.

Bintu's initial refusal of Musa presented the sticky financial problem of how to return the marriage payments, and she threatened family harmony by calling into question the authority and legitimacy of those who had arranged the marriage and who had received a portion of the payments. Her refusal also revealed generational tensions concerning ideas about love, matrimony, and the rights and obligations that are imposed by kin. Bintu's recourse to the idea of love rejected the maneuverings of the senior family members altogether and thus challenged their ideas about familial obligation, social virtue, and respectability. Bintu's protest was an assertion both of her inner feelings, which ran up against family commitments, and of the desires of the self in the face of community, and thus she astounded her seniors with what they took to be a shocking display of selfishness. Furthermore, because she made recourse to the idea of love as a personal right, senior women in particular responded that she was capricious, that she had her head *jaxas* (mixed up), and that she was *jaxasoo* (mixed up) with someone else. In choosing to frame her rejection of Musa in terms of her love for another, Bintu indicated to those senior to her that their investment in social relations through marriage payments and the rights and obligations that they conferred were not meaningful to her.

Bintu's protest went to the very heart of gendered and generational ideas of love, romance, and desire in Senegal. Her story pointed to the degree to which young women's expectations in love and matrimony were at odds with senior women's ideas about women's worth and marriage prestations. Bintu, Abdoul Aziz, and the ill-fated Musa shared a generational consciousness of romance and an ideology of *noppante* (romantic love). Though senior men and women also talked about romantic love, invoking the showing of Indian films in Dakar in the 1950s and the impact that this had upon ideas of courtship and desire,[4] Bintu and her *masse* (agemates) read French romance novels, followed the soap operas *Luz Clarita* and *Marimar,* and, in the year of her arranged marriage, fell in love with the Hollywood film *Titanic,* which was broadcast for the first time in 1999 on the local television station. Like the heroine in *Titanic,* Bintu spoke of love as a way of being in the world beyond cunning and calculating parents. Likewise, the plots of the soap operas she watched often involved wealthy men who fell in love with poor but virtuous women despite social pressure to marry within their own class. Love may have appealed to Bintu largely because she was acutely aware of her vulnerable position in a social landscape that was colored by what many saw as the inflation of social payments as a result of overseas remittances. Her recourse to love not only expressed a desire for autonomy, but also critiqued a system in which she, as a young woman from an impoverished family, was hostage to bridewealth prices set by her affluent, senior female relatives.

Though Bintu spoke of marriage as an affective connection between two autonomous individuals, she and her female cousins also talked about the institution practically as a means to personal sovereignty through the possibility it offered of obtaining homes of their own. Potentially, the matrimonial home offered women control over domestic space and the kinds of goods (housekeeping money, cloth, clothing, and housewares) through which they would construct their personhood, social worth, and relations with others. As a physical space, the home was a sign of male wealth and prosperity; junior men built homes with the aim of inhabiting them as elders in the future. Ideally, the home was also a form of value for women because of the relations it housed. Male transnational commodity circuits were driven not only by young men's hopes for salvation, but also by women's domestic aspirations. Though the home could be viewed as a constrictive space in which women's domestic labor sustained male productive efforts abroad, the home was also a node in women's circuits of exchange. These exchanges included family ceremonies, rotating savings and credit associations, and trading and were the arena in which women implicitly reconfigured relations of gender and generation within their communities.

By telling the story of an exchange of marriage payments that did not secure a lasting marriage alliance, I show how men and women, young and old, developed different ideas about selfhood and social circulation. It is also a story about the rights and duties that characterized kinship relations in the context of increasing migration abroad and the deep structural changes in the Senegalese economy. The introduction of remittances from long-distance trade networks into Murid households transformed cycles of domestic production. In this case, the promise of marital payments contained the potential to shift authority over the household and the relations it contained from senior men to senior women.

Local discourse concerning bridewealth payments often focused upon their inflation, and commentary on the marriage process centered upon the elaboration of certain rituals, such as the *céet,* carrying the bride's trousseau into her new home. It was generally agreed that the marriage prestations were important forms of mutual aid among women. In their lifetimes, senior women had watched the content of those prestations change from locally produced or sourced objects, such as woven cloth, mats, calabashes, and pottery, to manufactured goods that were often obtained abroad, such as enameled bowls, plastics, glasses, and other housewares. These household objects signified hosting and feeding others and producing social relations. They stood for the depth and breath of the social networks through which senior women acquired these valued objects and the productive potential of young brides. For this reason they were marched into the bride's new home in an elaborate procession of female kith and kin and celebrating griots. Women lined the tops of their armoires, headboards, and

A bride's céet, Dakar, 2000

étagères with large numbers of these wealth objects, especially bowls, along with porcelain figurines and glasses, to demonstrate their worth to their matrimonial home. In the late 1990s in Senegal, as Barbara Cooper (1997) so strikingly points out for Niger, the way in which women went about acquiring these goods changed. No longer the product of their own labor in the fields or creative work (such as decorating calabashes), wedding goods were obtained through women's engagement or that of their relatives in the cash economy, overseas trade, and microfinance projects. The provenance of many of these manufactured goods became increasingly important; for example, a set of insulated bowls that was said to be available only in Jeddah became popular in 2000.

Prospective brides and senior women were said to demand status items and to expect what seemed to young men like larger and larger payments of cloth and cash. Social commentary also focused upon the inflation of marriage payments as senior women, and even in some cases young women, seemed to delay the process in order to extract further gifts from the groom. Additionally, the very language used to refer to these social payments had changed as well. What was once called the *ndaq far,* the gift given by the groom to chase away other suitors, had come to be called the *may bu njekk* (first gift) by young women; they referred to these as the *first* gift with the assumption that others would certainly follow but that none would bind the young woman to the groom. Young men joked that courtship with gifts did little to guarantee a union; a man had to wait until the wife had actually entered his home to be sure that he was married. Young men often spoke bitterly of the inflation of bridewealth prices to levels that many found untenable.

Was the inflation of bridewealth prices actually new, or had young men always found it difficult to contract marriages? As I mentioned in chapter 2, by the 1940s in colonial Senegal there were indications that bridewealth prices were inflated as a result of the monetization of the economy, the spread of cash crop agriculture, and the availability of wage labor and trading opportunities in urban areas. As young men began to be able to accumulate the resources necessary to enter into marriage negotiations themselves, without relying on their fathers, the marriage market became more competitive (Robin 1947:201). Additionally, Meillassoux (1972, 1975) argued that in the mid-twentieth century senior men withheld assistance to young men to control their labor as dependents while extracting the highest sums possible for their daughters, perhaps to gain access to the earnings of junior men who were engaged in the cash economy.

These two important periods of flux in the price of bridewealth, the timing of the marriage process, and the forms of payment raise the important question: What was the value of bridewealth? Or, rather, what strategies did people employ to control the value of bridewealth despite a long history of volatility? If the value of bridewealth payments in this region has always been unstable, as in other regions of West and Central Africa, then how do we understand the value of bridewealth payments (cf. Guyer 1995:114)? Clearly, in Senegal there was not a steady rise in bridewealth prices from the precolonial era to the present, but rather there were changes in the "cultural topography of wealth" (Ferguson 1992) and in "the social geography of the channels through which money moves" (Guyer 1995:115). As new crops, new markets, new means of production, new currencies, and new commodities emerged, so too did debates about how to secure meaningful forms of value. These debates over the meaning and value of bridewealth payments and marriage manifested in the late 1990s in renewed calls by the state and the Muslim clergy to reform the Family Code which was passed in 1972 (and has been revised at least twice since then) to, among other things, codify marriage, divorce, and inheritance and to cap social payments.

As much as social commentary focused upon the inflation of bridewealth payments in relation to the changing economic conditions wrought by overseas migration and local fiscal austerity, this discourse was above all not about prices in and of themselves but about the changing nature of social relations (see, for example, Grosz-Ngaté 1988). As young men scrambled to garner cash and commodities to meet escalating bridewealth demands from senior female kin who controlled the domestic sphere, their marriages were delayed and young women continued to reside in their mothers' homes, their own entry into social adulthood postponed. Meanwhile, the absence of male kin from their homes was prolonged by the demand for their remittances in ritual and domestic spheres, which kept them tied to their overseas lives while elder placeholders occupied their homes. Consequently, many commented that social reproduction had been delayed (Antoine et al. 1995) as the tensions between men and women and between young and old mounted and these relations were no longer worked into alliances, but rather became disarticulated. Focusing, then, on the experience of the marriage process and the forms and timing of marriage payments illuminates how women are valued, how they create social value, how these exchanges produce sociocultural difference, and how they actualize or fail to actualize potential social relations.

THE MARRIAGE PROCESS AND WOLOF BRIDEWEALTH PAYMENTS

For Wolof families the English term *bridewealth* encompasses a series of payments that are made over time; the term is often translated into the French-language legal system as *la dot* (dowry). Although the French term *la dot* is used in Senegal, there is no payment on behalf of the wife's family to support her and her new family; rather, it is the groom who must give the bridewealth payments to the family of the bride (Kane 1972:717). There are transfers of gifts from the bride's mother to her in-laws, which mostly take the form of cloth for the in-laws and furnishings for the bride's room. But, for the most part, the prospective groom is responsible for making a series of marriage payments over the duration of the courtship from which the bride's mother purchases the trousseau. Broadly speaking, there are three instances of marital payments: payments made to the father of the bride or a male relative, which would be returned to the husband in case of divorce if there were no children; payments to the bride herself (which are also often given to her parents); and payments to the bride's mother to cover the cost of her trousseau, which would ideally go to furnishing the matrimonial home (Irvine 1974:387).

Wolof marriage payments begin with a *nuyoo* (greeting) of kola nuts and a small sum of money that are given to a young woman's family to signal interest and to initiate marriage negotiations (Diop 1985:100).

The young man may then begin courtship by offering a first gift (may bu njekk) to his prospective fiancée; as I said above, this was once called ndaq far, meaning to chase away other suitors, usually other cousins who were in competition for the young woman. The young man then undertakes a series of visits to the young woman's uncles and aunts, bearing gifts, while he continues to court his prospective fiancée with offerings, none of which obligate the family to accept the union. At this point, if the young woman breaks off the courtship, she must return the gifts, but if the young man does so he cannot reclaim what he has given.

Another series of gifts is offered to the young woman, which is called the *can,* which in some sense symbolizes repayment to her family for the investments that they made in rearing her. Can once referred to heads of livestock exchanged, which could also be called *jur* (livestock), as well as cloth, gold bracelets, and slaves, but now, as is the case with other exchanges, this has become monetized and is rarely distinguished from other gifts (Diop 1985:92). The spread of Islam in the region introduced the *alali-farata* to modify the can; this was given directly to the young woman to be disposed of at her discretion (94). The term derives in part from the Wolof *alal* (wealth) and the Arabic *fard* (divine prescription) (106). This process could unfold over many years, although the Family Code as it was proposed in 1972 initially limited this period to one year (Kane 1972:717). Over time, these gifts have become monetized for the most part, but also include clothing, jewelry, and other valuable objects.

The marriage is concluded without the presence of the bride and groom by the *takk* (tie), a token sum that is exchanged in the mosque between male representatives of the two families, often the paternal uncle of the groom and the maternal uncle of the bride, to signify that the marriage has been made legal according to Muslim law. The success of the marriage is then celebrated with the céet, the entry of the bride into her husband's home followed by her female kin and her trousseau (Kane 1972:719). The céet is an elaborate display of the strength of women's networks. Female kin and associates often arrive in large vans and buses that have been commandeered for the celebration with enormous stacks of plastic washtubs, bowls, and even mattresses tied to the top. These gifts are carried into the home on the heads of the women or their dependents, including griots and those of former slave status who are often also strong men, distinguished by the belts tied around the waists of their boubous. Drummers, singers, photographers, and videographers accompany them.

Not only is the céet an important display of women's material wealth and worth, it is also a visible display of women's "wealth in people"

(Cooper 1997:94). As Cooper argues, this display of valued objects (usually too numerous to actually be used on a daily basis) and of people is central to women's demonstration of productivity and reproductive potential (95). Moreover, the repetition and addition of similar objects, like bowls, glasses, and porcelain figurines that are displayed in sets, speak to women's searches for religious merit, which are seen as a series of repetitive and similar acts of feeding and hospitality that accumulate in value over time. The quantities of the gifts, in this case, are as important as their quality. Containers for food and drinks are some of the most valuable for they symbolize the bowls of cooked food that the wife will send to her kin and exchange partners at future feasts and family ceremonies.

There are many more exchanges that take place throughout the marriage process, including offerings that are made by male kin in addition to the bridewealth payments, such as grains and the slaughtering of livestock, which are symbolic of their hopes and good wishes for the couple and their families, and their desire for religious merit. Women also receive and bestow large amounts of locally dyed boubous, woven underwraps, and machine-made fabric that symbolize the ties between the two families and that become important stores of wealth to be exchanged at future family ceremonies, especially naming ceremonies for newborns.

I have briefly sketched the major payments that take place throughout the marriage process because it is difficult to speak of bridewealth, or indeed marriage, as a singular institution or practice. Examining marriage as a process enables one to focus on moments of "disaggregation" of the payments as well as on the process through which one enters into social adulthood (Comaroff 1980:7; Guyer 1995:121). Rather than charting the rising or falling bridewealth payments, it makes more sense to concentrate on the "partial and inventive transformations" of each of the parts (Guyer 1995:121) and the discourse surrounding the marriage process to understand the meaning and experience of these transactions. In Wolof bridewealth transactions in the late 1990s the ndaq far, the takk, and the céet were at the crux of the debate over social production. Since young women now regarded the ndaq far as a may bu njekk, rejecting the former's emphasis on eliminating competition among male cousins for the bride and embracing the latter's focus on possibilities for accumulation and the bride's right to reject suitors, senior men claimed that the only social payment recognized by Islam was the takk. This exchange, between male representatives of the bride and groom at the mosque, conferred the rights of the patrilineages over future offspring and was considered the only legally binding aspect of the marriage process.

While men struggled to regain control over social production through recourse to Islam, senior women sought to exercise control over volatile times by altering the forms of marriage prestations. Through changing what constituted the céet, women sought to maintain the crucial equivalencies in social life and thus they desired commodities that signaled ties to long-distance trade rather than locally produced goods that would have at one time symbolized agricultural productivity, the fertility of the land, and the control over dependents that were necessary for family-based agriculture. More important, senior women's exchanges, more so than those of men or young women, created social obligations that had future worth. The creation of these social obligations did not derive from the intrinsic power or sacred quality of the objects themselves, as proposed by Marcel Mauss (1990[1950]), but rather from the social context in which they were circulated (Cooper 1997:91).

Hospitality, feasting, and giving constituted relations of mutual obligation over time between kin and affines and extended the rights and obligations of kin to non-kin. These obligations underpinned the financial, social, and spiritual prospects of men and women. Descent, affinity, and exchange are central, then, to understanding both how social worlds are experienced and the debates that surround them. Marriage exchanges do not reflect a hierarchical structure of relations of gender, generation, and other forms of social rank; they are one of the very processes through which these relationships are constituted (Comaroff 1980; Evans-Pritchard 1940; Goody 1958). As I mentioned, in the past senior men perpetuated the dependency of junior men through their control of marriage payments, and these exchanges were central to producing sociocultural difference and subordination (Meillassoux 1972, 1975). At the same time, it was through the marriage process, including the formation of new households and the independence of sons, that parents became elders (Comaroff 1980:26). Marriage prestations, therefore, are central to understanding the reproduction of the social system over time. I focus on the social experience of the marriage process and its related exchanges, considering the key concepts of volatility and value, in order to understand the discourses that point to a crisis in social production as marriages are delayed and the marriage process is attenuated, forestalled, and incomplete.

Ideally, a young man ascends to the position of head of household through bridewealth exchanges while simultaneously constituting his father as head of the lineage (Turner 1984). Both the nuclear and the extended family are produced through the matrimonial process, which relies on a series of monetary transactions and counteractions between the families that will increase in value over time. Participants are brought into relationship with one another as full social beings bearing a particular kin relation that is recognized through these exchanges. In chapter 2, I discussed that in the past, the father of the groom helped his son to marry by giving him land. Sons could farm cash crops to earn money for marriage payments (Copans et al. 1972). Beginning in the early twentieth century, the Murid shaykhs made it possible for sons to acquire bridewealth independently of their fathers by encouraging young men to cultivate communal plots. In the 1970s, Judith Irvine's interlocutors reported that the bridewealth payments were distributed to the father of the bride, his brothers, the bride herself, or the mother of the bride, but in no particular order of preference (1974:387).

Sons now earn cash abroad as traders (often independently of their fathers), frequently with the sponsorship of a Murid shaykh rather than a male relative (though the latter may also be the case). Because of this, marriage has become a competitive market. Whereas fathers once controlled the marriage process through their provision of land to their sons and their receipt of bridewealth payments for their daughters, today's sons are more likely to make senior women the sole recipients of the bridewealth payments.

In the case of Musa and Bintu, Sokna Géer was the recipient of the marriage payments due to her role in fostering Bintu, which was related to her maternal kin's position in Mbacke. It was therefore within her authority to redistribute those payments to Bintu's kin in Mbacke. Because the marriage negotiations took place among Sokna's kin, Demba Géer had a limited role. In general, senior women are more likely to receive marriage payments for their daughters because of their efforts to find wives for their overseas sons. Perhaps payments are largely given to women since they are seen as having more authority in the ritual sphere and thus as having control over young women's productive and reproductive potential. Whatever the reasons for this shift, senior women are widely viewed as the culprits behind what many claim to be inflated bridewealth prices, and senior men are more likely to proclaim that the only part of the process that is recognized by Islam is the payment of the takk in the mosque, which contributes to their quest for moral renewal.

In the marriage of Musa and Bintu, Sokna Géer was the recipient of the entire sum of money that was intended both for the family and for Bintu because she was Bintu's foster mother. Sokna then redistributed the money both within the family and to individuals and groups beyond it with whom she sought to create good relations, such as her neighborhood ritual association, rotating savings and credit association, and other friends and associates. When Bintu said that she did not want to marry Musa, as in the case of a divorce that is initiated by the bride, the bridewealth payment ought to have been returned to Musa (Ames 1953:47). The legitimacy of the union itself was at stake, as well as the legitimacy of the rights and responsibilities of the family members who had arranged it and who could, when pushed, enforce it. Additionally, because marriage payments would be made over many years, the funds were important for the financial prospects of the family as well as for the aura of prestige and authority their receipt would convey on the various households involved.

Sokna Géer had eagerly accepted the initial payment and even went so far as to divert portions of it to her own ends since she was confident that the remaining installments would be forthcoming. The initial payment and those that would follow were counted on to create obligations, which would form the basis of affinity. Increasingly, however, bridewealth payments have become important as objects in and of themselves as Senegalese households have come to rely on receiving ritual payments like these to meet their obligations and daily needs (see, for example, Hutchinson 1996). The fact that these ritual payments are now more widely regarded as burdening the debtor households with hardship, rather than generating positive social ties over generations, is a fundamental feature of the neoliberal moment.

Through this marriage, Sokna Géer reckoned that she would instantiate her authority as an elder and thus draw upon the productive capabilities of the young household. Due to this reasoning, she racked up extensive social and financial debts during the marital transaction by promising gifts at family ceremonies and buying new housewares and cloth in anticipation of the wedding feasts, a portion of which would take place in her home. However, those future payments from Musa never arrived because Bintu ran away several times in the course of the marriage proceedings and because Musa was not creditworthy; he was never able to deliver the gifts he had promised.

The exchange of cash and gifts during the matrimonial process (or their failure to materialize) can be taken as a moment in a process of social transformation; the meaning of these exchanges derives from their relationship to wider processes of social and cultural production and reproduction. Marital exchanges simultaneously illuminate the surface features of the social landscape and the concomitant symbolic meanings that are embedded in these exchanges, bringing into relief the source of these surface forms and meanings. Exchange as a system of moral obligation not only mediates social relations but also generates them. Fundamental transformations in the structure of households can be gleaned from the changing relations of their inhabitants to the objects that they exchange, such as marriage payments coming to be made in the form of money. Within the context of increasing male migration, social payments such as bridewealth potentially reinforce the dominant social position of senior women and, when directed toward elders, these monetary exchanges also reduce the possibilities for autonomy that are available for junior women. Thus, it is not a coincidence that the increased monetization of bridewealth has gone hand in hand with an increasing emphasis upon an ideology of love. Nor is it surprising that there is a generational struggle over the sexual and emotional desires of young women and their reproductive capacity as mothers often seek to further their own moral, political, and economic objectives through their daughters' marriages. In Wolof society in particular, marriage alliances offer a crucial arena in which class-based ideas about proper social relations play out.[5]

ISLAM, THE STATE, AND FAMILY LAW: CONTROLLING WOMEN'S WEALTH AND WORTH

Although Bintu and Musa's marriage is a particular story, the politics of their courtship and the failure of their marriage alliance speak to wider transformations in Senegalese Murid households in relations of gender and generation, and to shifts in household production and reproduction in remittance economies in Africa and elsewhere. Their story demonstrates the politics of the domestic, including kin and family relations, and the politics of the neoliberal state. Shifts in the nature of social production relate to several transformative factors, including structural adjustment programs, the devaluation of the currency, the declining political and economic significance of the nation-state, and the implementation of neoliberal economic policies. Women's domestic practices are both informed by and seek to reform gendered and generational ideas of home, homemaking, and family and, consequently, are the site of some of the most creative and conflicted endeavors. As feminist critiques of kinship theory have shown, the domestic sphere is also a space of critical social, economic, and political practice (Collier and Yanagisako 1987).

Under French colonial rule, family law was adjudicated in the urban areas by the Napoleonic Code and in the rural areas by customary law, including Islamic (Maliki) law (Schulz 2003). Through this dual legal system, the colonial powers sought to limit interfamilial transfers by codifying limits to these practices into law. The colonial powers were, however, largely unsuccessful in controlling the inflation of bridewealth payments or the lengths to which young men would go to acquire the means to marry (Kane 1972:718). In 1943 a Muslim group known as Fraternité Musulmane set out to limit bridewealth payments and other ritual exchanges that were associated with the marriage process. They disliked the inflation of bridewealth prices and women's efforts to postpone the closure of the marriage process to extract additional marriage payments (Robin 1947:201). After 1945 the French also prioritized controlling the high cost of marriage in the colonies (Cooper 1997:16). In Senegal, both Muslim and French colonial authorities codified these social payments as early as 1946 in an attempt to limit them.[6]

The postcolonial Senegalese state also sought to regulate social payments that it saw as being detrimental to national development by reforming the Family Code to address marriage, divorce, and succession. This code abolished customary family law and sought to do away with the dual legal system that had been introduced by the French colonialists (Camara 2007:787). Though Senegal became an independent secular republic in 1960, it took until 1972 to enact the family law through which its architects attempted to follow the principle of one nation, one law, in spite of vast religious differences across the country (ibid.). The Family Code was based partly on French civil law and partly on Algerian customary law, the latter of which drew on the Maliki-Sunni school of law and sharia principles (Creevey 1996:296). From its inception, Muslim groups opposed the Family Code. They argued that it was incompatible with sharia. Sufi leaders banded together into the Superior Islamic Council to issue statements on their religious positions and most notably condemned the Family Code as the "women's code" to signal their opposition to the idea that it sought to ameliorate the condition of women (297). In the rural areas, especially in the Murid zones, the Family Code was not enforced, and disciples were discouraged from formally registering their marriages (298). Religious leaders saw family law as falling under the domain of religious authorities and resented the intrusion of the state.

Although the state intended the Family Code to ameliorate the position of women commensurate with a secular, modern, and democratic republic, many female intellectuals also came to oppose the law because they viewed it as legalizing an inferior status for women (Creevey 1996:298).

Fatou Camara argues that, although the Family Code required that a marriage be recorded at the civil registrar's office, the groom retained the right to choose the option of monogamy and, in the absence of having recorded such an option, the union was by default recorded as polygamous (2007:789). The husband also had the right to choose the matrimonial home and the wife's leaving the home was considered grounds for divorce, in which case she forfeited all marriage-related gifts and had no right to alimony (790). Under reforms to the code that were instituted in 1977 it became a criminal offense for a wife to leave the conjugal home for more than two months (791). Divorce by repudiation, in which the husband could renounce the marriage under Islamic law, was also no longer recognized and this act had to be adjudicated by a civil court (Creevey 1996:297). Yet, most women were reticent to approach the civil courts when problems such as a lack of financial support, abuse, and adultery plagued their marriages. Rather, they turned to alternative sources of authority within the family.

Camara argues that while the Family Code and case law stipulated the ramifications of a wife's leaving the conjugal home, women continued to return to their natal homes when they were dissatisfied with the conditions of the marriage, an action in keeping with their "indigenous right" to *fey* (leave the husband's home) (Camara 2007:792, 795; Kane 1972:720). They did so, she argues, because they preferred recourse to kin and elders to the convention of bringing marital disputes before the authority of the courts. Leaving the home, then, did not necessarily signify divorce if the elders could mediate an acceptable solution for both the husband and the wife; a wife would only return to the conjugal home after the husband agreed to the mediated solution and brought her gifts (Kane 1972:720). Bridewealth payments in this context signified the ongoing relationship between the two families as well as the woman's consent to the marriage (Camara 2007:794). In most cases in which a marriage was dissolved after women returned to the conjugal home following a dispute, the divorce was enacted without legal recourse to the state or the marriage was dissolved by a *qadi* (Muslim judge) (Kane 1972:721). In this context, the woman had a right to the conjugal home's furnishings (Camara 2007:796) and, if the children were young, they might reside with their mother and be financially supported by their father (Kane 1972:722).

In 2003, a group of Islamists and leaders of Sufi congregations, the Comité Islamique pour la Réforme du Code de la Famille au Sénégal (Islamic Committee for the Revision of the Family Code of Senegal),[7] responded to the state's renewed attempts to modify the Family Code by demanding the implementation of an Islamic family law in the national assembly (Bop 2005; Camara 2007; Sow 2003). In this context, female virtue and respectability came to be increasingly discussed through a discourse of moral and fiscal austerity that was promoted by Muslim groups (for an example from Niger, see Masquelier 2004:225).

Yet it seems as though women rarely were concerned by these attempts by central authorities to regulate interfamilial matters. On the one hand, although Bintu would ultimately leave her husband's home after her marriage, she never sought recourse in the civil courts perhaps because, as Camara suggests, women rarely have knowledge of the rules of the Family Code and often are seeking mediation on the part of elders rather than divorce (2007:797). Musa, on the other hand, could have benefited from pursuing a divorce under the Family Code since he would not have had to pay alimony or fulfill the promise of bridewealth payments. Yet he did not, perhaps because ultimately he sought to remain married to Bintu. Senior women who were engaged in the system of gift exchange rarely adhered to the limits set by the state and advocated by Muslim groups. These women understood the important role that such exchanges played in securing their own respectability and the honor of their families as well as in forging intergenerational ties between themselves and their daughters (see, for example, Masquelier 2004:242).

COURTING BINTU

Senior women are blamed for the rising cost of marriages, many of which go awry, and are criticized for transforming an exchange which was once meant to help defray the costs of the wedding feasts into a conspicuous display of banknotes. Sokna Géer arranged Bintu's marriage in the hope that an alliance with a prosperous Murid merchant would contribute to her own prosperity and good name. Although the marriage that Sokna arranged was by no means noble (though it was one of *set derat* [pure blood], as Bintu and Musa were both *géer* [freeborn] and therefore were considered to be of higher social status than casted artisans), she hoped to profit from the alliance by commanding a high bride price at the outset, and she banked on the continued flow of wealth from Musa's trading activities abroad in the future. Musa had little choice but to comply; he was largely dependent on the labor of women, especially senior women like Sokna Géer, to embed himself in the domestic sphere from afar. He relied on their social labor to arrange his marriage and redistribute the bridewealth payments that would constitute his relations to kin at home. Without entering into the marriage process, he could not establish his own household and reach social adulthood.

The politics of marriage, however, do not rest solely with the role that senior women play in the manipulation of monetary exchanges. Many allege, for example, that young women will ignore a suitor who is not an international trader; they are charged with having a dominant interest in the affluence and social position that such marriages promise. Young men bemoan the expansive and expensive demands for gifts that they receive from those whom they court; they must provide porcelain figurines, insulated bowls, richly embroidered cottons and brocade silks, and imported Italian furniture. Although senior women provide these furnishings for young women, the means to do so comes in part from the money given by prospective grooms. On the one hand, young women contend that they prize unions with a migrant because they allow for more autonomy since the husband is often away and the wife is able to put his remittances, which arrive monthly, to her own use; the possibility of control over remittances of cash and goods (such as cloth and cosmetic products) is appealing in the context of an inadequate local economy. On the other hand, young women resist the idea of a marriage that is based on the amount of bridewealth because the money rarely falls into their own hands. Furthermore, they fear the possibility that they may be placed under the care of their in-laws in their husband's absence, a situation in which feelings of abandonment and loneliness can be intense. Although young wives may benefit from what a husband sends, more often than not these payments are bundled with those that are intended for the mother-in-law, who is in charge of redistributing them and running the household. Since they are aware of the high incidence of infidelity, brothers-in-law will monitor the new bride's movements; and, dependent on her care, her in-laws will stand in the way of her demands for a divorce. Thus, the idea of love appealed to Bintu as a means of conveying her desire for an autonomous union in which she, not her elders, would be the major agent and beneficiary.

For junior men, marriage also involves important political considerations. For example, although Abdoul Aziz worried about Bintu's future, he was also cognizant of his obligations toward his mother's family. He relied on these relations to support his overseas trade since they assisted him in obtaining capital and securing clientele. On many occasions he said that he also felt obligated toward his younger cousin Bintu, since she had been the one to prepare his morning coffee and his afternoon tea and she had always remembered to reserve a bowl of food for him when he missed lunch. He respected her deference and gentle nature. He also admitted to a few close associates that he was in love with Bintu; however, he said, to declare such feelings openly or to act upon them would be tantamount to cutting himself off from his mother's relations, upon whom he relied for the success of his import-export business. Marriage to Bintu would mean defying his parents and blocking the path of the bridewealth that had already been circulated, and it would force him to choose between two very different social landscapes, between which he oscillated uneasily. At issue, then, were the changing forms of personhood, relations, and social production in a moral and mobile economy of global scale.

Musa and Bintu were raised in the same Murid village of Mbacke and were aware from an early age of the arrangements concerning their future marriage. By the 1990s, Musa had moved his parents to a wealthy Dakar suburb that was populated by emigrants and into a villa that Musa had built with his brother for their respective wives. When Bintu's parents could no longer count on the agricultural output of their land, they sent her to live with extended family members in Khar Yalla, where she became a shy outsider in the Géer home. In this household, Bintu assumed the obligations of a dependent niece: she cooked two meals a day, cleaned, and performed other domestic chores. Although she participated in the social and religious life of the family, her aunt and uncle did not send her to school with her cousins and they limited her outings to the markets in the highly populated urban neighborhood to protect her reputation.

As Bintu matured, she thought of her marriage to Musa. It was with great shock that she learned that he had taken her older cousin as his first wife and that she was now living with him in Italy. Her cousin was the daughter of her mother's sister and they had been raised in the same household in Mbacke where they came to relate as sisters. Musa now sought Bintu as a second wife who would make a home for him in Dakar, managing his social and business relations in his absence, and so he greeted Bintu's uncle and aunt with two kilos of kola nuts upon his return. This opening exchange of kola nuts, or the nuyoo, marked the beginning of his courtship of Bintu; her aunt and uncle accepted the gift and, in so doing, the offer of courtship.

Bintu seemed conflicted about Musa's courtship; though she saw the prospects for autonomy that marriage offered, she also considered what her situation would be as a second wife in general, and to her older cousin in particular. Her ambivalent position pointed to her vulnerability in the current system of social relations. Each time she was congratulated on her engagement, Bintu responded, "*Dafa new* [He's ugly]." From others' reactions it was not clear to me if this was an appropriate response. It could be understood as a classic joking reaction or an attempt to avoid witchcraft by denying her good luck. She also could have been speaking either literally of his physical appearance or figuratively of his comportment and behavior toward her, for some women had gossiped about his proclivity for domestic violence. Many people remarked on the unusual circumstances of the marriage, particularly the fact that Bintu and Musa's first wife lived in the same home in Mbacke when she was very young, which conflicted with an Islamic prohibition against a man marrying two sisters. Musa, however, continued to court Bintu aggressively, bringing her a bedroom suite and housewares from Italy. In conversations with her female cousins, Bintu began to consider the fact that Musa was a prosperous trader abroad and that, in the immediate future, marriage to him would change her condition entirely since she could escape the control of her relatives and hope for the possibility of future remittances from her husband. In her aunt and uncle's home, she slept on a foam mat on the parlor floor with the young children and grandchildren; marriage held the promise of her own room in a spacious villa with a European-style kitchen and her own Western-style bathroom.

Musa was not discouraged by Bintu's initial refusal to go along with the marriage, and he continued to send jewelry in lieu of visiting her. Bintu had not received much in her life and became fond of these presents as she slowly acquiesced to the idea of the union. Musa also sent small symbolic payments of cash to her aunt, uncle, and cousins, and by accepting these gifts Sokna and Demba gave the suitor the sole right to court their foster daughter (Diop 1985:103). In the past the ndaq far had been largely symbolic in the overall ritual process and signified a joking relationship between the suitor and the other male cousins who lost out to him; however, Bintu and her age-mates scoffed at such a notion, instead calling this exchange the may bu njekk. Bintu expected that, unlike the ndaq far, this was only the *first* gift; others would follow and be presented directly to her. Moreover, her use of the term may bu njekk suggested an emphasis on the thing itself as a kind of value that can be diverted into personal consumption. It was increasingly common for young women to accept such overtures without fulfilling the obligation to marry, making this process more like a courtship with consumables; and if a suitor failed to display extreme generosity during this period, the bride and her mother might call off the wedding. The increasing use of the term may bu njekk by junior women signaled a significant change in the nature of social relations. It suggested that the first gift was not in itself a symbol of acceptance and obligation but rather a competitive bid for the potential marriage, which may or may not ever take place. Because men travel for so long and because they cannot always sustain the relations that they initiate, young women hesitate to take their interest seriously.

TYING THE MARRIAGE AT THE MOSQUE

Musa's and Bintu's uncles participated in the tying of the marriage at the mosque. The takk signified the legal completion of the marriage according to Islam. The uncles exchanged the modest sum of 25 CFA francs, which was fixed by the clergy. If the marriage money had been paid in full at this time, the bride would have followed her husband to their new home; however, this is unusual and was not the case with Musa and Bintu. It was almost a year after Musa greeted his prospective in-laws with kola nuts that he offered the bridewealth payments, including the can and the alali-farata for Bintu, to her aunt Sokna. Musa gave Sokna Géer cash, a radio, and a gold wristwatch. The money was to go toward providing a trousseau for Bintu (clothing, household utensils, etc.) and toward a host of gifts for Bintu's in-laws. Sokna Géer accepted this money and proceeded to manage its distribution among the various households who held a claim to the bridewealth payments, including Bintu's natal household. Sokna called the members of her neighborhood ritual association to her home and they collectively appraised the value of the offerings and planned for a grand event.

After Musa returned to Italy, Sokna Géer began making preparations for a *xew bu mag* (big feast) at her home and for the céet, which would take place at Bintu's mother-in-law's home. Sokna telephoned her sons overseas to inform them of the modifications and improvements that she wanted to make to the house to accommodate the guests honorably and she demanded contributions from each of them. She used some of the bridewealth payment to purchase a cow, which would be slaughtered on the first day of the ceremony to feed the guests, and she also began to prepare Bintu's trousseau and to invest in her neighborhood ritual association, which also would help finance the event and prepare the feast. Sokna Géer purchased bowls, hung new curtains, and sent satin fabric to her tailor to be sewn into bed coverings. The cement courtyard of her home was transformed from a space of household work to a receiving area, where broken ceramic tiles were laid in a colorful mosaic pattern.

Not all of the household members agreed with this usage of the bridewealth and with the domestic preparations. Sokna Géer asked her adult children to contribute to the cost of tiling the courtyard. Rama agreed to the arrangement; however, Jigeen refused to contribute money to the wedding preparations and argued that she needed the funds to pay the school fees of her three daughters. In return, her siblings invoked her two failed marriages and her recent loss of the trading fortune that she had amassed in the Ivory Coast to her last husband, a Murid shaykh. She was roundly criticized for having returned to the already overcrowded family home with her children, impoverished and unwilling to contribute to the household expenditures, and her siblings told her that she added no njariñ (value) to the family circle. Thus, her value and status were measured by her ability and willingness to fund kin-building rituals, such as Bintu's marriage. In fact, Jigeen's younger sister Rama was chosen to be the honorary *ndeye* (mother, an institution that I discuss further in chapter 7) at Bintu's feast and reception, an honor that conventionally would have gone, according to age seniority, to Jigeen.

In the months prior to her disclosure of her love for Abdoul Aziz, Bintu ran away several times to her parents' home in Mbacke. Each time, she said that she did not want to marry Musa Mbacke. On three occasions, maternal and paternal kin persuaded her to return to Dakar and to continue with the nuptials: first her aunt, then her great-aunt, and finally Abdoul Aziz, who struggled to reconcile his feelings for Bintu and his respect for those senior to him. Following her third flight, Bintu's aunt, great-aunt, mother, and mother's brother met in Mbacke to discuss what should be done with respect to the bridewealth payments since her behavior had exhausted their patience. The elder women and the maternal uncle admitted that the bridewealth payments could not really be returned since the parties concerned had already consumed them. In addition to the modifications that had been made to the maternal home, Sokna Géer had already skimmed from the payments to cover her obligations to rotating savings and credit associations and to her neighborhood ritual association; she hoped to use her payout to finance the wedding feasts. She had also made appropriate exchanges with the groom's family, buying cloth for two boubous and many bowls for the groom's mother, in whose home the bride would reside.

In the end, Bintu's great-aunt (Sokna Géer's mother) and her mother's brother decided to force her to accept the marriage. The maternal elders thus told the bride that, since she had initially consented to the marriage by accepting the ndaq far, she could not go back on her word, especially since the marriage had already been tied at the mosque. Though Sokna sympathized with Bintu's plight, she could not return the bridewealth because it was no longer in her hands and she was already deep in debt preparing for the feasts. With the exception of Jigeen, Sokna Géer's daughters had not married by this point, and she and Demba looked forward to the day when their daughters would bring wealth into the house through marriage payments rather than relying on their parents for support.

Bintu began to slowly accommodate herself to the idea of marrying Musa, and two older female cousins took her to Marché HLM, a cloth market in Dakar, to choose her trousseau. At first she refused to select any cloth; she sat in silent defiance, barely glancing at the fabric that the sisters picked for her as they bargained with the vendor. Her cousins purchased the cloth for her, including one grand boubou and a peach satin skirt with a layer of peach lace that was embroidered elaborately and sewn with crystal beads to be worn over the boubou for the reception with her age-mates. Another aunt, a trader in France, sent a deep green-and-blue brocade cloth with gold embroidery for two additional grands boubous which would be worn at the *fête* at her aunt's home and on the following day at her husband's home. Bintu's three boubous were a modest number; Murid *commerçant* brides change their clothes as many as five times during a single gathering. In addition, Bintu's cousins bought cloth for five *complets,* each consisting of six meters of high-quality wax cloth that was manufactured in Nigeria, Mali, and the Ivory Coast, which would be sewn into dresses with skirts underneath to be worn during her first week in her new home. At the end of that first week, she would give her clothes away to her husband's sisters.

Bintu's cousins intended her to have a grand boubou sewn not by her mother's tailor, but by a couture seamstress who was known for her cutting-edge fashions; however, Sokna Géer refused to release the bridewealth for the seamstress, arguing that the dress would be too ostentatious. Rama fumed about the possibility that Bintu's lack of couture or unique design would reflect poorly on her since she was to stand with the bride during the event, and she also fretted about the possibility that a guest might appear in dress more elaborate than Bintu's, which could damage the family's pride. Unmarried, Rama relied on such occasions for her value to the family to be realized; thus, she had a stake in ensuring that the marriage not only proceeded, but proceeded well. She alleged that her mother had appropriated the marriage payments for her own use and that she had not set enough aside for Bintu's trousseau and reception.

Caught up in the preparations for the event—planning her clothing, her coiffure, and the food for the reception with her age-mates—Bintu uneasily consented to the final two stages of the marriage process while her future husband remained in Italy. These events might be stretched out over years but, in Bintu's case, they took place in two days, during which Musa remained abroad. While Bintu was preoccupied with visits to the tailor, the salon, and the photographer, female kin assembled at her aunt's house on the appointed morning for *lakk* (sour milk and millet porridge) and the slaughtering of a cow for the afternoon feast. In the evening, Bintu gathered with her age-mates for a Western-style reception during which she received gifts of housewares and cash in envelopes. That night she prepared to enter her in-laws' home in an elaborate ritual called the "covering of the bride." Sokna Géer and other senior women dressed her in white and sat her on a mat where, together with Demba, they administered marital advice. After prayers were said, her age-mates and a few senior women took the bride to her in-laws' home. There she was presented to her in-laws, who were asked to treat her like a daughter, and offerings were made of salt, cool water, and grain, which are symbolic of cool relations and are supposed to ensure a marriage that is free from quarrels and to encourage her in-laws to develop a taste for the bride (Gamble 1957:67). In Bintu's case, these rites were performed while her husband remained in Italy. In the morning the céet was celebrated with the arrival of an elaborate entourage of vans, griots, and female kith and kin, who carried her goods into her new home. There was lakk, *sabar* (drumming and dancing), and exchanges of meat among her female elders throughout the day.

THE UNRAVELING

Although Musa intended to build a home in Tuba, he had not yet begun construction. Consequently, Bintu was moved into his house in Dakar, which was occupied by her in-laws and her brothers-in-law's wives and where she was obligated to show elaborate forms of deference and symbolic submission to her elders. As the most junior woman in the household, she shouldered a share of the burden of domestic labor, preparing meals, cleaning the house, and performing child care even though she did not yet have children of her own. Though these activities conventionally fell under the responsibility of a new wife, Bintu did not receive her own home within a larger compound inhabited by the extended family, as was frequently the case in rural areas; rather, all family members shared a single urban house. Moreover, Bintu did not receive housekeeping money from Musa since he sent this money directly to his mother who, in turn, apportioned it among the junior women of the household, which meant that Bintu was forced to ask for market money each day that she cooked, taking turns with his brothers' wives. Her many responsibilities prevented her from engaging in her own market activities, attending family ceremonies and celebrations, or entertaining guests in her home. Thus, she was not able to establish her own social networks, which forestalled any social ambitions on her part. Bintu gave her mother-in-law money and occasional offerings of cloth and other forms of material assistance that were required of a good daughter-in-law in order to avoid her wrath, and she refrained from speaking too loudly, too much, and too aggressively. Bintu thus passed several months performing daily household chores so that her mother-in-law could participate in ritual work.

By the time that Musa returned to Senegal several months later to consummate his marriage, Bintu had fled again. Musa went to her parents' rural compound, endeavoring to woo her back, and after three days he finally convinced her to return to Dakar with him, not to his parents' home, but to a large hotel for the weekend for what Bintu's cousins called a Western-style *lune de miel* (honeymoon). She consented and he remained in Dakar for the duration of Ramadan, during which she cooked elaborate dishes for her in-laws—grilled chicken and lamb and okra stew—to show her deference and respect. During this time, embarrassed by her running away during her nuptials, Bintu's foster family shunned her by not visiting or receiving her. Toward the close of Ramadan, Musa and Bintu made an official visit to the home of her aunt and uncle. Sokna Géer received them in her room but did not offer the usual forms of hospitality, such as a special plate of chicken or large bottles of soda; rather, she complained that she had no bowls for guests since so many had gone out during Bintu's marriage celebrations full of meat and rice and sour milk and millet, and none had been returned. After an awkward wait, Rama finally sent a child to the shop on the corner to buy four small bottles of soda. After consuming the beverages quickly and in silence, the newlyweds went home, at which point Bintu's aunt exclaimed, "He is too cheap [*nay*]. He did not even offer to purchase a soda. He just returned from Italy and what did he bring me, the mother of his bride? Nothing. Cheap."

GENDERED AND GENERATIONAL TENSIONS AND THE POLITICS OF VALUE

In telling Musa and Bintu's story, I have tried to convey how Senegalese discuss their experience of marriage payments with respect to their age, gender, and social position in order to suggest the affective, emotional, and meaningful aspects of these exchanges and to address their political and material implications. Bintu's spoken thoughts and actions expressed her conflicted and contradictory view of her position in the marriage negotiations, and her experience was representative of profound changes that are occurring in the marital process in Senegal. Though prospective grooms have always been expected to court young brides and their families with goods and services, grooms today court women by sending gifts and cash to convey their intentions while they remain abroad to fulfill work obligations or because they are unable to travel due to their often undocumented immigrant status. The crisis of social production that is evidenced in this narrative revolves not merely around the failure of Musa to secure a lasting marital arrangement, but also around his inability to sustain the relations of kinship and alliance that are created through the marital process.

Musa and Bintu's eventual failure to continue their marriage speaks to the way in which the appearance of wealth that is produced by large feasts and generous prestations is at odds with the actual ability of household members to maintain the social relations that engender wealth. It also signifies a dangerous gap between the inflated expectations of young women and their relatives, and the ability of traders to deliver in the neoliberal era. In addition, the dissolution of their marriage speaks to the gendered and generational issues that are emerging out of a globalizing economy that draws young male workers abroad.

For Musa, the marriage was an important part of making his claim, in absentia, of being a head of household in his homeland. He understood that he needed to work through senior women to embed himself socially in Senegal; however, the role of his parents in his stead and the material impossibility of financing a second home forestalled his intentions. Musa, eager to assert himself as the head of a prosperous household with two wives, rushed into a marriage which he did not have the means to sustain, as was evidenced by Sokna Géer's comments that he had not continued to make the bridewealth payments, nor did he offer her gifts upon his return from Italy. Moreover, he had been caught between two sets of generational expectations. Whereas Bintu desired her own home, something that he had already provided for his first wife, and valued a marriage based on mutual love, Musa's parents expected that he would bring a wife into their home who would care for them in their son's absence. Musa expected that Bintu would adjust to his being gone; Murid women who are raised in *commerçant* families accustom themselves to these long absences, being told to have *muñ* (patience).

Bintu's sense of abandonment and disappointment remained strong and, shortly after the new year, she left the arrangement. She contended that she did not benefit from Musa's remittances (a common lament among Murid wives), that she saw no prospects of receiving her own home, and that she felt less autonomous in the house of her mother-in-law than in that of her aunt and uncle. Had she loved Musa, she said, she would have cared for his in-laws out of respect for him, but she did not. As I mentioned, as soon as he left a room she never failed to point out that he was ugly; though a joking relationship exists between cross-cousins, Bintu's expression conveyed her bitterness concerning her marriage. Though she had hoped that her status would change completely after marriage, it had not. If her husband had been the boroom kër ga (head of the household), then she would have had a socially sanctioned means of asserting her desires. But her situation was worsened by the fact that Musa, like many Murid traders overseas, pooled his remittances with other traders and made one transfer of money to minimize the fees, which led Bintu and her mother-in-law to argue over the portion of the remittance to which each was entitled. Like other Murid wives, Bintu resorted to asking her husband to send her remittances secretly and thus aroused hostility and discontent within the household.

Sokna Géer expected that the bridewealth would initiate a series of exchanges that would tie the two households together and enable each set of elders to profit from the trade of the *commerçant* son. The elders of both households, eager to constitute themselves as such through the receipt of his payments, were angered that Musa contracted the marriage without due attention to the exchanges that would be necessary to sustain the alliance. Sokna in particular refused to acknowledge the first visit of the couple to her home following their marriage because Musa's inability to continue to support Sokna meant that she would have to defer requests from others who had also counted on her receipt of the marriage money. Thus, Musa threatened her reputation of liberality and reciprocity; a deficit in her receipt of marriage money meant that she would have to come up with the money from another area.

Though young men may build houses, senior women control the production of households through their management of the rituals and exchanges of domestic life. The construction and production of these households exploit the labor of junior men whose willful activity brings them into being and who count on the houses to reflect their prosperity to the community in their absence. In this way, the work of male traders overseas fosters the creation of social hierarchies that drive production at home. Senior women control the means of production and, since they are tied into a ritual economy of prestige production that requires resources, members of the nuclear family are obligated to produce for them in addition to generating enough to reproduce themselves. Women's large feasts and ostentatious social prestations are made possible by access to cash that is earned by male labor abroad. In particular, the remittance of a monthly lump sum as housekeeping money (in addition to social payments) makes it possible for women to spend in capitally intensive ways. In general, a remittance of cash from afar affords women opportunities to divert sums of money that are intended for specific purposes by males; for example, women often invest a portion of men's remittances into rotating credit unions and ritual associations through which they finance their own local trading activities, the purchase of housewares, and family ceremonies.

With these remittances, female elders also acquire the clothing and the coiffures that index their prosperity and draw newcomers into their networks of exchange. Clad in the cargo of their male kin, female elders participate in exchange contests that are driven by ostentatious displays of wealth and conspicuous consumption. During these *fêtes,* women enhance their roles as powerful members of the lineage and the community through ostentatious displays of sañse (multiple changes of clothing)[8] and offerings of food, drink, and cash. Commodities are also important in that they index the depth of people's networks of exchange. The form of Murid trade is salient; their trading activities provide cosmetic products, cloth, and accessories which play into the promotion of female beauty as a social value and which women circulate as an important form of social relations. Murid traders thus provide both the means for and the forms of new economies of prestige.

Remittances have utterly changed the status of households and neighborhoods and have given new life to the domestic sphere of life-cycle rituals and exchanges among female elders; however, commercial families are vulnerable to countless claims on their prosperity, which often leave them heavily indebted. Strapped for cash, elder women face the immense social labor of delaying demands on their revenue while maintaining amicable relations with kin and community. They shoulder the burden of upholding their family's good name to ensure their financial solvency by promoting the family business, by judiciously extending credit, and by taking on debt to fund not only their commerce, but also the massive social prestations in the domestic sphere.

Not only have there been fundamental shifts in the symbolic and material bases of gender relations across generations in Senegal, but blood, money, and food are experienced and valued differently along the axes of gender and generation. While women's experiences of personhood and sociality in the present are tightly bound up with the circulation of cash among them, senior men's autonomy has been sharply reduced. In the past, male control over the allocation of land was one of the central factors in determining their dominance over the definition of kinship ties and marriage alliances. Today, senior men's control over the setting of bridewealth payments for their daughters is largely symbolic. As their control over land and thus dependents has eroded, senior men have had to grapple with the increasing power of junior men as the primary holders of wealth (i.e., cash), the increasing monetization of social exchanges, and the declining systems of patronage as a result of an ever more impoverished state. The hold that senior men used to have over the productive capacity and earnings of junior men has, since the 1990s, become largely symbolic. Junior men often give money to their mothers to cover the household expenses—gas, water, electricity, and foodstuffs—in the place of their fathers, and actual gifts to their fathers have become primarily symbolic in nature and include items such as kola nuts, tobacco, religious paraphernalia, and upgrading their living accommodations. Senior men are thus symbolic placeholders, occupying land in Dakar and Tuba to prevent it from reverting to the national government under the National Domain Law of 1964.

In the case of Bintu and Musa, their respective families not only fought over the distribution of the bridewealth payments and the practicality of returning them when the marriage failed, but they also questioned the value of bridewealth as a social practice and institution. On the one hand, bridewealth payments bring disparate households into relation with each other across space and over time and, for senior women, these marriage payments are part of a social system that is based on mutual obligation and responsibility. On the other hand, for junior males, bridewealth payments impose a financial burden and support what young men consider to be an outmoded and impractical system of exchange that depends on wealth in people and gift giving. This structure of relations, they contend, inhibits their attempts to manage their incomes, savings, and investments and prevents them from achieving a desired mode of being in the world, which is signified by investment in their own homes and endeavors.

Intense public debate surrounds the private and domestic sphere in Senegal and it often coalesces around the practice of social payments. Junior and senior men often invoke Islamic principles to argue that practices such as gift exchange are not a fundamental aspect of life-cycle rituals such as marriages, naming ceremonies, and funerals. Both the state and the Muslim clergy have attempted to reform this particularly Wolof practice of hefty and highly competitive ritualized exchanges among female kin.

Senior women recognize that the success of male commerce abroad has reinvigorated prior systems of exchange by making them highly monetized, a process that has imbued them with more authority despite a faltering economy. I have argued that there is a disjuncture between men investing in homes and not households, and women investing in households through ritual activities that are viewed by young men as being socially counterproductive. Though young male traders take advantage of overseas commodity networks as a way to extract themselves from lineage obligations, the incorporation of their cash remittances into the domestic sphere serves to reformulate the relations of gender and generation that drive social production. Likewise, young women's ideas about love are at odds with senior women's conceptions of the nature and significance of bridewealth transactions and marriage alliances. The domestic and money-making labor of unmarried adult daughters and married daughters-in-law supports the ritual activities of elder women.

I have considered the changing perceptions of courtship and marriage through the prism of the conflict that the marriage payments aroused between Bintu and her maternal kin; however, the idea of marrying for love is not new to this generation of young women and Bintu's case is not an isolated one. Mariama Bâ in *So Long a Letter* (1981) tells the story of Ramatoulaye, an aging schoolteacher who steadfastly remains married to her husband even after he has taken a second wife, a schoolmate of their daughter, because "the truth is that, despite everything, I remain faithful to the love of my youth" (56). Her statement is doubly meaningful, for the love of her youth is, first, her husband and, second, her belief in the power of individual choice over the machinations of others.

Ramatoulaye has only pity for her husband's new wife, whom she portrays as "a lamb slaughtered on the altar of affluence" (Bâ 1981:39). The second wife is the victim of her own mother's maneuverings to acquire a SICAP villa in a middle-class Dakar neighborhood and a fancy car; the mother is "swallowing up double mouthfuls from the trough offered her" (49). The young girl is mocked by her baccalaureate-bearing age-mates for having dropped out of school to wed such an old man. She frequents the nightclubs of her age-mates with her new husband, sitting at the most visible tables with bottles of beverages lined up to display her success, "but when the moment of admiration passed, she was the one who lowered her head at the sight of couples graced with nothing but their youth and rich in their happiness alone" (50). The young girl is eventually left destitute when the husband dies suddenly of a heart attack. For her part, Ramatoulaye rejects a subsequent offer of marriage made by her deceased husband's brother, as is the custom (i.e., the levirate), saying, "You forget that I have a heart, a mind, that I am not an object to be passed from hand to hand. You don't know what marriage means to me: it is an act of faith and of love, the total surrender of oneself to the person one has *chosen* and who has chosen you" (58).

SIX

HOME ECONOMICS

SOKNA GÉER SPOTTED the greasy chicken carcass lying on an aluminum platter near the stacks of enameled bowls that remained unwashed after the previous day's feast. Still stinging from the expense of the celebration, she was puzzled by her discovery of the costly meat. "Who bought this?" she wondered aloud. Then it dawned on her that these were the bones of sacrifice. They spoke to her son's flight from their Dakar home during the night, maybe this time for good.

Sokna said that she understood the forces behind and motivations for her son Abdoul Aziz's silent departure. After he left, she kept saying, "*Xaalis rekk menn naa faaj gacce* [I took on too much debt, only money will take care of shame]." She recounted how she had prepared, provisioned, and provided money to celebrate her husband, Demba Géer's, hajj to Mecca. The night before her husband left, she organized the ritual slaughter of a lamb and invited his friends and associates to their home for a feast to pray for his safe return. When he returned from the hajj a month later, she threw a lavish *fête* for the whole neighborhood, and his relatives came from their rural villages to welcome him home and congratulate him on completing the religious rite. She was now uncertain how she would disentangle herself from the debts she had incurred, and suspected that she had leaned too heavily on her son.

Despite her best efforts, Sokna's family had finally succumbed to the monetary troubles most everyone in the capital city faced. Her husband's spiritual journey had put her family in serious financial straits. Rather than being the house that neighbors flocked to because of the television and the social banter about the latest fashions, imports, or society events, the Géer home looked as worn and washed-out as any other home on their street in Khar Yalla. Her family slumbered, she entertained few friends, and no one seemed to notice that the same bland dish appeared before them daily—broken rice and *yaay boy,* a type of sardine whose thin bones often lodged themselves in one's throat.

She leaned against the doorway of the pantry as her energetic granddaughter tugged her white scarf to the floor, wrapped it around her own bare waist, and scampered off. Sokna looked after her and sighed, lacking the energy to scold her. Visiting family had finally returned to their villages; Sokna Géer had seen them off with handshakes that contained a number of small bills. Visits from acquaintances and business partners who wanted to pay homage to her husband and to benefit from his spiritual grace had also dwindled, and she was relieved to finally be alone in her home. Sokna eyed the sacks of onions, rice, and potatoes now lying empty on the concrete floor and was reminded of the tab to be paid at the corner store. She wearily turned to the young girl working in the cooking area and snapped at her, "*Eh yow,* pack your baggage, you are going back to your family in the Casamance. I no longer have a place for you here."

Her daughter Jigeen emerged from her room wearing only a *pagne* wrapped around her chest and exclaimed, "*Laay,* what are you doing? Who will cook and clean and do the laundry?"

Sokna Géer replied, "You and your sister can't cook?"

"Say that again!" exclaimed her daughter. "Me, I am not cooking."

Sokna turned away, saying to herself as she walked, "I have so many debts." Thinking of her son Abdoul Aziz's absence, she said again, "Only money heals shame." Then Sokna heaved a sigh and headed back to her room. She found her husband sitting alone in the dim room on his sheepskin prayer mat, dunking French bread into a tall glass of sweetened Nescafé. She stretched out on her bed, one hand propping up her head and the other drooping toward the floor. She tried to tune the radio to better hear the news: a meningitis epidemic had been spread throughout Senegal by pilgrims who had been on the hajj.

In the quiet of her room, she calculated and recalculated her obligations and the possibilities of honoring them: the many trips she had made to the market to prepare for her husband's hajj, the serving platters she had bought, the home improvements, the new gown she had made of a brilliant white *darou khoudous* cloth with a damask weave composed of layers of white lace embroidered in pink. She had also repainted her husband's room and hung new curtains across the walls and over the doorway, and she had had a chocolate satin bedspread made with matching throw pillows. These were all necessary expenses. A wife was expected to create a space that was pleasing to guests and that showed the family's best face.

Her thoughts returned again to yesterday's feast. She had attempted to give each guest a gift, a souvenir from Mecca brought back by her husband. The family had sorted the gifts—silk scarves, prayer beads and mats, Muslim hats and garments—into piles reflecting the status of each recipient. She winced as she recalled how she had sorted, counted, and

Pot belonging to an mbotaye, Dakar, 2000

attempted to make equivalences among the items designated for each person and how she had come up short each time. How grateful she had been to Rama for purchasing additional gifts at the cloth market in Dakar. She laughed as she remembered how Rama explained her actions, "Look, it all comes from Mecca anyway." Before her husband's departure, they had received so many gifts of cash that she felt obligated to return double what she had received, as was honorable among Wolof women.

Sokna Géer now needed to figure out how to face her neighbors, to whom she felt she hadn't done justice in terms of the gifts she was able to give them. The neighborhood women had helped her to finance and prepare for her husband's pilgrimage. They had brought themselves, their money, and their enormous cast-iron pots engraved with the name of their ritual association and the date of its founding. Through their help she had performed the hajj herself ten years earlier. Her pilgrimage had raised her status among her friends and enabled her to finance a number of new projects with her newfound spiritual capital. But things had certainly changed in the intervening years. Feasts no longer put one at the top of the social hierarchy. Her husband's trip had impoverished their family and emptied their home of its possessions—her woven wrappers, enameled bowls and platters, glassware, and the intimate feelings she associated with these valued objects were all gone.

The celebration of Demba Géer's hajj should have raised the family's standing in the eyes of their neighbors. Sokna had an impressive reputation in her community as a mother of twelve *bantu yalla,* or sticks of wood, as she often referred to her children, four of whom studied or worked abroad and supplemented the meager family income. It seemed as if she was always announcing her election to lead this or that women's group. She recognized that welcoming neighbors and rural relatives into their home brought daraja to the family. Yet such dignity demanded constant demonstration. As she endeavored to renovate and expand her cinder-block and pink stucco home floor by floor, room by room, and balcony by balcony, she was unable to turn away rural relatives who sought her help. There were the youths who wanted a French education in Dakar, young girls who came to work as maids, and adults who needed medical attention at the country's main hospital. Many of the relations who passed through their home commented about Sokna Géer's son Abdoul Aziz. "He is a *thiouf,*" they would say, "a prize fish." Neighbors would often say the same thing as they watched the cars, washing machines, and computers that Abdoul Aziz imported from Milan make their way into the Géer home.

It was no surprise when Sokna Géer announced that another of her sons had sent money to finance her husband's hajj. Neighbors flocked to the home the day before Sokna's husband departed, including the *ancien combattant* who arrived in a sapphire-dyed khaftan and red fez with the members of the neighborhood mosque to pray for Demba's safe return. They took their places on the woven mats laid out on the broken-tiled mosaic floor in the entryway of the home, which served as the garage at night and during the daytime afforded shelter from the sun and a cool breeze. The men chanted Qur'anic verses in unison with the guidance of their imam, praying on Demba Géer's behalf. At the same time, members of Sokna Géer's ritual association arrived and climbed the stairs to the unfinished second floor to cook the freshly slaughtered lamb sacrificed for his journey. They were entertained by the neighborhood griot, a tall, lanky woman dressed in a gold wax boubou with large birds printed on it and tied with a scarf at the waist. As she stood over the large pot of steaming millet porridge, stirring, she laughed and gestured wildly with her arms to punctuate this or that story that the women were telling as they peeled onions and potatoes, dropping them into plastic tubs of water. The telltale bloodstains in front of the home and the smell of a wood fire on the roof drew neighbors, relatives, and business partners who sought to wish Demba Géer a safe journey.

The women ladled *lait caillé,* sour milk scented with vanilla and orange blossom water, over steamed millet to thank the mosque association and

Men's mosque association, Dakar, 2000

bring the Qur'anic chanting to a close. The home filled with excited and talkative guests, including beautiful women who complimented one another on their dress and praise singers who went into raptures over those who were willing to pay.

"Madame Diouf," one praise singer cried out, "a *lingueer,* a princess from Sine."

From their pockets and wrappers the women withdrew small gifts of cash to help Sokna Géer, who would go without her husband's salary for the month-long pilgrimage. These visitors came to ask God's blessing for Demba's journey and, by giving these gifts, were asking to be remembered in his prayers in Mecca where he would name each person individually, as prescribed by Islam. Their foster daughter who had married and left the family home several years ago brought sour milk. A man who drove one of Demba Géer's taxis (who sought to take his third oldest daughter as his second wife) brought several sacks of baguettes. Relatives from Tuba brought bags of dried millet and roasted *café Tuba.* Even Demba Géer's religious guide donated a substantial sum for the journey. As guests presented Sokna with folded CFA bills, she scowled at them and said somewhat jokingly, "Why are you bringing money to a woman meant for a man?"—and tucked the bills into the money belt between her two woven wrappers.

When Demba Géer returned from Mecca, at least a hundred friends and family immediately surrounded him, crying, laughing, and trying to touch his person to absorb his newfound grace. As the video camera rolled, he made his way from the garage entrance to the living room where he sank down into a chair, barely visible in the crowd. As his family surrounded him, he opened his hands in prayer, something he would repeat throughout the night each time a new guest approached him. A quiet man who rarely spoke to his family except in authoritative tones, admonishing his sons to wake up at dawn and pray or his daughters to wrap their *pagne* cloths over their jeans in the home, he smiled grandly and nodded his head in appreciation.

Again, Sokna Géer's thoughts returned to Abdoul Aziz. He had not even tasted the roasted meat that he had provided for the feast. When he returned from work in the afternoon, all of the meat had been eaten. What a dismal discovery. The son who had provided the lamb to be sacrificed for his father's journey did not receive a share of it. Sokna should have been honored to have so many friends share in her husband's spiritual journey, and yet she recoiled at her guests' voracious appetites for roasted meat, iced drinks, and kola nuts. Her daughters seemed to run from room to room as guests called out for more ice or a bowl of water in which to wash their hands, oily from the meat they had consumed. She dared not think of the condition of her plush upholstered couches lining the walls of her living room or the new covers on the beds, where guests sat as they leaned down and ate rice from large platters and bowls on the floor.

Sokna Géer sighed as she thought of Abdoul Aziz, who had now emptied his wallet three times at the livestock market on the outskirts of Dakar. He had provided the cow for the marriage of a daughter fostered to the Géer family, a sheep for the celebration of Korite (the feast marking the close of the month of fasting), and this animal for his father's departure. Not only that, he had surprised her during Ramadan with cases of chicken and frozen fish, which she cooked into delicious stews to be shared with neighbors and delivered to her parents. She knew that he would not be able to provide a ram for the upcoming Tabaski celebration. In years past, this had been a particular honor for him; in the days leading up to Tabaski, one could look up and down the narrow roads of the neighborhood and compare the sizes of the sheep that were tethered outside the homes as indications of the families' means and potential in the year to come. She knew then that he would have to return to Italy, where he would get by selling imported African art, working in a factory, or taking up odd jobs. Last night, after her guests left, she had noticed that his car was not parked under the shade of the single tree in front of her home. She wondered if he had sold it to pay for his flight.

THE HAJJ

Embarking on the pilgrimage to Mecca and enacting the rites associated with it is a spiritual obligation for those who have the means to pay for it. The hajj, which takes place during the twelfth month of the Islamic year, is a *fard* (duty) and one of the *rukn* (five pillars) of Islam. As a condition of departing on this journey, a pilgrim must reconcile debts and leave sufficient means to finance their dependents' care in their absence (Hussain 1997:7). Pilgrims are instructed to put their affairs in order and to secure a living for their families should they die en route due to the physically demanding rites that are associated with the hajj and the challenging conditions of travel and residence during the month-long observance. The pilgrimage also entails assuming complex social responsibilities among kin and community. Prior to undertaking the journey, those who aspire to be an al Hajja or an al Hajji ask kin and community members to pray for God's blessing, and they are obligated to return these blessings after completing the hajj.

Prior to the twentieth century, religious travelers accumulated wealth over their lifetimes to finance their pilgrimages. The worldly possessions then were relinquished to pay for the journey through which they would acquire the honored title of al Hajji or al Hajja and the baraka that accompanies this. When, at advanced ages, the exalted devotees returned to their host communities after having taken the overland journey to Mecca, they were often financially and physically frail; their authority no longer rested on their accumulation and distribution of wealth objects but on their morally elevated position, which obligated others to care for them (Trimingham 1961). Whereas in their youth their social payments had been subsidized by their elders and in middle age they had invested heavily in exchange relations, when they returned from the hajj they lived on the donations of those below them (Berry 1989). Where women had once distributed cloth, they were now solely its recipients; and where men had fed others, they now had the right to be fed.

In general, Senegalese men and women who embark on the hajj today are younger than pilgrims were in the past. They enjoy the improved conditions of airline travel and expanded possibilities through which they may finance their journeys. Many rely on funds that they have saved through rotating savings and credit associations and the wages of sons and daughters abroad. Upon their return, family and friends flock to the newly titled al Hajji or al Hajja to benefit from their grace, often by imbibing water brought back from the Well of Zamzam or receiving gifts of religious paraphernalia from the holy city, and to heed the pilgrim's new understanding of Islam (cf. Bernal 1997; Ferme 1994; Kenny 2007). The returning pilgrims become part of the circle of senior members in the community who have also made the pilgrimage and who share a bond of suffering, and they are also accorded a degree of deference usually given to religious dignitaries (Ruthven 1984:24). Certainly the anticipation of an augmented stature in their communities, in addition to the religious prescription, motivates individuals to undertake the hajj.[1] One returns as a "new kind of globally implicated person" whose status encompasses household members and close associates (Kenny 2007:364).

Today, for those who have the means, embarking upon the hajj no longer requires that pilgrims devote a lifetime of savings to the religious journey. Thus the hajj, rather than marking the transition from taking care of others through reciprocal obligations to being taken care of through gifts that are no longer returned, has become a marker of elite status and a sort of fame whereby the expectations in reciprocal exchange are heightened. The new regard that peers have for those who hold the title of al Hajji or al Hajja is accompanied by increased expectations of these individuals' financial capabilities. How do families sustain the social relations engendered by undertaking the hajj and the feasts associated with this rite?

MICROFINANCE AND THE FINANCING OF FEASTS

During the hajj feast, members of Sokna Géer's ritual association discussed the religious implications of offering hospitality to neighbors and relatives. They said that to show teraanga (hospitality) to a guest, one needed to *teral* (honor) them by providing food, drink, conversation, rest, and peace and, if one had the means, one should also escort guests to transport and pay for them to return home as, the association claimed, the Prophet Muhammad had instructed. They repeated a commonly told story about the Prophet to exemplify their point: he offered his last date to a hungry stranger whom he encountered on a journey and, by sundown, he was blessed to find more dates. "It's in God," members of the ritual association explained. If one is short on cash, then one should offer the guest a boubou or a *sër* (underwrap); and, if nothing else, one should go to the corner store and make use of one's monthly tab to get two kilos of rice to offer to the guest for use in sweetened porridge for the children. Each of these women had brought something to Sokna Géer's feast, including cases of soda and bags of candy, to show their respect for her and to assist her in extending hospitality to her guests. In return, they each received

Mbotaye association, Dakar, 1999

tuyaaba (religious merit) directly from God for their good acts. To receive tuyaaba is to be a recipient of good things, of God's thanks, one could say. As one woman definitively explained, one should not pocket wealth, one should spread it around to *gërëm yalla* (please or thank God), and by doing this "you will be pleased, your family will be pleased, God will also be pleased with you, and this is the essence of hospitality."

Although the Géer home had been inundated with well-wishers, Sokna had prepared for the feasts and, along with contributing their labor to prepare the meals, the members of her mbotaye had pooled their money to acquire provisions such as onions, grains, and spices and had also brought soda and sweets as gifts. The griot who belonged to the association had cooked superbly, seasoning the dishes well, and Sokna Géer's family griot had presided over all of the gift exchanges, extolling the family's honorable genealogy and conduct in poetic verse. Though Sokna's adult children and kin provided liberally for the event, she had initially tried to keep the number of guests to a minimum. She did not rent a tent or a public address system, both of which would have signaled the occurrence of a large feast to her neighbors, nor did she call the members of the dahira to recite the Qur'an for Demba since they would have to be thanked, which would mean more cash, milk, and meat. Sokna tried to keep the celebration as low-key as possible because she knew that she had overextended herself during the feast preceding her husband's departure. Yet upon Demba Géer's return, guests flooded the house, and in the frenzy to serve everyone the most significant of relations were served equal amounts to the most distant. The lack of distinction, special attention, and recognition meant that Sokna had failed to produce the hoped-for feelings of reciprocal obligation that would signify future returns.

The Géer family sought to create relations of reciprocity among kin, neighbors, business associates, and members of their dahira by sharing in meals and giving gifts. Feasts and family ceremonies were therefore important venues not only for constituting lineage relations, but also for entering into relations with neighbors. Through these events, the Géer family extended the rights and obligations of kin to non-kin and thereby enlarged themselves in space and time, "initiating a spaciotemporally extending process" (Munn 1992:50) or a "mode of self expansion" (Weiner 1980:82). They gave food to guests to extend themselves beyond the space of the house and the moment of the feast. They entered into social networks that were vital to their productive activities, including trade and ritual exchanges; constructed their individual and collective honor in this life, an "extrabodily component of the self" (Munn 1992:50); and received religious merit directly from God for their good acts that would secure their salvation in the next life. These social networks afforded them credit, trading capital, and security against future ills, and, most important, established their reputation for honor and generosity, central to their receipt of religious merit. Through the sacrificial slaughter of an animal and the offerings of hospitality to guests, including kin and non-kin, the Géers had the potential to achieve a positive value transformation (see Munn 1992).

The opposite of a positive value transformation achieved by feeding others would have been to consume the food themselves. But this would have been viewed as a negative act; persons would have said that the family was *nay* (selfish) and potentially *dëmm* (witches), though the latter accusation is rarely, if ever, spoken aloud. Therefore, when the meat ran out during the feast, the Géers were deeply concerned that their moral standing in the community and their prospects for attaining religious merit were threatened. They articulated their despair over the value transformation that they had aspired to achieve, which would have taken place not in a series of distinct acts of giving and receiving, but rather would have unfolded over time and through which they would have achieved social production (cf. Weiner 1980). Consequently, rather than generating the good will and generosity in their guests that would carry over to future exchanges in business and in family ceremonies, household members dolefully found themselves unable to secure future replacements for their outlays.

During the hajj feasting, Sokna Géer attempted to control the exchange of food and wealth objects to avoid moral reprobation and a loss of future returns. She also tried to prevent the potential loss of lineage identity through the loss of honor. This is the danger of exchange and the problem of objects, including money, which Keane (2001) identifies. Not only are these subject to loss and decay, but they are also subject to misreading. Therefore, exchanges must be accompanied by a discursive frame through which their meaning is established.

Sokna Géer aimed to fix the meaning of gifts, which could have been perceived to be of inferior quality or quantity, as promises on future replacement by articulating an assurance that more milk, meat, or cloth would be provided the next time. Through complex modalities and contexts of exchange with her ritual, religious, and rotating savings and credit associations and with political organizations, Sokna sought to weave her obligations over time. In so doing she attempted to retain her honor as she distributed wealth in the form of gifts, a strategy known as "keeping-while-giving" (Weiner 1992). Despite her efforts, her guests interpreted these exchanges negatively as attempts at closure, signs of eating, or signals that she did not value the relationship. They complained about the lack of utensils and napkins, as well as food. Sokna Géer was unable to return the gifts that she had received with interest, and she could not extend the time interval between exchanges to a point where she could return double or at least more than what she had received. As a consequence, she lost both honor and wealth.

But other problems were afoot as well. People's expectations concerning social exchanges had not adjusted to the new economic realities. A neoliberal ethos of efficiency, transparency, and a balancing of accounts had influenced the give and take of social life over time. Nongovernmental organizations had promulgated an emphasis on repayment and had turned women's mbotaye associations into rotating savings and credit associations. The hajj gifts that Sokna Géer gave at the second feast were not intended as repayment for the gifts that she received at the first feast. If so, she would have used the Wolof word *fey* (to pay). Sokna Géer called the food and gifts *teraanga* (hospitality), *may* (gift), *njukkal* (countergift), or *dolli* (to add to). Through these gifts, Sokna attempted to invest value in others by putting her guests in the position of debtors. This strategy is called *lebbal-bor* (to lend a debt). It means that Sokna Géer could recover that debt at a later time in a process called *lijjanti xaalis* (to untangle or get to the bottom of a financial situation). These efforts to invest value in others were central to the processes of social production and regeneration whereby women were able to demand replacements in the future for items that had been given in the past for either themselves or their offspring.

In addition to the transformations wrought by NGOs, women were also confronted with generational differences. Since many young men and women had chosen not to place themselves on exchange paths, women risked seeing the loss of their lives' work. In particular, the gifts that they had given over a lifetime, which in the past would have been returned to their daughters, would be lost as these young women would look to salaried jobs and real estate speculation as means of creating value, rather than family ceremonies.

Importantly, Demba Géer's standing in the community depended upon Sokna Géer's capacity to hold a fine feast. As is generally the obligation of adult men, their sons had provided the livestock that had been ritually slaughtered by the imam, and Sokna's ritual association had performed the labor of transforming the sacrifice into cooked food and distributing it as hospitality through which they achieved religious merit and future good will.[2] Sokna's enterprising daughters had also provided additional religious paraphernalia for distribution at the feast to protect the family's honor. In bestowing upon guests articles from Mecca, members of the family planned to fulfill their sense of honor, demonstrate their baraka, and amplify their religious merit as any act of giving, liberality, and generosity would. The exchange of inalienable objects, such as religious paraphernalia from Mecca, would create an obligation between giver and receiver over time (Mauss 1990[1950]). These objects transmit part of the giver, such as one's baraka. Religious gifts therefore offer the opportunity to transform one's social persona and to amplify personal piety (Soares 2005).

Through these transactions, persons sought to create an asymmetrical relationship between the giver and receiver. For women in particular there were important ramifications to their skillful displays of hospitality since these displays had the potential to yield future gifts of cloth at family ceremonies. Through acts of hospitality, women strategized to persuade and influence recipients to bestow on them in the future first-quality cloth, especially locally woven strip cloth and dyed cotton damask. Women were seeking to alter others' views of them and thus were extending their control beyond themselves; they were crafting reputations (see Munn 1992:61). Women were assisted in this endeavor by their griots, who recited their genealogies and projected their reputations for generosity and liberality in public forums that involved gifts of food and cloth.

Women create asymmetry by not only returning the gifts that they receive over time, but also by returning them with interest. At a minimum, one aims to return double what one receives. Women call this strategy of gift giving lebbal-bor; it is the interest that compels a future replacement. To lebbal-bor is to act as a creditor by putting another in the position of debtor. This word comes from *lebbal* (to lend credit to someone) and *bor* (debt) (Mottin-Sylla 1987:21). In the case of the second hajj feast, celebrating Demba Géer's return from Mecca, the exchange of food and religious paraphernalia would have created an asymmetry because these gifts ought to have surpassed what the family had received at the feast prior to Demba's departure. That amount of interest would then be returned at subsequent feasts and family ceremonies. In other cases, women would often bestow cloth and trade merchandise upon associates and kin on the basis of credit. As a family ceremony or other occasion loomed, the donor would approach her recipients and seek replacements for items that she had previously bestowed upon them so that she could make her social payment at the family ceremony. One "lends debts" with the aim of recovering credit. As Mottin-Sylla describes it, one sows debts with the intention of harvesting them in time for a family ceremony (1987:21).

Although gifts at feasts and family ceremonies are presented, counted, and recorded publicly, usually with the aid of a griot, women are discreet about how they garner the means to make these prestations. Certainly, men assist women in their ritual endeavors, but many women supplement the men's contributions. In cases where their male relatives are not able to contribute, they must garner the ritual prestations themselves to protect the family honor. The process of "harvesting" debts for a family ceremony is called *lijjanti xaalis. Lijjanti* refers to a sorting out, an untangling, or getting to the bottom of a matter, and *xaalis* is the word for silver or money. Women frequented each other's homes to borrow money from their network of kin and confidantes. Though a welcome obligation that embodied the good will of the family, social calls could be dreaded by debtors. Women traveled great distances and spent entire afternoons convincing their friends and family members to pay for merchandise that they had extended to them on credit. Installment selling is increasingly the norm in Senegal as families are strapped for cash and unable to pay for goods in full. This kind of credit is essential to building up a culture of consumption (Calder 1999:9). Social visits require not only teraanga in the form of beignets and drinks to *sawar* (activate) latent relationships but also the initiation of gan (strangers or guests) into one's networks.

Importantly, Sokna Géer did not merely fail to secure a future return from her guests during the second hajj feast, but she articulated bewilderment with what seemed like unreasonable expectations on their part. Many guests came to the feast with the hope of receiving an entire boubou, or ten meters of cloth, and left with only a string of prayer beads and dashed hopes. Yet exchanges are often intentionally asymmetrical, either due to one party's limited capacities, as an attempt to extend the obligation into the future, or as a strategy to avoid unworthy recipients. People often count on these kinds of inequalities to elicit assistance (money, labor, mutual aid, etc.) over time. Moreover, persons enter into such exchange relationships with the assumption that they will be perpetuated by asymmetry, as an equivalent gift would, in effect, act as closure and end the relationship (Munn 1992:55). The latter is characteristic of market transactions and is the reason that market traders often offer their clients a small gift at the end of the transaction: to persuade them to remain clients in the future.

Why Sokna Géer's guests expected a return with interest rather than an equivalent return and why they hoped to obtain this at the very next event rather than over the course of the next year are important questions about the nature of financial repertoires. Social payments are central to financial repertoires because they hold persons in relations of reciprocity over time. For example, Evans-Pritchard argued that Nuer bridewealth in the form of the exchange of cattle held families in relations of reciprocal obligation indefinitely (1951:84). The groom often promised that additional cattle would be exchanged upon the marriages of his daughter and granddaughter. These enduring obligations were a source of social solidarity among persons and collectivities (Mauss 1990[1950]). Moreover, Evans-Pritchard observed that, although not every Nuer had the cattle necessary to pay bridewealth in its entirety at one time, this did not prevent alliances from being established (1940:180). Similarly, Wolof bridewealth payments were meted out over a lifetime and held the groom in a relationship of obligation to his in-laws whereby he would provide them with labor and any number of services in addition to the bridewealth payments.

Yet, in the case of the hajj feasts, Sokna Géer articulated fear for her own honor and that of the family because they had not been able to accomplish an immediate return with interest. In part this may have had to do with the fact that people's expectations had not adjusted to the decade of economic turbulence that had been wrought by economic liberalization in Senegal. However, fiscal changes, such as increasing prices and the devaluation of the currency, were not the only sources of instability, which "has arisen not only from changes in prices and the purchasing power of money, but also from the legal, judicial, and political processes through which 'contracts' were defined and enforced" (Berry 1995:308). Glickman (1971) argued that, for the Nuer, asymmetrical relations in gift exchange were challenged by parties who were seeking the assistance of the colonial courts to adjudicate disputes over unpaid social obligations, such as bridewealth. Courts enforced the idea that these were financial obligations that required closure in the form of repayment of the entire sum for the resolution of communal conflicts. Likewise, in Senegal during the colonial and postcolonial periods there have been numerous attempts by colonial officials, Muslim clergy, and the state to reform the Family Code in order to limit or even to abolish social payments altogether, because they consider obligations like these to create social disharmony and block development since they reinscribe hierarchical relations between kin and between members of hereditary occupational orders, or castes.

Although economic liberalization introduced specific forms of precariousness and what many analysts of Senegal called the crisis period of the 1980s, rather than focus on this period of austerity as a crisis or as a short-term phenomenon, I suggest that "the most important aspect of the currency interface over the longue durée [is] namely its instability" (Guyer, ed., 1995:3). Although women's gift giving during the 1990s and the early twenty-first century took place in this context and certainly became the subject of intense debate, their strategies were not merely a response to crisis at a critical moment. Nor were they episodes of relatively short duration, or coping strategies. Rather, women's gift-giving strategies were indicative of the ways in which African people had "honed their skills at rapid adjustment to maintain the crucial equivalences in social life" (5) over the long haul. Gift-giving strategies are crucial ways of understanding "how personhood and its inevitable growth and decay over time are conceptualized . . . in relation to the timeless value of assets and the conceptual stabilization in African modes of exchange" (26).

Just as these contemporary financial strategies cannot be thought of solely as coping mechanisms in times of crisis, they also cannot be viewed as merely timeless, traditional, precolonial, pre-Islamic, or rural holdovers. One could presumably find complex precolonial models of financial management that resemble contemporary rotating savings and credit associations. Yet many of these institutions emerged at the interface of Atlantic and African economies throughout the colonial period and after, and they have always been dynamic. These monetary practices took place in the context of "multiple currency economies in an expanding and inflationary, externally oriented, commercial economy" where "difference was thereby a resource to be cultivated" (Guyer 2004:42). These institutions expanded and contracted at different historical moments and operated in a context in which African men and women performed a vast repertoire of monetary management strategies. What these practices signify, however, is the desire to translate money into long-term stores of value, such as investing in associational life, titles, home building, cloth, and other forms of wealth that hold value.

Contemporary manifestations of these associations emerged in tandem with the shift in development away from large-scale infrastructure projects that were levied through the state to projects that centered upon women with an emphasis on microfinance (cf. Kane 2002:296). In part, these projects emerged from the incorrect assumption of international donors that Africans lacked financial management strategies (Stiansen and Guyer 1999:1). This misperception derived partially from these organizations' focus on formal banking institutions and credit, to which most African men and women have had little access.

Many of the guests at the feasts that celebrated Demba Géer's pilgrimage belonged to one of Sokna's ritual, neighborhood, religious, political, or credit associations. Through these associations she established social connections that were based on mutual interest and benefit and on favors and obligations that created reciprocity to yield future returns. At one time Sokna Géer had belonged to upward of forty associations. The financial strategies that women developed through these associations enabled them to create and sustain social relations with non-kin in an unstable state economy characterized by a frequently devalued currency. Particularly through the strategy of lending debts, women fashioned complex networks of obligation where money rarely changed hands. In times when social relations were difficult to contract, given the dearth of resources in inadequate local economies, this wealth, in the form of the elaborate borrowing of consumer goods, often manifested in bodily adornment. Such adornment conveyed the depth of women's social networks, which were in themselves forms of social value. These associations not only assisted in the performance of rituals and the holding of feasts, but the membership also became a client base for women's trading ventures, including the commodities that they imported through Murid transnational networks. Overseas traders found prosperity abroad not only because their warsek (luck) was always located elsewhere, but also due to the efforts of their maternal kin to promote their business interests by producing a strong family network, ensuring that filial obligations were met, providing credit, honoring debts, keeping the family's *sutura* (discretion), keeping their financial foibles private, and maintaining their solvency.

As Abdoulaye Kane has argued, the complexity of women's financial management strategies surpasses the brief description of rotating savings and credit associations that one often encounters in development literature (2002:295). Here are just a few of the strategies that members of the Géer family practiced and that were common in urban Dakar. Young married and unmarried women often organized a tuur (rotation) along the lines of matrilineal kin: each woman contributed a fixed amount at each gathering, and one woman would win the pot. These meetings might take place at the home of a family member who, as host, provided a DJ and music, food and drinks. Older married women often organized into mbotaye associations; in rural areas where extended kin resided nearby, the mbotaye consisted primarily of matrilineal kin. Other exchanges included *ndeye dikké,* which means the "mother of my choosing" or "twin," which is a relationship of patronage that is established between two women. Rotating savings and credit associations are referred to as *natt* or *tegg,* and through these associations women were able to save while deferring the demands of kin without moral reproach (Guérin 2006:557). When approached for aid or loans, women could defer requests by indicating that they were obligated to make their contribution to their natt, but next time they would certainly try to assist. Women collectively determined the order of rotation, how often payments would be made and the amount of those payments, and the time frame for the rotation and life of the union.

Sokna Géer's largest rotating savings and credit association met every Wednesday at her house; she was the president of this union of about sixty women, which received matching funds from the nongovernmental organization ENDA T.M. One of her sons was paid a small amount to keep the accounts for these women, who were largely illiterate, and a griot collected the money in a calabash, a symbol of fertility. Women often belonged to multiple natt, which permitted them to always draw on the pot of one of their credit unions, to buy and sell merchandise as quickly as possible, and to have ready access to cash for their ritual payments. Many women were said to divert a portion of men's remittances into these types of associations, and male kin often disdained such activities as *gaspillage* (waste) because the money was taken out of general circulation and put into a specialized circuit where men could not claim it. When a woman was in arrears to several of her unions it was not uncommon for her to telephone her spouse or brother abroad and claim that a child was sick and that he must send money immediately for hospital attention and medications, since shame and gossip follow the woman who does not honor her obligations.

Not only did women have incredible memories for gifts received and owed, they also often recorded these transactions in notebooks, which were frequently stored under their mattresses. Most of the women in Sokna Géer's neighborhood and age group were illiterate and thus their sons kept their various notebooks and were paid small allowances for the recordkeeping. One such son remarked with astonishment that his mother could remember who gave her what as many as five years ago, but she would still ask him to check the notebook to make sure that she was correct to avoid the great shame of miscalculation. Such mistakes were the subject of vicious gossip among women and could lead to the breakdown of social relationships. The ledgers contained the name of each woman who belonged to a particular association—ritual, family, rotating credit, etc.—and in one column listed the items that she had been given on a particular date, such as meters of cloth or amounts of cash, and often, but not always, another column recorded how much she gave in return at the next event. The names were listed vertically, and events and payments were listed horizontally. A woman would often have a notebook for each group with which she was involved. Though women tended to keep their notebooks over time, such groups could be ephemeral and notebooks could be lost, destroyed, or worn out.

Women reported using these notebooks as long as they could remember, which often meant as many as thirty years, beginning at the time that they entered into marriage. Yet it seemed as though this kind of accounting had "a social presence [of] a new kind" (Strathern 2000:1). The overt emphasis on recordkeeping stemmed in part from women's involvement with the NGOs and foreign lenders who organized and supported their mutual aid associations. Not only did these organizations provide matching funds for women's economic ventures, but they also offered classes in business management, Wolof literacy, and accounting. An ethos of accountability, as well as feelings of private shame and individual inadequacy, began to permeate social exchanges as NGOs emphasized balancing accounts over perpetuating asymmetries. Although NGOs may be less accountable to representative democracy, they bring with them their own "audit cultures" (Strathern 2000) through their monitoring and evaluating of program outcomes to meet the standards of accountability and transparency that are set by the international humanitarian and religious organizations that fund them. These audit cultures have implications for the people the organizations set out to serve; they establish a different set of moral expectations that are framed as financial efficiency, which they see as being essential to development.

FINANCIAL STRATEGIES, NGOS, AND THE STATE

When wealth trickled down from the Senegalese state, often through large-scale development projects that were aimed at agricultural inputs and infrastructure, it followed well-established lines of distribution. The money often worked its way through the Murid hierarchy and into the hands of male heads of household, who managed the distribution of land and fed dependents. Gifts were used to incorporate oneself into the paths of wealth, and they became a way of accessing and negotiating the bureaucracy (cf. Apter 1999; Bayart 1993, 2000; De Sardan 1999; Eames 1992; Yang 1994). Presenting gifts on the occasions of religious and family ceremonies was an intrinsic part of the patron-client relationship, and chains of indebtedness were created to reach up through the hierarchy, to obtain resources from the state, with everyone struggling to become lenders as well as debtors. As I have argued, Murid success in agriculture and, later, in trade, real estate, transportation, and cement had to do with the ways in which they successfully intertwined personal and political relationships and moved between the regulated and unregulated spheres of the economy. Gifts were an important means of converting transactions from short-term market exchanges into long-term value.

As the nature of production shifted from agriculture to transnational trade, and the position of the state as a locus of patronage eroded due to the way that it was scaled back through neoliberal reforms that were mandated by international lending organizations, the nature of exchange shifted as well. State functionaries began to be seen as less likely to offer patronage, while new patrons were emerging in the form of Murid shaykhs and businesspeople. Also emerging were powerful female entrepreneurs and money lenders, many of whom benefited from the shift toward financing women's organizations by international donors (cf. Perry 2002). The research emphasis on the economic crisis in Senegal from the 1980s onward has not yet come to terms with the presence of these NGOs as an indicator that the country, while being largely excluded from the benefits of globalization, is still at the very heart of neoliberal global capitalism (Ferguson 2006). While these organizations provide the social services that the Senegalese state is no longer able to bestow, they are not subject to processes of representative democracy (12). Substantial government functions have been outsourced to NGOs, many of which have absorbed unemployed government workers or lured away others with high salaries and benefits (38). It is for this reason that I argue that the spread of women's associations cannot be simply understood as a coping mechanism that is rooted in traditional practices, but rather that the prominence of these organizations has been at the very center of the process of neoliberal reform in Senegal since the 1980s.

Women's ritual associations gained increasing attention in the 1980s from international organizations that considered them as possible conduits for grassroots development schemes. In part, development ideology rested on the assumption that a bloated state bureaucracy impeded development and led to corruption, and NGOs thus promoted the idea that development could encourage gender equity, which might also lead to greater democratization. Microfinance projects began to be seen as a way of reaching those who did not have access to formal financial and banking institutions and those who lacked access to the property and literacy that they needed to obtain guarantees (Guérin 2006:549–50).

The impetus for the emergence of this culture of projects in Senegal was the idea that income generation projects for women would increase their influence within the household (Venema and van Eijk 2004:52). Yet women in Senegal already exercised autonomy over the proceeds from their employment and contributed to the well-being of household members. In development policy, however, the notion persisted that women in Senegal and elsewhere were lacking in experience regarding financial management and that this knowledge might be key to their empowerment.

The state under the Partie Socialiste organized mbotaye and rotating savings and credit associations into *groupements féminins* (women's groups). These groups organized registration and voting for elections and provided audiences for the Partie Socialiste officials. When women's mbotaye became *groupements féminins* they acquired the status of civil society organizations whose recognition by the state was indicated through its financial support and the matching funds that it provided for their rotating savings and credit associations (Patterson 2002:5). The state recognized the women's groups that had registered with it and paid a fee as *groupements de promotion féminine*. In return, women in these groups received access to bank credit, government technical advice, and recommendations from state officials for international donor projects (Patterson 1999:12; Patterson 2002:5).[3]

Women's groups also organized as *groupements d'intérêt économique* through the chamber of commerce, which enabled women to receive loans and aid from the state or from an NGO (Venema and van Eijk 2004:58, 66). These groups were formed as part of the new agricultural policy in 1984 and were aimed at reducing the risk involved in lending to individuals by lending to groups of women with similar interests. Many women relied on these organizations and their access to resources from the state and NGOs to supplement men's earnings or even to replace them as the prospects for male employment in agriculture and urban trades declined.

Changes in the nature of women's associations under President Abdou Diouf unfolded in relation to the decentralization and feminization of development that had already been taking place in Senegal. The *groupements féminins* that were created by Diouf in the 1980s became part of his decentralization reforms, which aimed to increase efficiency and limit corruption. Decentralization of the Senegalese state intensified in 1996 as power was transferred from the central state to locally elected government institutions. Through these reforms, in effect, the state abrogated its responsibility to provide for the welfare and well-being of its citizens (Simone 2006:137). As the global market prices for Senegal's primary exports of peanuts and phosphates declined and state revenues decreased, Senegal borrowed from the World Bank and the IMF. In exchange for these loans, the Senegalese state adopted free market reforms, such as the privatization of a myriad of state functions, the devaluation of the currency, and the liberalization of trade. Though, in theory, decentralization moved both the resources and the political authority to local institutions, Brett O'Bannon (2006) has shown that for the region of Bakel in the early twenty-first century, those resources had yet to be transferred from the state to the local level. As a consequence, many local groups turned not to local or state structures for assistance but rather sought to foster links with international donors through NGOs, which gave women's groups in particular special access to resources.

Women mobilized their associational membership in varying contexts, and some political parties encouraged women to organize as voting blocs (Venema and van Eijk 2004:62). Through their associations, women assisted each other with ceremonial expenses, offered loans to members, and collectively invested in productive projects such as agricultural inputs or consumer goods that they purchased wholesale. Following the currency devaluation, women's groups began to buy items in bulk, such as rice, bouillon cubes, milk, sugar, soap, and cloth, and then reapportioned these items into smaller packets and sold the smaller quantities, which reflected consumers' newly limited means (63). Members often called on each other to circumvent the state bureaucracy to obtain a *carte de commerçant* (a permit to sell and import merchandise, usually a prerequisite for obtaining a five-year multiple-entry visa to the United States for the purpose of trading) or a visa, or to resolve disputes (especially if a fine was involved). These networks were mobilized to obtain loans and start-up capital, and the relationships formed the basis for a system of social security to which people could turn if they needed financial help in an emergency, including hospital stays, deaths, boat crashes, and so forth.

In one case, Sokna Géer called upon her network of women's associations to assist her in seeking medical treatment for her oldest son, who needed kidney dialysis, which was not available in Senegal at the time. With the members' help, she was able to send him to Paris for medical treatment. Over time she also managed to send two more sons to see if they might be matches as kidney donors. A third son was finally determined to be a match through testing that had become available in Senegal, and to get him to Paris for the operation she worked through the members of her *groupement féminin* to secure him a seat on the state aircraft that was carrying the minister of women, children, and the family to Europe. This son now works in a glass factory in Italy. Her fifth son, who is also abroad, is the only one who succeeded in obtaining a student visa; however, in order to get that visa he needed a bank statement demonstrating that he had access to adequate funds to finance his education. As I mentioned, his oldest sister, Jigeen, mobilized her social network, especially the business partners of one of her ex-husbands with whom she had worked in the Ivory Coast, to obtain these papers.

The shift to a focus on women in development in Senegal and elsewhere on the continent reflected the assumption that providing resources for women would lead to their emancipation. Proponents argued that access to resources would result in the greater political participation of women and, ultimately, to development and democratization. These programs were part of the main thrust of development thinking in the 1990s that emphasized good governance, democratic elections, neoliberal reform, and free markets. Nongovernmental organizations transformed women's associations in part by introducing a notion of membership as voluntary, thus replacing kin- and caste-based reciprocal obligations and assuring equal rewards and sacrifices for each participant (Kane 2002:298). The associations that registered as *groupements féminins* were sometimes caste-based, that is, groups of freeborn or groups of artisans, although others were mixed (Venema and van Eijk 2004:58). Interestingly, Sokna Géer's mbotaye and her main rotating savings and credit association, sponsored by ENDA T.M., were both composed of freeborn persons and artisans.

Despite their aims, NGOs found in Senegal that, rather than promoting democracy and equality, investing in women's projects often resulted in reinscribing caste-based relations as women invested these funds in relations of reciprocity through family ceremonies. Moreover, as these groups became more accountable to the state and to the NGOs that were funding them and were held to Western standards of efficiency, divisions developed within the membership, and the associations became steadily less democratic. As they became more vertically organized to link to the state and international donors, their membership also became more hierarchical, and power was distributed less equally among members (Tostensen et al. 2001:23). The culture of accountability that went hand in hand with NGO microfinance programs also introduced the notion of the audit, which included auditing not only the performance of the NGO and its funding organizations, but the performance of the women themselves. As NGOs encouraged women to check themselves through an ethos of responsibility and civic duty, and in the name of development, an element of mistrust began to permeate women's exchange relationships. It was this lost trust that in large part led to the failure of the Géers to ensure future returns from those upon whom they bestowed hospitality and gifts.

GIFT EXCHANGE AND THE POLITICS OF SOCIAL PRODUCTION

At the feast marking his father's departure for the hajj, Abdoul Aziz stood outside his family home, leaning on his black Renault sedan with his arms folded across his chest, the silky, pale blue sleeves of his khaftan flapping in the wind. With a nod toward the confusion of voices coming from the home, he said, "*Gaspillage . . . jel rekk* [Waste . . . people only come to take]." Abdoul Aziz explained that the problem was not teraanga and showing respect for others through hospitality; rather, he said, many of the recipients of the Géers' hospitality had come to benefit from their prosperity but contributed little to the overall strength of their network. Abdoul Aziz's comments revealed his frustration with a system of exchange that was ideally based on an investment in social relations but that, in practice, potentially divested families of their wealth and productive capacities. From his perspective, this system of exchange divested junior men of their assets in order to support elders. Similarly, even after his younger brother had sent money for the hajj that he had saved working as an engineer in the United States, their mother pressured him for additional remittances for the feasts. Reading his adverse reaction as the austere comportment of an emigrant male, Sokna Géer did not know that her son had his own cycle of debt in the United States, including credit card and car payments and a mortgage.

Through exercising the rights and obligations of kin, many Senegalese have survived and even thrived in the turbulence that has characterized the urban economy of Senegal since the 1990s. Yet, it is those same obligations, as Abdoul Aziz pointed out, that have been nearly impossible for the great majority to meet (Simone 2006:138). Women and men, young and old, have varying views of the value of the gift economy because they occupy structurally different positions. Men and women have different expectations, desires, and strategies with regard to spending priorities because they may at certain times in their lives hold different values and because they are in different structural situations (Guyer 1988:160). For women, marriage, bridewealth, and the system of rights that are associated with kinship are the primary means through which they have acquired resources (163). In many ways, women have also seemed to have more access to men's resources than the reverse. As I have argued, wives earned their own income through farming and trade and had autonomy over its expenditure in addition to commanding a portion of men's resources for housekeeping and ritual expenses. However, these gendered responsibilities have shifted under changing seasonal and long-term economic conditions, and the process of provisioning the household and meeting ritual expenditures now involves an ongoing negotiation among family members.

As much as men's and women's urban livelihoods shifted with changing economic conditions, so too did their repertoires for meeting and maintaining crucial values in social life. Although women were criticized for drawing resources away from the home by their participation in the gift economy, at the same time, given the high rate of men's unemployment and retirement, they often financed the household. In theory, men as husbands and heads of household or as adult unmarried sons were responsible for feeding dependents by providing housekeeping money; purchasing grains, fish, and meat (often in bulk if refrigeration were available); paying the monthly tab at the store where spices, oil, coffee, sugar, and other foods were purchased; financing medical expenses and school fees; and maintaining the home, which included paying utilities. Men were also expected to provide livestock and cloth for ritual events and religious holidays; to supply bridewealth to their in-laws or for their sons; and to, at times, assist women in their ritual payments, although this was certainly a point of contention. Both men and women provided for their parents, had financial obligations toward other children among their kin, gave offerings to religious guides, contributed to religious associations, and offered alms.

There was a gendered disjuncture not only in the management of the household economy, but also in the very nature, purpose, and idea of the home itself. Abdoul Aziz sought to accumulate wealth by constructing a home, an inheritable form of value that could not be easily liquidated or claimed by his future in-laws, while Sokna Géer spent her earnings on displays of wealth during family ceremonies to protect and promote the honor of her lineage. With fluctuating exchange rates and the devaluation of the currency, putting her money toward the creation of social relations was a realistic hedge against instability. why?

The forms and signs of wealth are visible everywhere in the Senegalese communities from which male migrants originate. It is not uncommon for women to wear *broderie* or imported African voile, to have at least one male relative dealing in imported automobiles, and to carry 10,000–60,000 CFA francs a day to family ceremonies. At the same time, such households bemoan their high levels of obligation, including merchandise taken on credit, monthly tabs to be paid at the boutique and the corner store, and social payments that are promised or expected. Elders complain that bridewealth payments, which were once intended to cement relations between families over a lifetime of exchanges of labor, goods, and persons, are now made too slowly or not at all. The social aspects of debt are an underexplored feature of economic liberalization and the rise in household debt in many parts of the world. These household stories about debt were as much critical narratives of the neoliberal moment as were the more direct and public arguments of NGOs calling for relief of the national debt to free up state money for investment in "human development" at the turn of the twenty-first century.

SEVEN

ONLY TROUBLE

SOKNA GÉER'S SON Abdoul Aziz drove her to a naming ceremony one morning in February three weeks before her husband would depart for the hajj to Mecca. An early morning haze surrounded the neighborhood homes, which marched up the side of a russet-colored sandy bank. These square cement homes were half-built icons of the wealth that could be made abroad.

Abdoul Aziz stopped his car at the bottom of the hill and shut off the engine.

"*Waay,* Abdoul Aziz, what is it?" Sokna Géer asked. "Why don't you take me to the door of the Caaya house?"

Her son responded, somewhat exasperated, "The car won't go. These Renault cars don't like the sand in Senegal."

Sokna Géer pressed him, "You want me to walk up the hill with my bad hip? A taxi driver would take me right to the door."

Abdoul Aziz helped his mother out of the car and held her elbow as she walked, barely lifting her feet across the sand, the arthritis in her hip giving her the appearance of having one leg shorter than the other. The deeply hued folds of her damask gown trailed behind her. As she approached the Caaya home, she nodded in approval and smiled at Abdoul Aziz upon hearing the Muslim singers' high-pitched chanting being broadcast throughout the neighborhood. She stopped for a moment and closed her eyes as she took in the sounds.

Entering through the front gate of the home whose rooms faced an inner courtyard Sokna took in the white tent erected in its center, the fat, fleshy sheep tethered tightly to an acacia tree, and several cast-iron pots communally owned by the women's ritual association lying about in anticipation of the feast to celebrate the newborn. She said to Abdoul Aziz, "*Xaalis le* [This is money]."

He responded with a grin, "*Yow, drinanke nge* [You are a social doyen]."

Normally, Sokna Géer looked forward to these ceremonies and could easily spend two or three days a week attending weddings, naming ceremonies, and sometimes funerals. The naming ceremony for a newborn baby was a joyous occasion, and the maternal grandmother would call all of her friends to her home to celebrate the naming of her new grandchild. She would receive numerous gifts of cloth that she would bequeath to her daughter, the new mother. She would enjoy the company of her friends, trade gossip, and have the opportunity to shine in new gowns sewn for the occasion. Her friends would help her to throw a good feast, papering over her financial shortcomings if necessary.

Sokna Géer replied to Abdoul Aziz's teasing, "*Deedet,* no, this ceremony is work." She explained the parents' shock upon discovering that their school-age daughter was pregnant. They had quickly tied the marriage at the mosque, but the girl hadn't departed for her new husband's compound yet. The naming ceremony was to coincide with this next step in the marriage process. It was, in effect, to serve not only as a feast to sanction the naming of the newborn, but also as the marriage feast.

Sokna continued, "The baby is my *turandoo,* my namesake. I am bringing wrappers for her today." Not only was she obligated to bring cloth for the newborn's naming day, but she would also provide her first headscarf at puberty. "I am going to teach her patience and restraint." For her work, Sokna would be honored with the payment of the *ndeyale* when the girl married. But she would also be expected to return five to ten times the amount to the Caaya women. Thus the Caayas had named their grandchild after someone whom they esteemed and whom they considered to be of superior social rank, moral character, and material assets.

Traversing the courtyard in her tall shoes, Sokna Géer stopped to rearrange the voluminous white headscarf that had slid down the back of the polished cloth of her boubou. Gathering the ample fabric under her arm, she headed toward Penda's room where she found the newborn swaddled in two pieces of stripweave. Penda's mother, Cora, placed the baby in Sokna Géer's arms. Sokna looked up to see that Abdoul Aziz had entered the room.

"*Assalamu alaikum,*" he said. "Peace be with you."

Cora returned his greeting, "*Walaikum assalam,* and upon you be peace."

He then turned to leave, speaking of some business contacts he had to make that morning, and chuckled to his mother, "This naming ceremony is truly women's business."

Cora then turned to Sokna and said, "It is time to prepare her for her naming."

Sokna Géer took a razor to the right side of the baby's head. "This will protect her from misfortune," she said as the tufts of hair fell into a calabash containing a small amount of water. She looked up and asked, "Where is the baby's mother?"

"Gone," said the grandmother. "She went to the salon with friends to have her hair and makeup done."

"Really?" Sokna asked. The tight bedroom was already crowded with friends, family, and business associates. The guests were becoming restless as the morning sun grew hotter, and some of them asked, "Where is the lakk? It's getting late." Knowing that the lakk would not be served until the naming had taken place, Sokna Géer continued to prepare the newborn. She asked where the millet, kola nuts, and salt were. These were the crucial symbols of good luck, long life, and reproduction.

Cora responded, "*Laay,* we forgot those things."

Sokna turned to two other women in the room and raised her eyebrows in disbelief as she handed the baby to them. "Tell the maid to go to the store," she said as she pulled several small bills from the folds of her wrapper. A turbulent discussion ensued among the women who were ready to get on with the ceremony: because millet wasn't normally found at the corner store, one had to go all the way to the market. "Okay," Sokna acquiesced. "We will just substitute rice then."

The baby was given back to Sokna, who poured a cup of water into a calabash and, placing a handful of rice into it with some salt, said, "*Ku xumbana nun nyep nyungi ko begg, bu bare warsek* [Those who are in motion are desired by all, this daughter will have a lot of luck]." She added, "*Xoorum, yengu moo saaf* [Salt bodes well for her movement in life]."

She worked quickly, conscious that the men had long been assembled in another room, but she was delayed by three griots who entered the room to sing her praises. Sokna Géer was ready to dismiss these griots as profiteers, as those who travel from feast to feast and praise people whose family histories they do not know, hoping to receive cash, or, worse yet, as urban griots who steal bowls of food from feasts. But when Sokna looked up, she recognized her own family griot standing among them. This woman would play an important role in facilitating Sokna's participation in this feast and protecting her reputation, and it was important that she take a moment to speak to her.

As people continued to push in and out of the room, Sokna Géer stood to leave, but turned first to some of Penda's friends who stood near the door and handed them a few bills to recognize their role in the day's events. To her shock, the girls pressed together, forming a barrier in the doorway against which the banknotes fell to the floor. They looked at Sokna, and one of them laughed, "That is not enough money."

They were interrupted by the appearance of Penda's father, Cheikh Caaya, who shouted over the din, "*Laa ilaha illa-ilah* [There is no God but God]." He then directed Sokna Géer, "Leave this women's business and bring the baby into the men's room."

Sokna handed over another few bills to the girls as she attempted to move through the doorway, but they did not budge. The older women looked at one another and one of them pulled three wadded banknotes from under her waistband and threw it in the girls' direction without looking at them. The girls shrieked and pulled up their wrappers, revealing their scanty *bethio* underwraps—made of handworked fabrics, such as cotton cloth, with cutwork or crocheting to reveal the upper thighs and often embroidered sexual imagery demonstrating their reproductive power and potential.

Sokna Géer pushed her way past the girls, saying, "You have no shame," and headed toward the parlor. The pile of sandals in the entryway spoke to Cheikh Caaya's stature in this community. Sokna moved between the men who were seated on the floor mats toward the maternal grandfather, who was seated on a bed in the center of the room. She sat below him, facing the imam; holding the swaddled newborn, she draped her own head and shoulders with her white scarf. The imam leaned over and blew the baby's name into its ear, then spat. The *adhan* was then whispered into the newborn's right ear and the *lihan* into her left. Sokna Géer circled the room as the name was announced aloud so that others could touch the newborn's head and then their own, followed by their hearts, thus exchanging blessings with the infant while kola nuts were passed as alms. Blessings were thought to flow through the blood, the saliva, and the practice of touching sources of grace, including new babies, returnees from Mecca, shaykhs, and their images.

As soon as Sokna Géer returned to the women's room, Cora carried in a lime-green plastic washtub containing a butchered lamb with its feet pointing skyward. A griot followed behind, holding the caul fat high over her head, announcing, "Teraanga [hospitality] for Madame Géer." A senior woman followed with a large plastic bucket of sour milk, and another brought Sokna an enameled bowl of millet porridge covered with a piece of cloth. The milk and millet were placed on top of the armoire, where they would remain until evening, and the meat, which was left lower down for guests to see, was protected from flies with the caul fat, which was laid across it. These items would return home with Sokna Géer after the feast. As the newborn was spirited away, lest she fall prey to bewitching eyes, Sokna Géer looked down and exclaimed, "*Laay,* in the mayhem I forgot to shave the other side of her head."

Several more women placed large bowls of lakk in front of the guests, who were gathered on the beds, in the courtyard, and in the men's room.

The more quarrelsome women, impatient in the confined room but reluctant to take the time to relocate to the courtyard, positioned themselves around the steaming porridge. As one woman drew a spoon out of her handbag, the others complained that the household was not providing all of the guests with spoons or at least napkins for their gowns. As they were eating, several of Penda's girlfriends returned with sullen expressions: "The father stopped our *sabar.* He said that dancing isn't part of Islam." When they finished, Cora brought in another bucket of sour milk and offered it to Sokna. Turning her head in the direction of the bucket on top of the armoire, Sokna Géer replied, "Thank you for your generosity, it is too much." A woman sitting nearby chuckled and said, "Yes, a woman doesn't want to appear too greedy."

By three o'clock the men began to disperse to perform their afternoon prayers. They had fulfilled their obligation of bringing millet and small amounts of cash to offset the day's expenses, assisted in naming the child, shared in the kola nuts, and eaten the slaughtered lamb. But the women kept arriving. They encountered rooms that were already full of well-dressed women whose garments were constructed of layers of flounces, laces, and embroidered and brilliantly dyed fabrics; their stacked hair-dos and pancake makeup were melting in the cramped, airless quarters. Several latecomers asked if the lunch of roasted lamb and garlic rice had already been served. As they waited to eat, they pulled various goods out of their bags—strands of waist beads, pots of hand-perfumed incense, skin lotions, and sandals—which were admired and tried on. Women without wares talked of the cargo that they had for sale which was stashed at home, naming scarves from Mecca, insulated bowls from Jeddah, and gold bracelets from India (which had probably been bought in New York). The guests also spoke of their various friends and family who had traveled abroad and the things that they anticipated they would receive when they returned. They discussed what was and was not selling, what was fashionable, and what was new on the market. What was not discussed, however, was that the number of gifts they imagined giving and receiving that afternoon would surpass their material ability to reciprocate. Or that the gifts that did materialize had been acquired through an expanding culture of credit.

Each woman also kept near her and out of sight the rolls of cloth and stacks of banknotes that she would present to Cora once the gift giving began. When they heard that Penda had arrived, they moved quickly to the courtyard with their gifts in hand. Sokna Géer approached Penda and embraced her, throwing her headscarf on the ground for the new mother to walk on. Several other women followed suit. Penda made her way through the crowd with her girlfriends on her heels, pushing their heads toward the various lenses of the cameras and video recorders pointed in their direction.

Sokna Géer led Penda toward her mother, who was seated next to a large suitcase at the center of a collection of mats that were laid out under the white tent. A circle of about eighty women closed in around them, with the griots working the outer reaches of the crowd. Guests leaned forward to catch a glimpse of the housewares and novel fabrics that were carefully pulled from the suitcase in order to never reveal its full contents. As Penda's mother received pieces of strip cloth rolled into cylinders with cash placed on top, as though the cloth were infusing the beholder's reproductive potential into the money itself, she opened the suitcase, placed the gifts in it, and then withdrew other gifts, which she then distributed to her guests along with cash. With each transaction, much debate ensued between Cora, her close friends and family sitting near her, and her daughter. Eventually an appropriate gift was chosen to return to the donor, who would likely not have heard the discussion among Penda's kin, as the din and crush of the crowd made it difficult to follow what was happening. One of Penda's girlfriends recorded these transactions in her notebook as a griot announced them loudly for all to hear.

As the sun began to sink on the horizon, several women pointed out, "It's dusk, we can't see very well. Let's call an end to the gift giving." The event wound down either because of the sheer exhaustion of the women or because of the descending darkness.

Sokna Géer recognized that the time had come for Penda to officially enter her husband's compound for the first time. As Sokna began to prepare Penda, looking for the piece of stripweave that would be used to cover her head and getting ready to speak to her about what was expected of a new wife, Cora stopped her.

"Penda is a child," she said. "She can't go to her husband's home just seven days after giving birth, especially since she should still be in school." Cora continued, "Penda is too young to handle the responsibilities required of a second wife. She is too new to motherhood and too new to marriage. A naming ceremony and a marriage shouldn't happen on the same day."

Sokna Géer replied, "Is Penda a child? Are these ceremonies happening too fast? Or is it that you did not get to have a marriage feast at your home the day before she was to enter her husband's home?"

The women assembled knew the implications of these questions. Sokna Géer was suggesting that Penda's mother thought she was entitled to more gifts than she had received during the naming ceremony. If Penda entered her husband's home that night, her mother would be expected not only to supply her trousseau, but also to bring gifts to her in-laws the following day, during another feast that would welcome her daughter into their home.

Sokna Géer remained silent for a moment, weighing the situation, turned to the woman next to her and asked, "Did the groom not pay all of the bridewealth? Surely it had been enough for Penda's mother to prepare a trousseau for her and gifts for her in-laws?"

It was well after 1:00 AM before Sokna Géer finally alighted from the taxi in front of her home. From the car, she withdrew cylindrical packages of cloth while the driver pulled out the large green plastic washtub of meat and bowls of millet and sour milk from the trunk. Sokna threw two pieces of the inexpensive, gauzy, summer-weight cloth called khartoum in her daughters' direction. As her son took the tub of meat from the driver and carried it toward the pantry, she admonished him, "Lock the door carefully. Given the opportunity, *bandit* are likely to make off with the meat during the night." She then lowered herself into a nearby chair to exchange her high-heeled shoes for plastic flip-flops to perform her ablutions, which she had missed in the course of the day's bedlam. After praying, Sokna Géer examined the two remaining pieces of cloth that she had been given. One was a manufactured wax print and the other a gown of damask cloth dyed in red and blue triangles. She unrolled the dyed piece, held it up, and then threw it toward another daughter who was passing by. The piece of cloth was a *petite boubou* too short and narrow for her matronly body and unequal to her social stature. "*Coow rekk* [Only trouble]," she said.

WOMEN'S WEALTH

On a Friday in March 1996, al Hajji Ousmane Gueye, the permanent secretary of the National Association of Imams and Oulémas of Senegal, distributed a sermon denouncing *gaspillage* (wastefulness) that was to be read simultaneously at the *xutba* (Friday sermon) in mosques throughout Senegal. "*Dieu proscrit le gaspillage* [God prohibits squandering]," the sermon read, condemning women's gift exchange practices during family ceremonies.[1] Gueye's denunciation, however, was not targeted at the countless symbolic gestures of mutual aid that are made during matrimonial and mortuary ceremonies; rather, he targeted the *ndawtal,* the competitive display and bestowal of cloth by women which takes place during *ngénte* celebrations, the Muslim naming ceremonies that are held seven days after the birth of a child. Rather than squandering their resources at family ceremonies, Gueye urged women to support the *zakkat,* funds that are collected by the Muslim hierarchy to support health clinics, classrooms, and the poor.

Gueye's sermon followed on the heels of a national declaration that also condemned excessive expenditures during family ceremonies. The 1996 declaration was issued by the participants in a forum that was organized by the minister of women, children, and the family, which commemorated International Women's Day and addressed the changing fortunes of Senegalese families following the 1994 devaluation of the CFA currency. Members of the forum resurrected the popular 1980s saying "*les Sénégalais sont fatigués* (the Senegalese are tired)," which had captured the national mood following the implementation of structural adjustment programs, this time applying it to the practice of gift exchange during family ceremonies. The forum faulted the uniquely Wolof custom of returning double the sums that one received at one's own feast at one's peers' celebrations. Attendees were reminded of the Family Code, which, since its implementation in 1972, has capped social payments like these.

Ironically, the same women who issued the declaration against gift exchange—leaders of women's rotating savings and credit associations—were largely responsible for the inflation of these gifts since, through their participation in these associations, which were sponsored by development organizations that matched women's investments, they gained access to lump sums of cash that they could circulate at family ceremonies. The central contradiction that they were facing, then, was how to work with the NGOs with their liberal, grassroots bias toward promoting women's groups, which had been a major source of women's political empowerment following state decentralization in the late 1990s, while also maintaining the *masla* (sociability, civility) needed to respect the tradition of gift exchange. After all, what better way to demonstrate masla than through dispersing the massive sums that were obtained from rotating credit unions, which enhanced the remittances of migrant brothers, husbands, and sons?

It was not only the Muslim clergy who sought to stem the circulation of cloth and clothing. As in the rest of the continent, the diminishment of the Senegalese state's power had been matched by the emergence of a vast NGO network to which former state functions had been outsourced

(Ferguson 2005:379). The NGOs singled out women as preferred recipients of development aid because of their organizational capacity and their status as long-term residents of the country in the face of male migration (see, for example, Patterson 2002; Perry 2002). Yet, women often distributed microfinance funds in ways that instantiated social asymmetries (Ndione 1989).

There had also been calls by a prominent male psychologist to hold an *ndëp* (exorcism) ceremony for women who continued to produce spectacular prestations during these events. An exorcism like this involves the appearance of a masked figure representing a lion, which is said to scare the transgressive behavior out of an individual in order to cure social, mental, and moral illness.[2] This seemed like a strange prescription since exorcism is rarely practiced overtly in the urban neighborhoods of Dakar. The *ndëp* has become more closely linked with youth associations, which often sponsor these events; the lion appears both frightening and comical, chasing disobedient children through the streets to raise money for local soccer leagues, which made appeals for this kind of ceremony to cure women of their financial ills seem rather condescending. By 2000, on the radio, in the print media, in religious sermons, and in the offices of nongovernmental development organizations, women were accused of inflating the cost of social payments and thus threatening the development of the nation (Ndione 1994; Patterson 2002; Perry 2002).

In 2003, leaders of Islamist movements and the Sufi orders demanded the implementation of an Islamic family law in the national assembly (Bop 2005; Camara 2007; Sow 2003; Villalón 2004). They aimed to limit the social payments made on the occasions of family ceremonies. They viewed these payments as relating to cosaan, or custom, rather than to Islam. The social commentary that condemned women's gift-giving practices suggested both moral outrage at these conspicuous and visible forms of exchange in a society where money conventionally changes hands in the famous closed handshake known as the *nuyoo murid* (Murid greeting), and also suspicion toward female circuits of exchange, which were closed and impenetrable to male clergy and elders, government ministries, and nongovernmental organizations. It is important to note, however, that these ostentatious displays were particular to the urban areas. In Murid villages and in Tuba, family ceremonies were accompanied by the exchange of coins, not numerous bills, with the exception being the Tuba households of prosperous migrant traders, which host many Dakar guests.

There had been significant attempts by the colonial state to control social payments, including bridewealth and those associated with naming ceremonies. During the colonial era, the government and the imams attempted to abolish these payments outright in a document, Réglementation Générale,[3] which permitted 500 CFA francs to be donated to the birth mother as "*frais de soins sanitaires* [fees for health care]." The document prohibited further payments and limited families' celebrations to slaughtering a single sheep and preparing two large bowls of porridge, two large bowls of beignets, and a pitcher of ginger beer. It also prohibited members of the *gewel* (praise singers) and *lawbë* (woodworking caste, also known for their erotic dances) from attending naming ceremonies during which they exacted significant payments for their praises and dances.

During the 1990s, women, however, rather than responding to the ongoing negative moral discourse, spoke of their fear that the visibility of their wealth made them targets of male youth who sought to steal from them during chaotic and crowded feasts. Thus, some women moved gift exchanges into closed bedrooms that were separated from the crowd attending the ceremonies. The thefts suggest that discontent with women's wealth was not just an issue for the male-dominated religious clergy, who were seeking to extend their influence over the domestic sphere, or for a declining state apparatus that was concerned with promoting development, but also for the youth who were deeply frustrated with the inability of elders to provide for them.

The circulation of cloth during naming ceremonies is linked to women's respectability, reproductive power, and ritual authority. Women employ strategies of display, bestowal, and concealment to control social renewal and produce sociocultural difference. For women, these textiles are tactile, sensual, and visual forms of wealth; thus, they have responded to social criticism concerning their exchange and sartorial practices by asserting that the clean and properly prepared body is beautiful and valued in Islam, as are displays of hospitality, mutual aid, and generosity; thus, such practices are expressions of tuyaaba. Although the Muslim clergy sought to locate these exchange practices outside of Islam as relics of a pre-Islamic past, they are modern, dynamic, and critical practices, forming part of women's financial repertoires over the *longue durée* and enabling them to maintain crucial equivalences in social life despite periods of economic volatility (Guyer 2004).

Although the households of Murid migrants, especially urban families, may appear more prosperous than those of their rural kith and kin, networks of obligation underpin such appearances. Therefore, women increasingly rely on qualities such as feminine beauty, underscored by conspicuous consumption, to convey the possibilities of engaging in reciprocal gift exchange and the social relationships that such reciprocity would engender.[4] In fact, many women are unable to match the inflationary sums that are set by their peers, which are triggered by the influx of remittances from overseas male kin and, consequently, they engage in elaborate social labor to defer expectations of reciprocity. Unlike the localized agricultural production and dry-season trading that characterized the early twentieth-century Murid communes, in which inhabitants knew with whom they were trading, business today occurs in distant locations that are invisible and misunderstood by those at home. Since housekeeping money appears in monthly lump sum remittances at the Western Union office or is delivered by visiting friends, families know little about the conditions in which it was earned abroad. The debate about women's wealth, then, was an attempt to render the relations between persons and objects visible and knowable (Foster 2006) in a time when the production of wealth abroad appeared inexplicable, even at times occult (Comaroff and Comaroff 1999). A complicated relationship has emerged between a concern for reciprocity in gift exchange during family ceremonies, which is based upon the assumption of debt, and the pretensions to consumerism in dress and other bodily practices, which are based upon the assumption of surplus. For example, the wealth that women display on their bodies is often borrowed from kin or obtained through credit; what this borrowing permits is the expansion of a vast culture of credit upon which men's trade networks depend. For the men, it is not actual wealth in the form of material objects that they are trading but, rather, their reputations. Money transfers often occur through informal networks of family and friends, and one's word, reputation, and honor, not one's material wealth, form the basis of credit.

The ndeyale, a gift that is given to honorary mothers during family ceremonies, is emblematic of female grace, honor, and reputation. In recent years, the Senegalese print media have been rife with negative representations of this particular form of women's gift exchange and it is not uncommon to read headlines such as "*Pourquoi de telles folies?*" "*Lekku-ndeye: Les dessous d'un commerce lucratif*," "*Une violence contre les démunis*," or "*La tyrannie du lekku-ndeye*."[5] The ndeyale is popularly criticized in Wolof by referring to it as the *lekku-ndeye* (what the mothers eat), which emphasizes the consumption rather than the redistribution of wealth; this word comes from *lekk* (food), *u* (the possessive), and *ndeye* (mother). Social commentary cites the lekku-ndeye as the paramount example of the perversion of the system of gift exchange, implying that what was once meant as a form of mutual aid has become a source of grave competition between age-mates and generational groupings. In the case of Sokna Géer and Cora, the lekku-ndeye was presented to the honorary mother: the newborn was to become her turandoo (namesake). This relationship imposed mutual obligations upon each party over time; for example, when the namesake became engaged, she presented her ndeye with 5,000 CFA francs, and when the namesake had her first child, her fictive mother reimbursed her five or six times that amount.

The inflationary practice of the ndeyale goes hand in hand with the emergence of the figure of the urban feminine ideal, or *drianké.* The word drianké is a slang term that is taken from the Wolof radical *diri,* which means to pull a load behind one or to keep on a leash, and the Pulaar suffix *yanke* (*nke* in Soninke), which means the person who does the action (Ndiaye 1998:274); together, they denote a woman who keeps others on a leash. The woman chosen to be the guardian of the namesake, and upon whom the lekku-ndeye will be bestowed, is often a drianké, an urban Wolof woman and a local socialite. She is usually a woman of beauty and largesse, and her girth is a sign of her wealth; she will incorporate the host family into the *jet-société.* T. K. Biaya, in an article on eroticism in Senegal, describes the drianké as "a titillating, plump, and mature woman expert at thiuraye [a kind of incense]" (1999:715). Her erotic arts involve the sensual deployment of incense and bethio, risqué, scented cotton underwraps that women embroider with vulgar imagery or enhance with elaborately skilled cutwork to reveal their bare bodies. Such erotic deployments do not necessarily run counter to Islam, where beauty and sexuality are not located in the nude body but rather in the body which is accessorized and properly decorated (Biaya 2000:788). Often, the drianké wears the latest fashionable cloth, European shoes, and enormous amounts of jewelry; carries a designer handbag; and appears at feasts only to encounter her hairdresser, manicurist, tailor, and cloth vendor attempting to reel in her line of credit. She may be guilty of what is referred to as *pukaare* (vanity), or of borrowing cash to fund her self-presentation rather than to participate in nesting hierarchies of patron-client relations. There is no real material basis underpinning her largesse. She comes by her wares from the men whom she knows. She is a Dakaroise, known for her leisurely attitude, whose days are filled with feasts and festivities.

The drianké stands in contrast to the ideal feminine type, the *sokna,* who is a senior woman: pious, virtuous, and of noble origin; the sokna displays the qualities of a woman in the post-monarchic, colonial, agrarian epoch

(Ndiaye 1998:274). It may seem like a contradiction, but for the woman who is generally regarded as a sokna among her family and peers, to be chided about acting or looking like a drianké, especially when she is en route to a feast, is almost a compliment. To be called a drianké is not only a form of flattery, it also plays on the inherent tension of gift exchange: Will the gifts she receives be redistributed or will she eat them?

RESOLVING THE CRISIS OF SOCIAL PRODUCTION

Days after the feast, Sokna Géer rehashed the events with her peers, who were at her home bringing the latest gossip, their newest trade wares, and pleas for aid. The senior women dismissed Cora's protests against the hasty marriage, for how could she expect a long and fruitful courtship for a daughter who was already pregnant? For Cora and other women, the marriage of a daughter in this way, rather than providing them with the opportunity to accumulate wealth and to display the strength of their social networks, served as a reminder that even completed processes of social production, in this case the success of Penda's marriage to the wealthy Modou Baxa, might not raise their status in the community. Instead, Cora was roundly ridiculed among her peers for her machinations concerning her daughter's unexpected pregnancy and swift marriage. As things stood, it was Sokna Géer who primarily benefited from the exchanges during the naming ceremony through the ndeyale, despite her dissatisfaction with the cloth that she received; therefore, it could be argued that it was she who ate Cora's portion of the marriage payment.

It is through symbolic means that crises of social production, in this case the naming ceremony that was held before the marital process was completed, are worked out. The coupling of the naming ceremony with the nocturnal rituals associated with entering the husband's compound for the first time suggests that, for Penda, the naming ceremony *was* the marriage. After all, both the naming ceremony and the céet, the carrying of a bride's trousseau into her conjugal home, are processes of enclosure that are central to the production of domestic space (Masquelier 2004:245). Filling the new bride's home with valued possessions such as cloth, cooking vessels, and other housewares creates a space of beauty that conveys respectability, prosperity, and future productive potential. This creation of enclosure or interiority through fashioning domestic space is essential to women's moral and sexual identities (247). Moreover, the naming ceremony marked Penda's first foray into the arena of ritualized exchanges as a married woman; the exchanges were recorded in a notebook as her first set of obligations, which she would endeavor to honor at subsequent feasts, a responsibility of married women.

The crisis of social production was also resolved through the display and bestowal of cloth, including cut and uncut cloth, locally woven and dyed textiles, and manufactured fabrics, among the women. Just as sañse shows respect for those with whom one endeavors to enter into relations of reciprocity, gifts *jottali* (convey, transmit) the prestige and the reputation of the giver as well as her esteem and respect for the receiver (Curtin 1975:287–88). By lending her presence to a family ceremony, a woman is participating in a kind of virtual exchange of reputation and creditworthiness. The latter can be expressed both by the bodily display of wealth, including clothing, coiffure, and cosmetics, which demonstrate the depth of the social networks through which one obtains consumer goods like manufactured cloth, and by exercising control over dependents who provide services, such as casted hair braiders, weavers, and tailors.

With respect to the figure of the driankė as well as to the forms of social critique that surround women's dress and exchange practices, the display and bestowal of wealth at family ceremonies can be dangerous:

> To have wealth and to dispense it generously are important elements of high social standing. To display it too ostentatiously, however, would run counter to the Wolof notion of *kersa* [restraint]. So it is that women, through *sanse,* may transmit [*jottali*; see Irvine 1974] the message that their male *kilife* are men of means, at the same time allowing the latter to behave with appropriate reserve. (Heath 1992:24)

That Sokna Géer expressed misgivings about Penda's overwhelming interest in sañse, the art of looking good, suggests that junior and senior women configure their social personas differently in this context. This disjuncture between age groups points to structural and generational shifts within a longer history. As I mentioned, sañse is about looking good to other women, showing respect for those with whom you are endeavoring to enter into relations of reciprocity, and conveying male honor. Sañse reveals the strength of women's networks, through which they acquire objects of adornment; the prosperity of their male kin, who also provide them with cloth and clothing; and the fact that they are themselves in positions to distribute largesse. Penda, as a young woman who was initiating exchange relationships for the first time, was held to a higher standard than the older women, who had already established their

Griot transferring manu-
factured cloth at an
ngénte, Dakar, 2000

Griot transferring two rolls of strip cloth at an ngénte, Dakar, 2000

credibility. Therefore, though attention to dress and other forms of display are highly valued as acts of sañse and of creating one's social persona, Penda's attention to her own style over showing deference to those senior to her undermined her attempts at sañse. She was seen as being too frivolous and too showy and not behaving with enough restraint.

Keeping the senior women waiting for her while she was at the salon, the disrespectful actions of her peers, and the way in which she understood hospitality as beauty and a nice bedroom rather than as generosity, all demonstrated a degree of self-interest on Penda's part. The senior women criticized Penda's actions as consumerist even though she was doing exactly what the senior women were doing at the naming ceremony; like them, she was creating a social persona. However, the senior women did not share Penda's model of beauty, which was not based upon a Muslim ideal of beauty emanating from the north. Rather, it was modeled after American pop stars and styles that she had seen on the weekly television program *Style et Mode* (Style and Fashion). As such, the consumerism of junior women like her referenced a world beyond Senegal. Sokna's exasperation with Penda suggested her own uneasiness with a shifting between consumption and reciprocity in the contemporary moment.

Sokna's and Penda's unease points to their fundamentally different approaches to sexuality, eroticism, and reproduction and to their conflicting ideas about the appropriate ways of attracting men and contracting alliances. I have discussed Sokna Géer as a kind of drianké. Though fashioning oneself as a drianké absent the means to pay for the goods one wears is thought of negatively by Senegalese men and women alike, there are also desirable aspects of the drianké figure (regardless of her means), such as her erotic mastery, as discussed by T. K. Biaya (2000). This is referred to as mokk pooj (large thighs) and denotes that women's power over men derives, in part, from their sexual mastery. For senior men and women, seduction and submission were two sides of the same coin. As I mentioned, women's erotic arts include wearing bethio, underwraps that they embellish with embroidery, appliqué, cutwork, hardanger, and vulgar imagery, such as an erect penis or a woman's vulva, to flaunt women's reproductive power. In addition, the drianké strings around her waist fragrant beads, known as *fer,* which are produced locally by casted women from clay, cinnamon, myrrh, frankincense, and other organic substances and sold in the market, and she deploys the incense that is used in Islamic healing practices in order to stimulate "creativity in the erotic imagination" (ibid.:714). These erotic deployments, Biaya argues, do not run counter to Islam, or at least certainly not to Sufi Islam. Indeed, it was

Bethio wrapper, Dakar, 2000

through Muslim trade routes that perfume and incense were introduced into the region and that the idea of the fully clothed body was introduced. In Islam, beauty and sexuality are not found in the nude body but rather in the body that is accessorized and properly prepared "in such a way that blurs the distinction of the cosmetic and the organic" (ibid.:708).

In contrast, Penda's sexuality was in her clothing, her walk, and her plastic waist beads, not in the realm of marriage, mutual aid, and support, and it was certainly not beholden to hierarchies of age and gender. Her sexuality was not linked to her submission; it was an image and an appearance instead of a sentiment or a passion which could lead to productive social relations. Penda scoffed at old-fashioned displays of sexuality, such as mokk pooj, that were employed by the drianké. Her age group was known as the *diskettes,* a word derived from disco music and used to describe the tall, slender, young beauties who could be spotted in the big discos in the urban center of Dakar (Biaya 2000:715). Biaya explores how the diskettes' sexuality was crafted from images that appeared in magazines such as *Ebony* and *Amina* and television shows, suggesting that "less expert than the mature, full-figured *drianké,* the diskette nonetheless carries a double erotic charge: a body type with global erotic purchase, stamped with the *thiuraye* [incense] seal of erotic sophistication and craft" (ibid.). Young women like Penda wear their sexuality not in hand-crafted clay beads that are strung about their waists but in manufactured, plastic, "shimmering, multicolored pearls [*bine bine*]" (716).

Although senior women preferred to exchange and wear locally woven and locally dyed cotton cloth, junior women sought out the latest global trends, which often included ready-made garments or local styles that were fashioned from manufactured cloth. Both kinds of cloth and clothing engendered social hierarchies. One could locate women based upon the style of their garments, including cuts and fabrics. If someone wore an out-of-date fashion, it was probably passed down from an older sister or a patron. If she were dressed in an *abaaya,* then one could presume that she had ties to a prosperous brother or husband. An abaaya is a more tailored version of the boubou and is seen as somewhat more modern for the way in which it emphasizes a woman's figure. At the same time, it is less open at the neck and sides than the conventional boubou. Vivienne Ndour made the abaaya popular by wearing it in her music videos. Ndour's were often made from imported cloth. The fabrics and their tailoring came into and went out of fashion on a monthly basis. For example, in January 2000 burned-out velvet was the style; by February women had discovered painted silks from India; and by the time the pilgrims returned from the hajj in late March, women were vying for gold, embroidered, sheer silks from Jeddah. During those three months, hand-cut voile came and went as well. Women's prestige lay in displaying these imported and often factory-made fabrics; their value increased due to their distant places of origin and whether they were seen on the person before they could be found in the market.

Women were drawn to objects that were unique in order to set themselves apart from others and to achieve distinction. Through the art of knowing what to consume, women set the terms of social relations. Those who honored each other and their families by dressing well objectified their high status but, in order to do so, they incurred debt. The fashion-conscious nature of a cloth's popularity suggests the growing role of conspicuous consumption and display in the creation of reputation and honor, in addition to one's capacity to give and to reciprocate what was received. Yet, this was not always the case, for these acts of consumption were also acts of production. These commodities were intimately linked to ideas about women's bodies and reproduction; they embodied a certain commodification of desire, class, status, and prestige, all of which were tied to esteem for large families and social networks. For example, upon her marriage, Penda received a set of three stacking insulated bowls with lids, which promised to keep food warm for up to twelve hours. These bowls, carefully and conspicuously placed on top of her armoire, were the subject of much conversation during social visits over the following weeks. Penda talked imaginatively of filling them with rice and fish and setting them in her husband's room for him to eat should he return late from the market and miss the family meal—despite the fact that, since he would be living abroad trading, he would not be eating his meals at home. Nevertheless, the bowls spoke to Penda's status as a married woman and to the strength of the female networks through which she had acquired them.

CLOTH, CASH, AND THE CRUCIAL EQUIVALENCES OF SOCIAL LIFE

In the case of Penda, I have focused thus far on the timing of the marriage process and of the naming ceremony as well as on the shifting forms of dress and social exchange. Through their attention to both the quantity and the kind of valued objects that they exchanged, women sought to maintain crucial equivalences in social life in an ever-turbulent economic context (Guyer 2004). Although Penda and Sokna Géer constructed their social personas through different sartorial practices that often related to the dissimilar fabrics that they favored, it is not the case that the prevalence of machine-made cloth has undercut the meanings associated with the circulation of cloth in naming ceremonies and thus the authority of senior women. Sër-u-rabbal, or woven strip cloth, is still considered to be the most honorable gift at a naming ceremony, although it is sometimes accompanied by factory-printed cloth and cash. This is due to its symbolic association with reproduction and its historical association with women's control over cloth through spinning. Though most women no longer spin cotton into thread and cloth is largely bought in the market, through its exchange during family ceremonies sër-u-rabbal continues to have symbolic meanings. Even after the popularity of machine-made cloth affected local cloth production in the wider Sahel region, and even after women shifted from exchanging regional textiles to exchanging global textiles, the exchanges still maintained crucial equivalences and women still maintained their control over the value that was produced through the distribution of cloth. Importantly, for Wolof women, the inalienability of cloth was not tied to their role in its production, but rather to its association with fertility and lineage identity and their control over its exchange.

While social critics of women's gift exchanges focused on the volume of gifts, the shifting forms of exchange, especially the replacement of cloth by cash and the supplementation of stripweaves with machine-made cloth, raise interesting questions about value over the *longue durée*. Historically, stripweaves were widely used in ceremonial and economic exchanges; they were forms of currency and commodities as well as inalienable possessions (Ames 1955b:1019; Curtin 1975:237). The cloth's ability to shift from currency to commodity to inalienable possession came not from its intrinsic qualities or the relations of production, but rather from its circulation, for "these terms are never fixed . . . they are always political" (Graeber 1996:12).

That women have sought to wear and to bestow a range of different social forms, including locally produced, manufactured, and imported objects as well as cash, is not a new strategy. Philip Curtin (1975) describes how precolonial Wolof gift exchange was based upon an idea of "one of each." At that time, the most prestigious gifts were composed of the greatest amount of different goods, and the specific number of them had an important "ritual significance, since it was often divisible by either two or ten, and the value of the multiple gift has extended down to the present, where a Senegambian gift consisting of two silver coins, two robes, two kola nuts and two sarooji [cloth] will carry much more weight than the same value in cash" (288). Today, substances of local production that are associated with the domestic sphere, such as millet, *and* prestige items, such as imported cloth which stands as a spatiotemporal condensation of global cities, are exchanged together. "One of each," then, suggests a synthesis within a dialectic. Imported consumer goods serve as a global map linking persons to worldwide trade networks, and locally produced substances locate men and women, young and old, within the domestic sphere. For example, men often bring *ruy* (millet porridge), a product of local agriculture commensurate with their role in feeding others, to naming ceremonies; these are pure gifts in the sense that they are consumables that are not reciprocated. Women also bring potent forms of exchange to these events, such as bath soap, baby cereal, sugar, clothespins, laundry soap, and other kinds of housewares, to aid the new mother and to symbolize her reproductive potential. The most prestigious gifts that women wear and bestow in naming ceremonies are the sër-u-rabbal wrappers, often in up to five layers, and women often sit with their legs splayed out in front of them to make the layers visible. The cloth is exchanged either as a long uncut roll of woven fabric or as pieces that are already cut and sewn into a two-meter underwrap.

Curtin argues that, in precolonial Senegal, equivalences were made between cloth and other marketable commodities, such as livestock and even bridewealth: "Taken as a whole, these systems of equivalences contained a suggestion of numerology, since the steps were almost always multiples of 2 and 10, but each was also a system of comparative values

A recipient of cloth and cash, Dakar, 2000

that linked food, labor and social values" (1975:239). Today, Curtin's characterization of Wolof gift exchange as "one of each" appears to translate into an upward-spiraling consumerist cult of gift giving, but it is actually a strategy of remaining productive. Not only are the varieties of gifts increasing, so are the numbers of recipients. The ndeyale, for example, can be divided among several women who have been chosen as the honorary ndeye. Its goods are portioned out to the honorary mothers in multiples of two, five, ten, or twelve, for which there is great competition.[6] The amount that each of these "mothers" receives will be returned at the next ceremony also in multiples of two, five, ten, or twelve (two is currently in vogue).

WOMEN'S WEALTH AND SOCIOCULTURAL DIFFERENCE

Cloth became a political object in Senegal at the turn of the twenty-first century because of its potent association with women's authority in the ritual sphere. By controlling the circulation of wealth in the form of cloth during family ceremonies, women competed with their peers for dependents, strived to control persons, and guarded against loss. Through these practices, they played an important role in the social regeneration of their lineage and in asserting its claim to high-ranking ancestry. In displaying or bestowing cloth on others, women transmitted jom (honor), which was linked to cosaan.

In the past, Wolof women did not accumulate cloth wealth through their own individual production; they did so by drawing upon the labor of dependents, including casted male weavers and slaves whom they supported. Today, though casted male weavers and those of former slave status still perform weaving that some women may support, women largely draw cloth from their networks of ritual, credit, and religious associations and from kin and affines, including men. Women's displays of accumulated cloth wealth during family ceremonies speak to the strength and scale of the social networks through which they procure cloth and to their control over its distribution.

Men disparaged women for spending excessively on family ceremonies in their absence—and many stories circulated about deviant wives who diverted money to family ceremonies that had been sent for household expenses or, even worse, feigned their own or their children's illnesses to extract remittances for medical prescriptions, which they would then spend on family ceremonies. Yet, ultimately, men assisted women in accumulating cloth wealth to distribute at the ceremonies of their relations and neighbors. Men participated in this process largely because they were concerned about the creation of alal (wealth) and its connection to the continuity of their lineage's identity. Through the circulation of cloth, an inalienable form of wealth, as ndawtal gifts at naming ceremonies, women ensured a replacement to themselves or their daughters that would ensure the future of the lineage (Weiner 1980).

Although Etienne (1980) focuses on women's cloth wealth in Baule mortuary ceremonial exchanges and Cooper (1993) suggests that cloth exchange among Hausa women in Niger is more prevalent during matrimonial ceremonies, the most significant exchange of cloth among Wolof women takes place during naming ceremonies. One reason is perhaps the strong association between the locally woven strip cloth, which is worn as an undergarment by Wolof women, and reproduction. It is not surprising, then, that both infants and the deceased are wrapped in this valued object, which ties the living to the dead and this world to the next.

As I described during Penda's daughter's naming ceremony, the exchange of ndawtal often takes the form of rolls of locally woven strip cloth underwraps, locally dyed cloth boubous, and manufactured cloth,

A mother and her newborn swaddled in strip cloth at an ngénte, Dakar, 2000

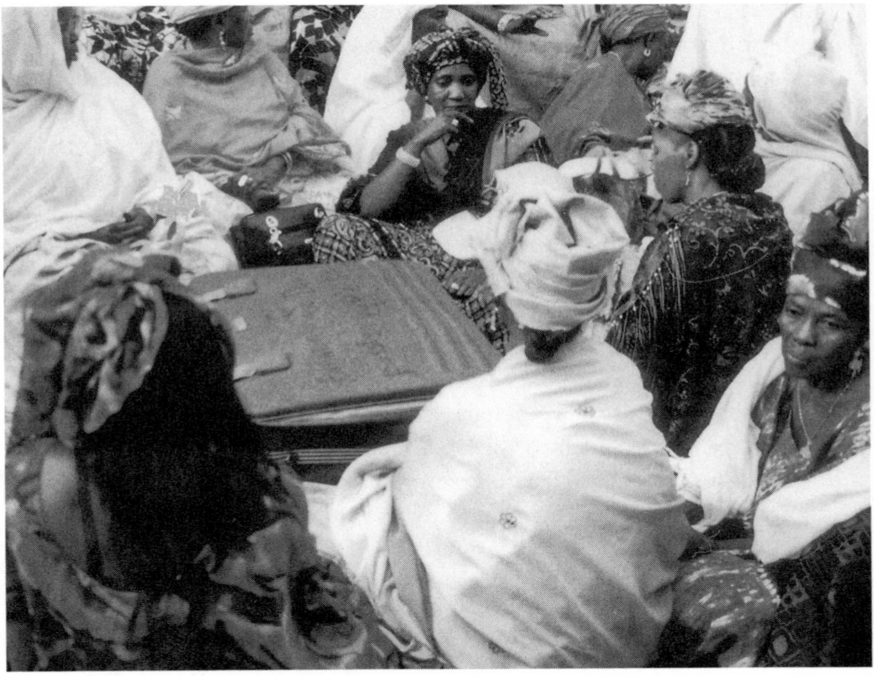

A suitcase full of gifts at an ngénte, Dakar, 2000

all with cash laid on top. Women often discuss their gift beforehand with their gewels, who mediate the exchange, announcing the quantity and quality of the gift and praising both the giver and the recipient; this praise is rewarded with cash. The gewel either moves from the outer sphere of the circle from which the gift originates to convey it to the inner sector, where the birth mother and her mother are seated, or forms a chain with other gewels to pass the gift to the center. In return, the birth mother and her mother will draw upon their own stores of cloth wealth and cash and upon what they have just received, and offer a return gift to the original donor, the njukkal. Whether an njukkal is made at this ceremony or at the next ceremony is dependent upon the relationship between the two women. Although all women in attendance offer ndawtal gifts, not all women receive a return gift at the same ceremony. This activity may take several hours in the late afternoon and, while it is occurring, women have their portraits taken by roving photographers, who develop the pictures at local photo labs within the hour and return them to the women for a payment of 500–1,000 CFA francs. In addition, women often carry smaller goods on their persons, including perfumes and waist beads, to show to their clients who are participating in the naming ceremony, who may make purchases on the spot.

A peer of the birth mother records the gifts in a notebook, which the new mother will refer to on future occasions. For example, if Penda received 5,000 CFA francs (a respectable sum, 2,000 CFA francs being the minimum that one would have given in 1999) at the naming ceremony for her child, she would record this amount next to the name of the woman who gave it to her. Subsequently, at that woman's next naming ceremony (or funeral or marriage), Penda will present her with 10,000 CFA francs in return: 5,000 CFA francs to repay the initial credit lent to her (lebbal) and 5,000 to begin a new debt (bor), which her age-mate will owe to her. If the recipient of the ndawtal is unable to reciprocate the sum at the next event hosted by the giver of the gift, the obligation is dealt with in various ways. Usually, the recipient will pay her friend's taxi fare or offer other forms of hospitality, including buying kolas, lending or donating clothing and jewelry, buying her friend's wares during social calls, or simply handing her small sums of cash for daily expenditures as the need arises. Moreover, leniency or forgiveness in the sphere of social obligations could spill over into women's mutual participation in a rotating credit union. For example, one woman could cover another's contribution as a gesture of friendship and as an implicit nod to the debt that has not been settled. Over time, these small gestures of respect and mutual good will

An ngénte, Dakar, 2000

could amount to more than the actual cost of returning the initial gift or its double in the context of the next family ceremony. Thus, the desire of women to return the obligation at the next ceremony if they are able stems from their desire to keep as many women as possible obligated to them so that the debts can be collected in these small ways, which make a difference in the difficult economic climate.

In addition to bestowing cloth on others during family ceremonies, women also perform the work of keeping objects out of circulation and of exacting replacements for others. Not all kinds of cloth are circulated; women often retain heirloom pieces of strip cloth that were obtained from their mothers and grandmothers since these are inalienable objects that represent personal histories. They may also keep some cloth out of circulation to use in bodily display, especially locally woven strip cloth that conveys their control over social dependents.

Weiner differentiates between two kinds of objects that are not circulated: those that never circulate and those that compel a replacement and thus are given on loan in exchange for an object of similar value later in time (1985:212). In Senegal, the first type of object includes cloth or, more frequently, clothing, which is called *may* (gift); in its verb form, *may* means "to give" and is often followed by what is given, such as *may yere* (to give clothing). Women offer these kinds of gifts as payment for labor at family ceremonies to cross-cousins, gewels, and those who used to be slaves, and they do not compel a return. The second type of object includes the ndawtal and the more substantial and visible gifts of cloth that are offered during family ceremonies to peers along the axes of kinship and filiation and, increasingly, to people who are connected to one's neighborhood or common religious and political realms. These gifts often do require a return, not usually of the original object but rather of a replacement of similar quantity and quality. During my fieldwork, women said that they "give" ndawtal, or *may ndawtal,* and that to give ndawtal is to lebbal (to lend credit to someone).[7] That women's gifts are thought of as loans is further demonstrated by the recording of these gifts in a ledger, which is consulted at future ceremonies. The recipient, usually the holder of the feast on the occasion of a life-cycle ritual for her daughter such as a marriage or a birth, records the gifts in a ledger, which she then consults prior to the next feast of the donor, and she would aspire to double the original gift. Whether or not the ndawtal is returned depends in part upon how it is given. Women often combine a number of valued objects when forming one of these gifts, including locally woven strip cloth, dyed boubous, manufactured cloth, and cash. Of these items, only the sër-u-rabbal and dyed boubous truly convey the heirloom qualities of inalienable possessions and thus require future replacements.

It is because of its association with generational continuity that cloth like this compels a replacement. Unlike commodities and other gifts that are given as hospitality and as payment for services, sër-u-rabbal given during family ceremonies are inalienable. Cloth embodies the reproduction of the essential ties of kinship through its close association with the female body, especially when it is used as an underskirt, wedding veil, baby blanket, or funeral shroud.[8] This association with fertility and reproduction makes cloth an inalienable object. Therefore, the "borrower" must return it at some point to its owner—if not the actual object, then some symbolic equivalent. Beyond the valuable gifts of strip cloth, women may also give hand-dyed boubous. Some women substitute for cloth substantial amounts of cash, which is still called ndawtal; early in my research, the term ndawtal was explained to me as cash given at a family ceremony by women. My examination of several ledgers of gift exchange revealed that most of the gifts were recorded in cash rather than in lengths of cloth, although the latter appeared occasionally as well. Increasingly, during 1999–2000, I noticed that women were also using inexpensive, summer-weight fabrics imported from Asia in place of the ten-meter boubous; these consisted of white rayon fabrics with small purple, orange, or red

African-inspired motifs, which were popular among older women in the hot summer months.

While cloth is no longer used for general-purpose exchange, it remains the central form of prestation for women. Mustafa's interlocutors indicated that cloth was the essential gift although they often supplemented it with cash (1998:124). Money contains what David Graeber calls "hidden capacities for action" (2001); indeed, cash, unlike cloth, more directly conveys the potential for future exchanges since it is so easily hidden outside of ritualized exchange. Unlike cloth perhaps, it might be more difficult to discern how much cash someone actually possesses, given that it is often not as visible. Cloth acts like an inalienable object in that it conveys the essence of the giver and therefore recognizes the status of the receiver. It also contrasts with the hidden power of money since, Graeber contends, as an object of adornment and a form of display, cloth persuades others of the value of both the giver and receiver; indeed, "by covering themselves with gold, then, kings persuade others to cover them with gold as well" (1996:9). Perhaps this is why Rama joked that her mother, Sokna Géer, thought she was a Wolof *buur,* or king. A woman both gives strip cloth as prestations at family ceremonies and wears many layers of it underneath her boubou. By wearing strip cloth in this way, she is not only like a king covering herself with gold, but she is also holding something back from the pressure to give; she is keeping while giving, well aware that "the things kept allow a person to circulate other things" (Weiner 1985:222). A woman adorns herself with cloth not as a form of conspicuous consumption, but as a strategy to encourage others to seek her out so that she will not be excluded from possessing the valuable resource. By keeping some cloth out of circulation for bodily display, she is ensuring that she will remain on the path of the circulation of cloth.

Through ritualized exchanges of cloth, women both perform the work of keeping some objects, like heirloom strip cloth, out of circulation since items like these define who they are in the present by reference to the past, and they exact replacements. Objects that women give to dependents as forms of payment for labor performed at feasts are not returned. Through these payments, women remain politically dominant. Conversely, items that are given to freeborn women and kin are thought of as loans that demand a future replacement. Women record the latter exchanges in ledgers because to lose in exchange cannot be understood as merely an economic loss for the individual, but as a lineage's loss of "its power to sustain itself for future generations" (Weiner 1985:212).

Given the pressure on high-status persons like Sokna Géer and Cora to give generously, how do they avoid depleting the forms of wealth on which their claims to status rest? How do they simultaneously accumulate wealth for future largesse and respond to pressure to distribute it in the present (Irvine 1974:220)? Up to this point, I have focused upon unequal relations between those of different social status, including freeborn persons and artisans, young and old, male and female. How, then, are asymmetrical relations created among women of the same status? How is rank produced among seeming social equals without disrupting the overall hierarchy of difference that separates the freeborn from the casted members of society?

Cheikh Caaya and Cora were of freeborn status, but they were relatively impoverished in that they could no longer count upon the agricultural output of their land to create dependents. Thus, they sought out Sokna Géer and named their grandchild after her, in effect becoming her clients. There is, however, a central contradiction in modern Wolof society in that, while the wealth of the freeborn has historically been based largely upon agricultural products, a fixed form of wealth in which there rarely has been a great surplus, the demands of dependents are ever growing. While freeborn persons must give generously in keeping with their status, in doing so they risk depleting the forms of wealth on which their claims to high status have rested. Judith Irvine observed in her fieldwork in rural Kayor in the early 1970s that there were freeborn persons who did not have many clients or great wealth, and who had not released themselves from the labor force (although they had the potential to do so), who became clients of other freeborn persons without relinquishing their freeborn identity (1974:204). The analogy between certain kin relationships and caste relationships made such a resolution possible. As I mentioned, the qualities defining caste, both high and low, are not fixed; instead, they are engendered in all social relationships, even among the freeborn. Freeborn persons, therefore, competed not only for dependents, but also for labor and political support within the freeborn caste: "he must, one way or another, cause other nobles to believe that by supporting him or becoming his clients temporarily, they increase their own chances for the future" (205). Freeborn persons might find supporters among their own kin group; for a Wolof male head of household, that meant the labor of his wives and children and the services of his younger brothers, nephews, and patrilineal cousins of the junior branches of the lineage (205). A freeborn person could also hire the labor of young unmarried men as surga for what was usually considered temporary contractual dependence, and one could acquire dependents by extending loans and credit to kin and non-kin (207). These loans differed from the public gifts given to artisans and were regarded with sutura (discretion). Thus, in giving cloth to Sokna Géer, an inalienable possession that must at some future point be replaced, they were also keeping-while-giving.

During feasts, women demonstrated largesse in the provision of food as hospitality, in their payments to gewels who amplified their reputations in these public forums, and in their gifts of cloth to non-dependents, including other high-status persons and kin, with the aim of creating inclusion and difference (Heath 1992:22), controlling persons, and guarding against loss. Along with the constant pressure to give is the fear of loss of that which is most valued: cloth and its association with generational continuity.

SYMBOLIC PRODUCTION

In the context of a naming ceremony, women's consumption becomes a form of production. The commodities do not stop at the receiver because women channel them into redistributive networks. Even if women cannot directly reciprocate the ndawtal gift at a subsequent feast, it exists as an obligation; people will talk about it as a real debt, and it will be repaid in lesser ways, such as through mutual aid by purchasing one another's merchandise. The kind of commerce that took place at the naming ceremony as the women waited for Penda to arrive, therefore, is an example of another form of sociality and working out of the relations of debt, obligation, and mutual aid. Forms of conspicuous consumption do not stop with the person to whom they are tied since they are also connected to notions of prosperity and baraka. Consumption at naming ceremonies makes one a magnet for social relations, but this is a double-edged sword because these relations have to be sustained.

In the context of family ceremonies, the promise of the gift, as conveyed through one's self-presentation, was sufficient to fulfill the indexical and performative aspects of gift exchange because gifts, rather than encoding social relations, constituted them through the promise of their delivery. Thus, in Senegal, it was not in the actual exchange of wealth, but in the performative moment that the structure of circulation was realized. This is a form of symbolic production. The images of wealth exist but real wealth is absent (for comparison with the Nigerian context, see Apter 2005). For example, in Senegal well-dressed women talked about obtaining cloth and objects of adornment from male kin who were trading abroad, which created an appearance of wealth that was at odds with their actual material situation. While debates about women's cloth wealth may have considered these practices to be forms of conspicuous consumption, this assumption of surplus is at odds with reality. In this way, the sign of wealth is detached from its referent, with money becoming less linked to the material substance of wealth. This fact that ideas about debt and surplus are at odds with reality is one of the fundamental features of neoliberalism.

Overseas migration has changed the nature and composition of families and of social processes like marriage and naming ceremonies. When they were part of an agricultural community, households depended upon their extended kin and the forging of alliances through marriage to cultivate the land. Today, however, families increasingly rely on remittances from men living abroad. As young men spend longer periods of time overseas in order to support their households in Senegal, their marriages are occurring later in life (Antoine et al. 1995), and naming ceremonies are often taking place outside of the marital process or before it can be completed. One reason that these social processes are not being finalized is that junior men lack the material means to sustain the exchanges that are required by these events, such as bridewealth. Due to these changes in the nature of work, commodities have come to play a major social role in Senegal as the home shifts from the primary site of production to the primary site of consumption. Furthermore, as the distance between wealth and work spreads, male productive efforts abroad become ever more distant, vague, and misunderstood.

EPILOGUE

THE 1990S AND EARLY 2000S saw an increasing number of migrants leaving Senegal for better prospects abroad. Senegalese men and women sought to improve their own lives and those of their families during a time marked by continued agricultural decline, rural-urban migration, massive unemployment, shortages of food and necessities, and insufficient resources for housing, health care, and education. Although many men and women traveled abroad on student and business visas, some found more precarious means of making the journey, from stowing away in airline wheel wells to crossing the Atlantic in unseaworthy wooden pirogues to reach Spain's Canary Islands. As I write this last chapter, Senegal is undergoing yet another transformation, this time in relation to the global economic recession. Although many African countries were less affected by the credit crisis, those countries dependent on remittances from migrants inhabiting global financial centers have felt the impact of the worldwide recession. The global downturn that has led to lower incomes and job losses in construction, tourism, and commerce in Western countries has made it more difficult for migrants to send money home. Declining remittances of cash have coincided with rising prices for food and other commodities, shortages of cooking gas, and cuts in electrical power for much of the country, making it harder for households to endure tough times. While many men and women returned to Senegal in the 1990s to engage in real estate speculation, many homes—and the social relations they house—remain unfinished projects in these precarious financial times.

Given the rate at which men were investing in new homes in Senegal in the 1990s, and women's concern that these buildings masked a lack of investment in family relations, how did social criticism in Senegal turn against women's role in life-cycle rituals? How did this criticism come to be articulated in relation to Islam? Were women's generous prestations during family ceremonies out of step with what many painted as an enduring economic crisis of the previous thirty years? If economic crisis spurred on by structural adjustment policies defined the decades of the

1980s and 1990s, how do we understand the ongoing conditions of fiscal austerity that continue to mark life in Senegal today?

One of the underlying goals of this book has been to understand the moral terms in which economic realities are apprehended. I have argued that exchange practices, and the debates surrounding them, ought to be understood as part of a repertoire of value creation under the conditions of volatility and turbulence that have characterized West African economies over the *longue durée* (Guyer 2004). Clearly, men and women found security in making offerings to religious figures, building family homes, and accumulating cloth wealth. It remains to be seen if men will continue to build homes and if women will continue to exchange cloth and if both will continue to patronize Murid shaykhs. Even if the forms and modalities of exchange shift over time to reflect changing productive possibilities, the practice of seeking the means to achieve value over the long term in spite of continued volatility in markets, the actions of the state, and the evolution of family relations, is likely to continue. In many ways, cloth became a placeholder for turbulent social relations as men and women attempted to create wholeness. Where others have argued that such creative practices were piecemeal attempts at making do in uncertain times, I have argued to the contrary: it has been the search for wholeness and continuity in the face of fragmented and fractured experiences that has been at the heart of men's and women's actions.

THE SOCIAL DISCOURSE OF EXCESS AND THE INFLATION OF SOCIAL PAYMENTS

By late 2000 women's exchange and dress practices were subject to a social discourse that valued modesty and restraint. This discourse unfolded in the context of inflation, unemployment, and increasing crime and corruption following the implementation of structural adjustment programs mandated by the International Monetary Fund and the World Bank in exchange for development aid and debt relief beginning in the 1980s. The election of the long-suffering opposition candidate Abdoulaye Wade as president in 2000 unleashed a wave of hope that his policies of economic and political liberalization would ameliorate the condition of many in Senegal, especially the youth who were being described as the "lost generation" (Cruise O'Brien 2003). Now, more than ten years later and into Wade's second term, it has become clear that the neoliberal economic agenda has not fulfilled its promises of job creation, economic growth, good governance, or transparency (Mbow 2008). Indeed, one need only witness the dangerous Atlantic crossing to the Canary Islands, stalled home building of both new villas and homes ravaged by floods, food shortages, and rising food prices. Although transnational migration in the 1990s led to consumerism, real estate speculation, and a growing divide between those with access to remittances and those dependent on local trade and declining agricultural production, today's remittances have dwindled with the global downturn.

This discourse of austerity also unfolded in the context of Muslim reform movements that sought to question not only women's ostentatious displays of wealth, but also what many religious figures saw as their lack of modest dress. For example, a small number of women associated with these movements abandoned boubous with low-cut necklines, which emphasized their back and shoulders, and the more tailored styles, which emphasized the waist, bust, and behind. A few even donned a white headscarf that entirely covered the hairline and neck, and clothing with longer sleeves (Augis 2000).

The reformist movements were not alone in employing a discourse of self-control and moderation. Murid clergy encouraged devotees to invest their wealth in the sacred center of Tuba. Religious devotion attracted many men, young and old, who saw the decline of the value of their agricultural land and thus the forms of authority they wielded over the household through their control of land and marriages (Perry 2005). In the immediate postcolonial period, senior men's authority was augmented by their access to national development programs that emphasized agricultural inputs and large projects like roads and dams. Inputs, labor, and profits were largely under the control of senior men (Perry 2009). With the liberalization of trade in the 1990s and the defeat of the Partie Socialiste, the position of senior men in particular became more fraught, and Islam provided new opportunities for achieving masculine virtue through moral renewal.

The Muslim clergy, Sufi and reformist alike, responded to fiscal and moral uncertainty by denouncing costly family ceremonies. They focused on women's practice of exchanging locally woven and dyed cloth, a measure of women's wealth and worth, and called for an Islamic family law, which would codify limits on these expenditures. Muslim clergy and many male devotees expressed disapproval toward women's ritual practices, which they described as cosaan, as pre-Islamic practices that were incommensurate with modern Islam. Although these practices were incompatible with the Muslim idea of equality before God, they were contentious as well because through these practices women established their ritual authority and their capacity as historical agents.

In the offices of nongovernmental organizations, researchers and policy makers argued that Senegal's economic development and the preservation of democracy depended on equal access to resources by women, especially women of low social rank. They appealed to women to practice restraint in their ritualized exchanges and feasts, which marked important moments in their lifetimes. Yet they often witnessed the instantiation of social rank as women turned credit and savings association funds to the ritualized exchange of cloth in family ceremonies. The Senegalese state thus also sought to limit these payments by reforming the Family Code.

Young men also appealed to women to slow down the pace of their spending on ritual activities. Those who had migrated abroad in search of livelihoods and those who stayed behind sought to cement marriages with social payments between families and were confronted with the escalating demands of prospective brides and their mothers. Many young women spoke of only accepting a marriage to a transnational trader. Many were seeking a way out of Senegal, and many more were thinking of their economic futures in Senegal, which they saw as tied to overseas remittances. Today, men and women who have migrated to New York City speak of a rather different situation. As marriages have continued to be delayed and polygamous unions have become less common because of the austere times, some men have said that fathers and mothers are more willing to allow their daughters to enter into the marriage process without making onerous demands on a prospective groom. It would seem that a marriage in which a modest amount of wealth is transferred is preferable to having many unmarried daughters about the house.

Yet the generous gifts that women bestowed on one another at lifecycle ceremonies and that they demanded in the form of marriage payments from men were not the sole sources of excess in Senegalese society in the 1990s. The postcolonial period has been marked by vigorous excess in political patronage (Cruise O'Brien 2003), and much of the academic literature and development specialists' reports have focused on the corruption of the state and the need for transparency and good governance, and much less on the predicaments of social production. Additionally, Sufi leaders have long relied on a performance of excess to attract and retain devotees. The large villas, cars, and numerous wives all attest to the baraka of the religious figure. Indeed, adherents of the Murid order are often subject to social criticism by Muslim reformists, members of other Sufi orders, and development specialists for donating large sums of money to religious leaders to develop the sacred capital of Tuba, at the expense of the nation and secular democracy. Young male migrants also engaged in extravagant displays of excess in the form of new homes, imported autos, being seen in casinos and restaurants, and, for the more religious among them, giving vast sums as religious offerings to their shaykhs.

ISLAM AND EQUALITY

Muslim texts emphasize equality before God, and in the colonial period the desire for social equality drew many new adherents to the Murid way. Social status was largely ascribed based on social rank, gender, and age, but could be achieved in the money economy through cash cropping and, later, trade (Berry 1989). In the late nineteenth century and early twentieth, young men and the colonial powers expressed dissatisfaction with what seemed like escalating demands for social payments for marriage and naming ceremonies. Changes in the colonial era also had a lasting impact on women's exchange practices insofar as the rise of a money economy, fluctuations in the value of cash crops, and urban migration sent women as well as men into trade to sustain their social and economic projects. As women became traders of cloth and household goods locally, family ceremonies provided opportunities for them to demonstrate their success and skill in trade, and their vast social networks through which they extracted clients, capital, and prestige.

Men and women alike sought to attain religious merit, or tuyaaba, which one received directly from God, and religious grace, or baraka, which was transmitted through shaykhs. Disciples made offerings to shaykhs in the hopes of receiving baraka in return. Religious offerings signified submission not to shaykhs, but to the divine in the hope of achieving salvation in the next life and prosperity in the present. Although Murid followers have been engaged in the money economy since the inception of the order at the turn of the twentieth century through cash cropping, urban economies, and global trade networks, market value has not replaced other values (Carrier 1991; Miller 1994; Zelizer 1994). The use of money is not inimical to the production of social and sacred value (Akin and Robbins 1999; Keane 2001). As I argued in chapter 3, these offerings and the moral discourse framing them are an essential aspect of Murid devotion to their spiritual masters and form part of their repertoire of economic practices. Through the practice of offerings and their redistribution by the clergy, Murids protect wealth from what has historically been a volatile market (Guyer 1999).

EXCHANGE AND DIFFERENCE

If exchange practices contravened both consumption practices and official discourses praising modesty, austerity, and restraint in dress, then why were well-dressed women admired for performing sañse, and why did men often exclaim with pride that cosaan mattered? Though many fieldworkers have dismissed the centrality of Islam to women's ritual roles based on men's descriptions of them as affaire-u-jigeen, or women's business, I have argued that men employ this phrase, often with a knowing smile, to acknowledge the complexities of women's exchanges and to indicate that if one wants to understand them, one ought to ask the women themselves. Why did men also continue to boast of their offerings to the Murid clergy and to acquire cloth for their mothers, wives, and sisters to distribute in family ceremonies? I have argued that Murids withstood the pressure to give to shaykhs by keeping certain wealth objects out of circulation. Men often invested in cement bricks for home building, which did not circulate, or they gave to their female kin wealth in the form of cloth, which did circulate but demanded a return.

Cloth demanded a return because it was viewed as an inalienable possession due to its association with reproduction. Woven cloth wrappers were worn as undergarments, used to wrap and carry babies on the back, and used to shroud bodies for burial. These same wrappers often covered a bride's head when she entered her groom's home. Over their lifetimes women accrued vast stores of cloth wealth, which they sought to bestow on women of similar social rank during family ceremonies and on their daughters to preserve and produce individual and collective identities related to notions of honor. These inalienable objects ensured an eventual replacement over time, either to the original giver or to her daughter. Thus, in circulating cloth wealth, women were keeping-while-giving; they gave cloth and kept honor (Weiner 1992). But cloth's value was endangered by young women's reticence to participate in continuing to build the social ties woven by their mothers. At stake was not only the loss of wealth, but also the possible loss of family identity.

Exchanges index individual and collective identities and create social solidarities among women of similar social standing as well as asymmetries among women of differing social rank. These exchanges continue to be valued, perhaps because they express the desire for the perpetuation of individual and collective identities based on ideals of beauty such as rafet judo (beautiful birth), jom (honor), kersa (restraint), and alal (wealth). As I have demonstrated, exchange events such as weddings and naming ceremonies provided women with the opportunity to make visible what was ordinarily not seen: the expanse of their social network, which was quantified by the amount and length of the cloth underwraps and boubous that they received; and their hidden stores of cloth wealth, which were made visible through dress and through bestowal on women of similar social standing.

Ambivalence about exchange practices reflects a fundamental tension in Wolof social and political life between adherence to Islam and its ideals of equality, and the perpetuation of inequality and the system of hereditary occupational orders. Exchange perpetuates inequalities at the level of lineages and families, between those of low rank and high rank, juniors and seniors, women and men, in contrast to an encompassing religious and political order that values autonomy and equality. Women sought to resolve this fundamental tension through the discourse of religious merit that accompanies exchange practices. Though men also sought religious merit, I have focused on women's discourses of religious merit in the context of their exchange practices to understand how they meaningfully reconcile the temporality of cosaan with Islam and with the global order. Women's exchange practices are not a residue of pre-Islamic tradition, but part of a large repertoire of meaningful and carefully formulated fiscal practices through which women have created value historically and through which they create social futures. They are critical practices because they are the ways in which women consciously reflect on their own histories and those of their families and construct their futures.

Exchange not only created reciprocal social obligations and fiscal relations of credit and debt, it also involved the crafting of reputations; women made themselves known through the responses they elicited from others (Foster 1995). Upon entering into marriage, women developed their opportunities to publicly demonstrate and constitute their value through gift exchanges during family ceremonies and feasts. During their married lives, women established their economic power and lineage identity through the distribution and recapturing of cloth wealth during these events. In tough times they retained value by bestowing cloth on women of similar social status, in effect becoming their dependents (Irvine 1974). Through their hidden stores of cloth wealth, women incorporated their ancestors' honor, authority, and rank into themselves, produced alternative centers of authority, and accrued religious merit. In all of these exchanges, cloth as an object of value was central to their desire to constitute their productive and reproductive power. Locally woven underwraps were particularly valued due to their association with fertility and reproductive power. For this reason, men provided women with cloth, which they in turn conferred on others on public occasions to demonstrate (and create) both female and male worth and value.

I have addressed the ways in which women's exchange practices merged with a neoliberal discourse learned from business management courses offered to women by NGOs and other development organizations. From their courses, women learned the individual accountability and entrepreneurial skills that are central to audit cultures (Strathern 2000), which impacted some of the ways in which they thought about credit, debt, and reciprocity in relation to ritualized exchange. The NGOs sought to offer these courses to augment women's economic productivity and as a source of empowerment, which program leaders saw as essential to the development of the nation-state as a thriving democracy. While these programs did introduce new forms of accountability among participants, they also reinforced hierarchies of social rank as women turned these funds toward ritualized exchanges as often as they used them for entrepreneurial projects.

The state's contradictory and partial intervention in Muslim family law impacted the way in which men and women sought to construct alliances and to maintain them over time. In the 1990s, generational tensions surrounding love, matrimony, and the rights and obligations imposed by kin led to the dissolution of many marriages. Today, the divorce rate has continued to rise. Lacking the support of kin at home, many overseas marriages fall apart. Tough financial times, squabbles over money, and gender roles are often at the heart of these failed alliances.

THE MEANINGS OF EXCHANGE

The anthropological literature on exchange has largely focused on its economic and social functions. Exchange has been understood in opposition to capitalist production and as a form of political and social organization, a means of reproducing relations of power over time. I have argued that it is not only women's worlds and their forms of wealth, but also their very words, that have been underanalyzed by scholars of the Murid order. Male talk has associated women's wealth with cosaan, the customs of the pre-Islamic world that had been under the control of women, and the system of social rank based on hereditary occupational orders. Scholars of Islam have taken male talk at face value and dismissed women's words and practices as folk beliefs. Yet women frame their exchange practices through a discourse of religious merit, which is as central to Islam as the practice of making offerings to shaykhs.

Attention to the ways in which women talk about their exchange practices takes the analyst beyond merely textual approaches to Islam. We can understand women's exchange practices during family ceremonies not as a pre-Islamic practice, or as merely local discourses, but as informed by a supralocal discourse of Islam in which the categories of local and global have never been fixed (Bowen 1993; Soares 2000). It was through social criticism and debate that men and women sought to determine whether women's ritual practices and their role in social reproduction were consonant with a broader scriptural tradition. For this reason, I have treated "Islam" as the discursive tradition that relates to a broader scriptural tradition of Islam (Soares 2000). Thus, the debate over women's cloth wealth was not just a debate over women's wealth and worth, but also a debate over offerings to spiritual masters, a particular obligation practiced primarily by followers of the Murid order that was thought to draw value away from the family. These debates are key to understanding the practice of Islam in Senegal not as a particular African Islam, but as historically constituted and partaking in global Islam.

The seemingly local contests over the nature and appropriateness of exchange at particular historical moments were not only about the microeconomic practices of women, but also shed light on larger transformations in the region, which in turn have affected men's and women's political and economic aspirations. Women's practices have important implications for our understanding of global Senegal in the twenty-first century and the particular history of Islam in the region.

By the late 1990s and early 2000s, households had become the site of some of the most creative and conflicted endeavors of the neoliberal moment. To the extent that the production of persons was embodied in the value form of the house, the scattering of homes in progress on the Senegalese landscape spoke well about the prospects for processes of social production. Yet today, many of these dwellings have yet to be inhabited, forming incomplete neighborhoods that are both the outcome and the inspiration for their owners' sojourns abroad. That the villas that characterize the landscape in Senegal remain largely unfinished speaks both to the projected prosperity of a globalizing economy and to the subsequent foreclosure of an array of intended social projects in the twenty-first century.

GLOSSARY

addiya (Arabic): religious offering
affaire-u-jigeen (Wolof): women's business
alal (Wolof): wealth
assaka (Wolof): payment; derived from Arabic *zakkat*
baraka (Arabic): grace, blessing, divine power
bor (Wolof): debt
boroom kër ga (Wolof): head of the household
boubou (French): *see* mbubb
céet (Wolof): the entry of the bride into her husband's home
cosaan (Wolof): custom
cuub (Wolof): dyed cloth
daara (Wolof): collective work group in service to a shaykh; derived from Arabic *daar* (house)
dahira (Arabic): circle; association of disciples
daraja (Arabic): dignity, respectability
dëmm (Wolof): witch
dimbali (Wolof): assistance
dolli (Wolof): strengthen
doom-u-benn tàngk (Wolof): child of one foot; refers to children of freeborn-slave marriages
drianké (Wolof): woman who keeps others on a leash; an urban woman and socialite
faj (Wolof): heal
fayda (Arabic): determination, importance
fit (Arabic): courage
gacce (Wolof): shame
gan (Wolof): guest or stranger
géer (Wolof): freeborn, nobility; those who have honor
gërëm (Wolof): thank
gewel (Wolof): casted bards or praise singers; the keepers of oral history

Source: Jean-Léopold Diouf, *Dictionnaire wolof-français et français-wolof* (Paris: Karthala, 2003).

hijra (Arabic): pilgrimage to Mecca
Islamists (English): generally, those who have sought to reorganize state and society under sharia
jaam (Wolof): slaves and descendants of slaves
jigeen (Wolof): woman
jikko (Wolof): character
jom (Wolof): honor
jottali (Wolof): convey
karamat: working of God through persons
kër (Wolof): household
kersa (Wolof): deference, restraint
khaftan (Arabic): tailored ensemble consisting of a long shirt over pants
khalifa (Arabic): successor, head of a holy lineage
khalifa général (Arabic): supreme head of the Muridiyya
khar yalla (Arabic): waiting for God
khassaid: litanies penned by Amadou Bamba
lakk (Wolof): a porridge made from yogurt and millet
laman (Wolof): representative; refers to the chiefs
leb (Wolof): to contract a debt
lebbal (Wolof): to lend credit to someone
Lebu (Wolof): ethnic group
lekk (Wolof): to eat
lijjanti (Wolof): sort out, untangle, get to the bottom of a matter
Màggal (Wolof): pilgrimage to Tuba
masla (Wolof): sociability, civility
masse (Wolof): age group
may (Wolof): gift (n); to give (v)
may bu njekk (Wolof): first gift
mbaseñ riche (Wolof): cotton damask
mbotaye (Wolof): neighborhood ritual association
mbubb (Wolof): minimally tailored cloth worn over wrapper
mokk pooj (Wolof): large thighs; coquettish behavior, feminine wiles
muñ (Wolof): patience
murid (Arabic): disciple
musóor (Wolof): head wrapper
natt (Wolof): rotating credit union
nawetaan (Wolof): seasonal laborers
naxari (Wolof): hard, inflexible
nay (Wolof): selfish
ndaq far (Wolof): the gift that chases away other suitors

ndawtal (Wolof): gifts given by women at family ceremonies, which are recorded in ledgers and repaid at a later date
ndeyale (Wolof): to take someone as a sponsor or godparent; a social payment representing such a relationship
ndeye (Wolof): mother
ndiggel (Wolof): command
ngénte (Wolof): baby-naming ceremony
njariñ (Wolof): value
njebbel (Wolof): submission
njukkal (Wolof): countergift
nuyoo (Wolof): greeting
nyenyo (Wolof): artisans and musicians
pukaare (Wolof): pose or present an appearance that is beyond one's means
rafet (Wolof): beauty
russ (Wolof): shame
sañse (Wolof): shine, fancy dress; to dress for a special occasion; from the French *changer*
sarax (Wolof): sacrifice or alms
sawar (Wolof): activate
sër (Wolof): underwrap skirt of two meters worn by women
seriñ (Wolof): scholar
sër-u-rabbal (Wolof): locally woven strip cloth
set setal (Wolof): renewal; to clean and make clean
sharia (Arabic): divinely ordained law of Islam
shaykh (Arabic): religious leader
sokna (Wolof): adult woman; also used to refer to female shaykhs
surga (Wolof): hired laborer; one who is filled up
sutura (Wolof): discretion
taara (Wolof): former slave of a ruler who became a fifth spouse
takk (Wolof): to tie; marriage performed at a mosque
talibe (Arabic): disciple or student
tarbiyya (Arabic): to sacrifice for a religious guide
tariqa (Arabic): a known way or path of achieving divine union
teraanga (Wolof): hospitality, honor
teral (Wolof): honor
timis (Wolof): dusk
tubab (Wolof): white person
turandoo (Wolof): namesake
tuur (Wolof): rotation

tuyaaba (Arabic): religious merit
wali (Arabic): friend of God, holy person
warsek (Wolof): luck
wecc (Wolof): exchange
wird (Arabic): litanies
xaalis (Wolof): money or silver
xew (Wolof): ceremony or feast
xutba (Wolof): Friday sermon
yaru (Wolof): respect
zakkat (Arabic): charitable payment given to the poor; one of five obligations in Islam
ziyara (Arabic): pious visit

NOTES

PROLOGUE

1. *Quartier populaire* is often translated as "working-class neighborhood," but might be better translated as "lower-class neighborhood" because it is usually a neighborhood with a high unemployment rate.

2. A *bidonville* is an unauthorized settlement of self-built dwellings. *Bidon* is French for "oil drum."

3. Young men apprenticing to be drivers.

4. Sow was largely concerned with a discussion of the Pikine neighborhood of Dakar. Similar land tenure arrangements can be found in Grand Yoff.

5. In 2003, S.C.I.'s two- and three-bedroom homes were listed on its website for 18 million to 25 million CFA francs, roughly US$25,000. See http://www.bhs.sn/sci-lalinguere.htm, accessed on April 1, 2003; and http://www.scilalinguere.com, accessed on June 24, 2008.

6. I am using the term *household* here following Irvine's (1974:20) definition: several persons who eat together, and the unit of greatest economic cooperation. This is in contrast to the compound, which in a rural context might be composed of several households, each of which would have differing levels of financial independence.

1. GLOBAL SENEGAL

1. Not to be confused with *ceddo* (pagan).

2. Sufism may be properly understood as Islamic mysticism, but it does not adhere to the notions of individualistic subjectivity that are prevalent in Christian mysticism (John Hunwick, personal communication, October 1997).

3. In Arabic, *tariqa* is synonymous with *sirat,* or path, but it has a wider meaning and can be translated as "ways and means" (Lings 1993:28). Some scholars have translated *tariqa* as brotherhood, or *confrerie*; however, this is misleading since the *turuq* include both male and female disciples. The tariqa has also been referred to in the literature as "order," but this is also not an accurate translation of tariqa, which refers to the Sufi path to divine union.

4. Eric Ross (1995) discusses the development of Tuba in relation to the *ndiggel* (commands) by Murid shaykhs to encourage their disciples to invest in Tuba in order to stem the flow of urban and overseas migration, in addition to Bamba's prophecy concerning the sacred city. For information on the growth and development of Tuba, see Gueye 1999.

5. Land privatization and titling were also central to the World Bank's agenda for some decades, though it has retreated somewhat on this subject while neoliberals continue to push for private property. See Boone 2007:558.

6. This is exactly the sort of rural despotism that Mahmood Mamdani describes in his book *Citizen and Subject: Contemporary Africa and the Legacy of Late Colonialism* (Princeton, N.J.: Princeton University Press, 1996).

7. See the World Development Indicators database, http://data.worldbank.org/indicator, April 2002.

8. See also some important work on dress in Senegal, which Konate draws on: Ousseynou Faye, "L'habillement et ses accessoires dans les milieux Africains de Dakar, 1857–1960," *Revue Sénégalaise d'Histoire* 1 (1995):69–86; and Djibril Seck, "Histoire des modes vestimentaires chez les jeunes filles à Dakar 1945–1960," master's thesis, University of Cheikh Anta Diop, 2000.

9. Mustafa suggests that the Wolof word *sañse* derives from the French *changer,* meaning "to transform" (2006:178). Senegalese women's performance of sañse to express individual and collective identities has been widely commented on. See, for example, Grabski 2009; Heath 1992; Mustafa 2002; Rabine 2002; Scheld 2003, 2007.

10. The notion of "women's business" is not peculiar to Senegal. In her monograph *Women of Value, Men of Renown,* Weiner recounts that she was told by a male Kiriwina informant that the exchange of cloth, here banana leaf bundles and fibrous skirts, was "women's business." She speculated that, among her predecessors, including the founding figure of anthropology, Bronislaw Malinowski, wealth objects circulated by women were overlooked because they misunderstood this statement as derogatory. Weiner argues that what her informant meant was that "women could tell me about their business much better than men because women were in charge of these distributions" (1976:12n4).

2. HOMES AND THEIR HISTORIES

1. In the Khar Yalla *mbotaye* (ritual association), nearly three-quarters of the women listed their husbands as retired, though the women themselves continued to garner an income.

2. For a detailed analysis of the use of the term *caste* in the West African context, see A. Diop 1981; Irvine 1974; Tamari 1991; and D. M. Todd, "Caste in Africa?" *Africa* 47(4) (1997):398–412. The use of the term *caste* and the portability of the term from India to West African societies was much debated in the literature throughout the 1970s.

3. Diop noted the contradictory claims by R. Rousseau, who argued that Wolof families practiced matrilineal descent prior to the spread of Islam; Fayet, who argued that patrilineal descent had been the norm prior to the introduction of Islam; the colonial Arabist Paul Marty, who argued that the Wolof practiced matrilineal descent but under Islam adopted a bilateral system of descent; the anthropologist David Ames, who claimed that Wolof families practiced double

descent (with patrilineages controlling status and property while matrilineages provided advice and economic aid); and the anthropologist David Gamble, who argued that Wolof families in the Gambia practiced unilineal descent with variations according to hereditary occupational groups. For a full discussion, see Diop 1985.

4. The first great Murid migration took place between 1904 and 1920 to the *arrondissements* of Darou Mousty, Kael, and N'Dame. The second major Murid migration occurred between 1930 and 1950 to the area of Kaffrine. See ANS 10 D1/15, Le Mouvement Mouride (1905–1945), Circulaires, Bureau Politique, Le Gouverneur des Colonies, Lieutenant-gouverneur du Sénégal à Messieurs les Administrateurs Commandants de cercle, May 28, 1912; ANS 10 D1/15, Renseignements sur la secte des Mourides, L'Administrateur en Chef, Thies, May 8, 1911.

5. David Ames (1955a:396) records that women who farmed peanuts in Saloum in the 1950s used the proceeds to purchase clothing and livestock and to hire seasonal laborers to work in their fields.

6. See ANS 13G 67, Paul Marty, Le groupement de Bou Kunta, Affaires Musulmanes, Politique Musulmane, Activité des Marabouts, 1906–1917.

7. On this point Searing (2002) and Klein (1998) differ considerably; Searing makes the case that slaves were able to join peasants in the production of peanuts as a cash crop, while Klein says that there were a large number of slaves in Wolof society overall and thus a more significant transition at the end of slavery.

3. THE PROMISE OF PARADISE

1. Even in the early twenty-first century, *sokna* (female shaykhs) did not commonly give radio addresses to their faithful.

2. For a discussion of the textile industry, see Boone 1992.

3. See the website of the Murid Islamic Community in America, www.toubamica.org, accessed on June 16, 2008.

4. A Sufi term meaning "remembrance," *dhikr* is the prayerful repetition of the name of God; see Mervyn Hiskett, *The Development of Islam in West Africa* (London: Longman, 1984), 327. Dhikr is practiced with *fikr,* or meditation. The two practices are complementary; see Lings 1993:88.

5. The equivalent of the miracles of the Prophet exists in the karamat of the saint (wali) because the latter is the heir of the former. The Prophet is proof of the existence of God, and the saints are the signs that his religion is the true one. The Prophet is spotless, and the saints are preserved and honored. Both share in divine immunity (*isma*), as shown by the Gnostics. But immunity is only necessary for the Prophet, not for the saints. Cheikh Amadou Bamba, Masalik-al-jinan, quoted in Monteil 1969:89.

4. A TALE OF TWO SISTERS

1. For an extended discussion of this phenomenon in relation to tailoring, see Mustafa 1998.

2. Suzanne Scheld (2003) says that *sañse* is Wolof for the French verb *changer* and that, in the Wolof context, it is employed to mean "changing outfits." She suggests that it refers to the last and most spectacular outfit worn at a family ceremony.

3. In February 2000, 700 CFA francs were equal to US$1.

4. Interestingly, the equivalent expression *ça ne marche pas* is common in French and is also used in Senegal.

5. For further discussion on rituals and power, see Comaroff and Comaroff 1993.

5. A LAMB SLAUGHTERED

1. The term *xaalis* is used both for silver items, like jewelry, and for money, including paper money.

2. Musa was the nephew of Sokna Géer, and Bintu was the daughter of Sokna's husband's brother, who was also the brother of Musa's mother.

3. For further discussion of marital payments and multiple kinship ties, see Comaroff 1980.

4. Ames' informants also spoke about the success of marriages based on love versus those arranged by family members. Additionally, men spoke about the incidence of women marrying for wealth and the pressures on suitors to provide sufficient marital gifts (1953:48–49). In 1999, Suzanne Scheld's informants also spoke about the impact of Indian movies on ideas about relationships (personal communication, 1999).

5. Georges Balandier distinguishes between castes, as professions (blacksmith, griot, leatherworker, etc.), and orders, as hierarchical relations between aristocrats, freeborn persons, and slaves, each of which has its specific forms of hierarchy and stratification in Senegal and Mali. See Balandier, *Anthropologie politique* (Paris: PUF, 1967), 100.

6. ANS 23 G/12, 17, Nouvelles clauses de contrat matrimonial, Section I: Etat civil, Gouvernement Général de L'AOF, Grand Imanat de Dakar, Réglementation Générale, May 15, 1946.

7. For further discussion of this debate, see Villalón 2004.

8. See, for example, Heath 1992.

6. HOME ECONOMICS

1. Mary Byrne McDonnell's research among hajj pilgrims in Malaysia reveals similar trends. Malaysian pilgrims today enjoy a higher status upon their return than they did in an earlier period. Moreover, state-sponsored savings and investment plans now enable pilgrims to finance their journeys without jeopardizing their financial stability. Pilgrimages are also less arduous than in previous eras due to air travel. Most important, Malaysian pilgrims who once were sent off with a feast and prayers for a safe return, due in part to the high mortality rate of pilgrims, are now feted with offerings of cash from those who hope to benefit from

the blessings of the newly honored al Hajji. See McDonnell, "Patterns of Muslim Pilgrimage from Malaysia, 1885–1985," in *Muslim Travellers: Pilgrimage, Migration and the Religious Imagination,* ed. Dale F. Eickelman and James Piscatori (Berkeley: University of California Press, 1990), 111–30.

2. Compare to Munn (1992:53), who reports that Gawan men distributed food cooked by women.

3. In her fascinating ethnographic study, Patterson looks at how women use these associations to pressure political parties to include women on the electoral ballots and to mobilize women to vote for female candidates.

7. ONLY TROUBLE

1. El Bachir Sow, *Le Soleil,* March 11, 1996.

2. For further discussion of ndëp, see A. Zempleni, "La dimension thérapeutique de culte des rab, Ndop, Fuuru et Samp: Rites de possession chez les Lebou et les Wolof," *Psychopathologie africaine* 2(3) (1966):295–439.

3. 23 G/12, 17, Nouvelles clauses de contrat matrimonial, Section I: Etat civil, Gouvernement Général de L'AOF, Grand Imanat de Dakar, Réglementation Générale, May 15, 1946.

4. Appadurai describes a trend in gift exchange in the West based on the mail-order catalog, "where gifts are imagined but never given or received . . . where all social reciprocity is imploded into the possible gift, and the possible relationship." See Arun Appadurai, "Things to Come: Emergent Regimes of Materiality," *CODESRIA Bulletin* 3–4 (1999):39.

5. "Why this madness?" "Lekku-ndeye: Beneath this lucrative commerce," "A violence against the destitute," and "The tyranny of the lekku-ndeye."

6. *Le Soleil,* August 19, 1993.

7. Some persons even suggested that gifts given by men at family ceremonies were also ndawtal, though they were never returned and were not recorded in a ledger nor given publicly.

8. For further discussion of this, see Annette Weiner's discussion of Mauss in "Inalienable Wealth" (1985:213).

REFERENCES

Abu-Lughod, Lila. 1993. Writing Women's Worlds: Bedouin Stories. Berkeley: University of California Press.

Adams, Adrian, and Jaabe So. 1996. A Claim to Land by the River. Athens: Ohio University Press.

Akin, David, and Joel Robbins. 1999. Money and Modernity: State and Local Currencies in Melanesia. Pittsburgh, Pa.: University of Pittsburgh Press.

Al-Hujwiri, Ali B. Uthman. 1911. The Kashf al-Mahjub [of al-Hijwiri]: The Oldest Persian Treatise of Sufism. Translated by R. A. Nicholson. London: Cosmo.

Allman, Jean Marie. 2004. Fashioning Africa: Power and the Politics of Dress. Bloomington: Indiana University Press.

Ames, David. 1953. Plural Marriage among the Wolof in the Gambia. Ph.D. diss., Northwestern University.

———. 1955a. The Economic Base of Wolof Polygyny. Southwestern Journal of Anthropology 11(4):391–403.

———. 1955b. The Use of Transitional Cloth-Money Token among the Wolof. American Anthropologist 57:1016–24.

———. 1956. The Selection of Mates, Courtship, and Marriage among the Wolof. Bulletin de l'IFAN 17:156–68.

Amselle, J. L. 1971. Parenté et commerce chez les Kookoro. *In* Development of Indigenous Trade and Markets in West Africa, edited by C. Meillassoux, 253–66. Oxford: Oxford University Press.

Antoine, Philippe, et al. 1995. Les familles dakaroises face à la crise. Dakar: ORSTOM, IFAN, and CEPED.

Apter, Andrew. 1999. IBB = 419: Nigerian Democracy and the Politics of Illusion. *In* Civil Society and the Political Imagination in Africa, edited by J. L. Comaroff and J. Comaroff, 267–307. Chicago: University of Chicago Press.

———. 2005. The Pan African Nation: Oil and the Spectacle of Culture in Nigeria. Chicago: University of Chicago Press.

Augis, Erin. 2000. Dakar's Sunnite Women: The Politics of Person. Ph.D. diss., University of Chicago.

Bâ, Mariama. 1981. So Long a Letter. London: Heinemann.

Babou, Cheikh Anta. 2002. Brotherhood Solidarity, Education, and Migration: The Role of the Dahiras among the Murid Muslim Community of New York. African Affairs 101:151–70.

———. 2005. Contesting Space, Shaping Places: Making Room for the Muridiyya in Colonial Senegal, 1912–1945. Journal of African History 46:405–426.

———. 2007a. Fighting the Greater Jihad: Amadu Bamba and the Founding of the Muridiyya of Senegal, 1853–1913. Athens: Ohio University Press.

———. 2007b. Urbanizing Mystical Islam: Making Murid Space in the Cities of Senegal. International Journal of African Historical Studies 40(2):197–223.

———. 2008. Migration and Cultural Change: Money, Caste, Gender, and Social Status among Senegalese Female Hair Braiders in the United States. Africa Today 55(2):3–22.

Bastian, Misty. 1996. Female "Alhajis" and Entrepreneurial Fashions: Flexible Identities in Southeastern Nigerian Clothing Practice. *In* Clothing and Difference: Embodied Identities in Colonial and Post-Colonial Africa, edited by H. Hendrickson. Durham, N.C.: Duke University Press.

Bayart, Jean-François. 1993. The State in Africa: The Politics of the Belly. New York: Longman.

———. 2000. Africa in the World: A History of Extraversion. African Affairs 99(395):217–67.

Bayart, Jean-François, Stephen Ellis, and Béatrice Hibou. 1999. The Criminalization of the State in Africa. Bloomington: Indiana University Press.

Beck, Linda. 2008. Brokering Democracy in Africa: The Rise of a Clientelist Democracy in Senegal. New York: Palgrave.

Behrman, Linda. 1968. The Political Significance of the Wolof Adherence to the Muslim Brotherhoods in the Nineteenth Century. African Historical Studies 1(1):60–78.

Bernal, Victoria. 1997. Islam, Transnational Culture, and Modernity in Rural Sudan. *In* Gendered Encounters: Challenging Cultural Boundaries and Social Hierarchies in Africa, edited by M. Grosz-Ngaté and O. H. Kokole, 131–52. New York: Routledge.

Berry, Sara S. 1989. Social Institutions and Access to Resources. Africa 59(1):41–55.

———. 1995. Stable Prices, Unstable Values: Some Thoughts on Monetization and the Meaning of Transactions in West African Economies. *In* Money Matters: Instability, Values and Social Payments in the Modern History of West African Communities, edited by J. I. Guyer, 299–311. Portsmouth, N.H.: Heinemann.

Biaya, T. K. 1999. Eroticism and Sexuality in Africa. CODESRIA Bulletin 3–4:41–45.

———. 2000. "Crushing the Pistachio": Eroticism in Senegal and the Art of Ousmane Ndiaye Dago. Public Culture 12(3):707–719.

Bohannan, Paul. 1959. The Impact of Money on an African Subsistence Economy. *In* Tribal and Peasant Economies: Readings in Economic Anthropology, edited by G. Dalton. New York: Natural History Press.

Boone, Catherine. 1992. Merchant Capital and the Roots of State Power in Senegal, 1930–1985. Cambridge: Cambridge University Press.

———. 2003. Political Topographies of the African State. Cambridge: Cambridge University Press.

———. 2007. Property and Constitutional Order: Land Tenure Reform and the Future of the African State. African Affairs 106(425):557–86.

Bop, Codou. 2005. Roles and the Position of Women in Sufi Brotherhoods in Senegal. Journal of the American Academy of Religion 73(4):1099–1119.

Bowen, John. 1993. Muslims through Discourse. Princeton, N.J.: Princeton University Press.

———. 2004. Does French Islam Have Borders? Dilemmas of Domestication in a Global Religious Field. American Anthropologist 106(1):43–55.

Buggenhagen, Beth. 2001. Prophets and Profits: Gendered and Generational Visions of Wealth and Value in Senegalese Murid Households. Journal of Religion in Africa 31(4):373–401.

———. 2008. Beyond Brotherhood: Gender, Religious Authority, and the Global Circuits of Senegalese Muridiyya. *In* New Perspectives on Islam in Senegal: Conversion, Migration, Wealth, Power, and Femininity, edited by M. Diouf and M. A. Leichtman, 189–210. New York: Palgrave.

Bugnicourt, Jacques. 1983. Dakar without Bounds. *In* Reading the Contemporary African City, edited by B. B. Taylor, 27–42. Singapore: Concept Media/Aga Khan Award for Architecture.

Burckhardt, Titus. 1995. An Introduction to Sufism. Translated by D. M. Matheson. London: Thorsons.

Calder, Lendol. 1999. Financing the American Dream: A Cultural History of Consumer Credit. Princeton, N.J.: Princeton University Press.

Callaway, Barbara, and Lucy Creevey. 1994. The Heritage of Islam: Women, Religion, and Politics in West Africa. Boulder, Colo.: Lynne Rienner.

Camara, Fatou K. 2007. Women and the Law: A Critique of Senegalese Family Law. Social Identities 13(6):787–800.

Carrier, J. 1991. Gifts, Commodities, and Social Relations: A Maussian View of Exchange. Social Analysis 6(1):119–36.

Carter, Donald Martin. 1997. States of Grace: Senegalese in Italy and the New European Immigration. Minneapolis: University of Minnesota Press.

Cochrane, Laura L. 2009. Senegalese Weavers' Ethnic Identities in Discourse and in Craft. African Identities 7(1):3–15.

Cohen, Abner. 1971. Cultural Strategies in the Organization of Trading Diasporas. *In* The Development of Indigenous Trade and Markets in West Africa, edited by C. Meillassoux, 266–78. Oxford: Oxford University Press for the International Africa Institute.

Collier, J., and Sylvia Yanagisako, eds. 1987. Gender and Kinship: Essays toward a Unified Theory. Stanford, Calif.: Stanford University Press.

Comaroff, Jean, and John L. Comaroff. 1999. Occult Economics and the Violence of Abstraction: Notes from the South African Postcolony. American Ethnologist 26(2):276–303.

Comaroff, Jean, and John L. Comaroff, eds. 1993. Modernity and Its Malcontents: Ritual and Power in Postcolonial Africa. Chicago: University of Chicago Press.

Comaroff, John L. 1980. Introduction. *In* The Meaning of Marriage Payments, edited by J. L. Comaroff, 1–48. New York: Academic.

Comaroff, John L., and Jean Comaroff. 1990. Goodly Beasts and Beastly Goods: Cattle and Commodities in a South African Context. American Ethnologist 17(2):195–216.

———. 1997. Of Revelation and Revolution: The Dialectics of Modernity on a South African Frontier. Vol. 2. Chicago: University of Chicago Press.

———. 2000. Millennial Capitalism: First Thoughts on a Second Coming. Public Culture 12(2):291–343.

Cooper, Barbara. 1993. Cloth, Commodity Production, and Social Capital: Women in Maradi, Niger 1890–1989. African Economic History 21:51–71.

———. 1997. Marriage in Maradi: Gender and Culture in Hausa Society in Niger, 1900–1989. London: James Currey.

Copans, Jean. 1980. Les marabouts de l'arachide. Paris: L'Harmattan.

Copans, Jean, et al. 1972. Maintenance sociale et changement économique au Sénégal: I. Doctrine économique et pratique du travail chez les Mourides. Paris: Travaux et Documents de l'ORSTOM.

Cotula, Lorenzo, et al. 2004. Till to Tiller: Linkages between International Remittances and Access to Land in West Africa. Paper prepared for the Food and Agriculture Organization of the United Nations, Livelihood Support Programme.

Coulon, Christian. 1999. The Grand Magal in Touba: A Religious Festival of the Mouride Brotherhood in Senegal. African Affairs 98(391):195–210.

Creevey, Lucy. 1970. Muslim Brotherhoods and Politics in Senegal. Cambridge, Mass.: Harvard University Press.

———. 1985. Muslim Brotherhoods and Politics in Senegal in 1985. Journal of Modern African Studies 23(4):715–21.

———. 1991. The Impact of Islam on Women in Senegal. Journal of Developing Areas 25(3):347–68.

———. 1996. Islam, Women, and the Role of the State in Senegal. Journal of Religion in Africa 26(3):268–307.

Creevey, Lucy, Richard Vengroff, and Ibrahima Gaye. 1995. Devaluation of the CFA Franc in Senegal: The Reaction of Small Business. Journal of Modern African Studies 33(4):669–83.

Cruise O'Brien, Donal B. 1971a. Co-operators and Bureaucrats: Class Formation in a Senegalese Peasant Society. Africa 4:263–78.

———. 1971b. The Mourides of Senegal: The Political and Economic Organization of an Islamic Brotherhood. Oxford: Clarendon.

———. 1975. Saints and Politicians: Essays in the Organization of a Senegalese Peasant Society. Cambridge: Cambridge University Press.

———. 1988. Charisma Comes to Town: Mouride Urbanization, 1945–86. *In* Charisma and Brotherhood in African Islam, edited by C. Coulon and D. B. Cruise O'Brien, 135–56. Oxford: Clarendon.

———. 2003. Symbolic Confrontations: Muslims Imagining the State in Africa. New York: Palgrave.

Curtin, Philip D. 1975. Economic Change in Precolonial Africa: Senegambia in the Era of the Slave Trade. Madison: University of Wisconsin Press.

Das, Veena, and Deborah Poole. 2004. State and Its Margins: Comparative Ethnographies. *In* Anthropology in the Margins of the State, edited by V. Das and D. Poole. Santa Fe, N.M.: School of American Research.

Davis, Mike. 2006. Planet of Slums. New York: Verso.

Depret, Roland. 1983. The Assimilation of Traditional Practices in Contemporary Architecture. *In* Reading the Contemporary African City, edited by B. B. Taylor, 61–72. Singapore: Concept Media/Aga Khan Award for Architecture.

De Sardan, J. P. Olivier. 1999. A Moral Economy of Corruption in Africa? Journal of Modern African Studies 37(1):25–52.

Dilley, Roy. 1987. Myth and Meaning and the Tukolor Loom. Man 22(2):256–66.

———. 2004. Islamic and Caste Knowledge Practices among Haalpulaar'en in Senegal: Between Mosque and Termite Mound. Edinburgh: Edinburgh University Press.

Diop, Abdoulaye Bara. 1981. La société wolof: Les systèmes d'inégalité et de domination. Paris: Karthala.

———. 1985. La famille wolof: Tradition et changement. Paris: Karthala.

Diop, Momar Coumba. 1981. Fonctions et activités des dahira mourides urbains (Sénégal). Cahiers d'études africaines 20(1–3):79–91.

Diop, Mustapha, and Laurence Michalak. 1996. "Refuge" and "Prison": Islam, Ethnicity, and the Adaptation of Space in Workers' Housing in France. *In* Making Muslim Space in North America and Europe, edited by B. D. Metcalf. Berkeley: University of California Press.

Diouf, Mamadou. 2000. The Senegalese Murid Trade Diaspora and the Making of a Vernacular Cosmopolitanism. Public Culture 12(3):679–702.

Diouf, Sylviane. 2004. The West African Paradox. *In* Muslims' Place in the American Public Square, edited by Z. Bukhari, S. Nyang, M. Ahmad, and J. Esposito, 268–98. Lanham, Md.: AltaMira.

Eames, Elizabeth. 1992. Navigating Nigerian Bureaucracy; or, "Why Can't You Beg?" She Demanded. *In* The Naked Anthropologist, edited by P. R. DeVita. New York: Wadsworth.

Ebin, Victoria. 1986. Commerçants et missionnaires: Une confrérie sénégalaise à New York. Translated by Dorothy S. Blair. New York: Longman.

———. 1992. A la recherche de nouveaux poissons: Stratégies commerciales mourides en temps de crise. Politique Africaine 45:86–99.

———. 1993. Les commerçants mourides à Marseille et à New York. *In* Grand commerçants d'Afrique de l'Ouest, edited by E. Grégoire and P. Labazée. Paris: Karthala-ORSTOM.

Eicher, Joan B. 2000. The Anthropology of Dress. Dress 27:59–70.

Etienne, Mona. 1980. Women and Men, Cloth, and Colonization: The Transformation of Production-Distribution Relations among the Baule (Ivory Coast). *In* Women and Colonization: Anthropological Perspectives, edited by M. Etienne and E. Leacock, 214–38. New York: Praeger.

Evans-Pritchard, E. E. 1940. The Nuer. Oxford: Oxford University Press.

———. 1951. Kinship and Marriage among the Nuer. Oxford: Oxford University Press.

Fall, Aminata Sow. 1986. The Beggars' Strike. Translated by Dorothy S. Blair. New York: Longman.

Feeley Harnick, Gillian. 1989. Cloth and the Creation of Ancestors. *In* Cloth and Human Experience, edited by A. B. Weiner and J. Schneider, 73–117. Washington, D.C.: Smithsonian Institution Press.

Ferguson, James G. 1992. The Cultural Topography of Wealth: Commodity Paths and the Structure of Property in Rural Lesotho. American Anthropologist 94:55–73.

———. 2005. Seeing Like an Oil Company: Space, Security, and Global Capital in Neoliberal Africa. American Anthropologist 107(3):377–82.

———. 2006. Global Shadows: Africa in the Neoliberal World Order. Durham, N.C.: Duke University Press.

Ferme, Mariane. 1994. What Alhaji Airplane Saw in Mecca and What Happened When He Came Home: Ritual Transformation in a Mende Community. *In* Syncretism/Anti-Syncretism: The Politics of Religious Synthesis, edited by C. Stewart and R. Shaw, 27–44. New York: Routledge.

Fischer, Michael M. J., and Mehdi Abedi. 1990. Debating Muslims: Cultural Dialogues in Postmodernity and Tradition. Madison: University of Wisconsin Press.

Foster, Robert. 1995. Social Reproduction and History in Melanesia: Mortuary Ritual, Gift Exchange, and Custom in the Tanga Islands. Cambridge: Cambridge University Press.

———. 2006. Tracking Globalization: Commodities and Value in Motion. *In* Handbook of Material Culture, edited by C. Tilley, W. Keane, S. Kuchler, M. Rowlands, and P. Spyer, 285–302. London: Sage.

Freund, Bill. 2007. The African City: A History. Cambridge: Cambridge University Press.

Galvan, Dennis Charles. 2004. The State Must Be Our Master of Fire: How Peasants Craft Culturally Sustainable Development in Senegal. Berkeley: University of California Press.

Gamble, David. 1957. The Wolof of Senegambia: Ethnographic Survey of Africa. Part 14. London: International Africa Institute.

Gamble, David, and David Ames. n.d. A Wolof Naming Ceremony: Human Interaction and Its Aesthetic Significance. Unpublished manuscript, Smithsonian Institution Library.

Gillow, John. 2003. African Textiles: Color and Creativity across a Continent. London: Thames and Hudson.

Glickman, M. 1971. Kinship and Credit among the Nuer. Africa 41(4):306–319.

Goody, Jack, ed. 1958. The Developmental Cycle in Domestic Groups. Cambridge: Cambridge University Press.

Grabski, J. 2009. Making Fashion in the City: A Case of Tailors and Designers in Dakar, Senegal. Fashion Theory 13(2):215–42.

Graeber, David. 1996. Beads and Money: Notes toward a Theory of Wealth and Power. American Ethnologist 23:1–32.

———. 2001. Toward an Anthropological Theory of Value: The False Coin of Our Own Dreams. New York: Palgrave.

Grosz-Ngaté, Maria. 1988. Monetization of Bridewealth and the Abandonment of "Kin Road" to Marriage in Sana, Mali. American Ethnologist 15(3):501–514.

Guérin, Isabelle. 2006. Women and Money: Lessons from Senegal. Development and Change 37(3):549–70.

Gueye, Cheikh. 1999. L'organisation de l'espace dans une ville religieuse: Touba (Sénégal). Ph.D. diss., University of Strasbourg.

———. 2001. Touba: The New Dairas and the Urban Dream. *In* Associational Life in

African Cities: Popular Responses to the Urban Crisis, edited by A. Tostensen, I. Tvedten, and M. Vaa. Stockholm: Nordiska Afrikainstitutet.

———. 2003. New Information and Communications Technology Use by Muslim Mourides in Senegal. Review of African Political Economy 98:609–625.

Guyer, Jane I. 1988. Dynamic Approaches to Domestic Budgeting: Cases and Methods from Africa. *In* A Home Divided: Women and Income in the Third World, edited by D. Dwyer and J. Bruce. Stanford, Calif.: Stanford University Press.

———. 1995. The Value of Beti Bridewealth. *In* Money Matters: Instability, Values, and Social Payment in the Modern History of West African Communities, edited by J. I. Guyer, 113–32. Portsmouth, N.H.: Heinemann.

———. 1999. Comparisons and Equivalencies in Africa and Melanesia. *In* Money and Modernity: State and Local Currencies in Melanesia, edited by D. Akin and J. Robbins, 232–46. Pittsburgh, Pa.: University of Pittsburgh Press.

———. 2004. Marginal Gains: Monetary Transactions in Atlantic Africa. Chicago: University of Chicago Press.

Guyer, Jane I., ed. 1995. Money Matters: Instability, Values, and Social Payments in the Modern History of West African Communities. Portsmouth, N.H.: Heinemann.

Hansen, Karen. 2004. The World in Dress: Anthropological Perspectives on Clothing, Fashion, and Culture. Annual Review of Anthropology 33:369–92.

Hanson, John H. 1994. Migration and the Political Economy of Meaning: Fergo Nioro from the Senegal River, 1862–1890. Journal of African History 35(1):37–60.

Heath, Deborah. 1992. Fashion, Anti-Fashion, and Heteroglossia in Urban Senegal. American Ethnologist 19(1):19–33.

Hesse, Brian J. 2004. The Peugeot and the Baobab: Islam, Structural Adjustment, and Liberalism in Senegal. Journal of Contemporary African Studies 22(1):4–12.

Hibou, Béatrice. 1999. The "Social Capital" of the State as an Agent of Deception. *In* The Criminalization of the State in Africa, edited by J.-F. Bayart, S. Ellis, and B. Hibou, 69–113. Bloomington: Indiana University Press.

Hopkins, A. G. 1973. An Economic History of West Africa. New York: Columbia University Press.

Hunwick, J. O. 1999. Islamic Financial Institutions: Theoretical Structures and Aspects of Their Application in Sub-Saharan Africa. *In* Credit, Currencies, and Culture: African Financial Institutions in Historical Perspective, edited by E. Stiansen and J. Guyer, 72–96. Stockholm: Nordiska Afrikainstitutet.

Hussain, S. A. 1997. A Guide to Hajj. New Delhi: Kitab Bhavan.

Hutchinson, Sharon E. 1996. Nuer Dilemmas: Coping with Money, War, and the State. Berkeley: University of California Press.

Irvine, Judith T. 1974. Caste and Communication in a Wolof Village. Ph.D. diss., University of Pennsylvania.

———. 1978. When Is Genealogy History? Wolof Genealogies in Comparative Perspective. American Ethnologist 5(4):651–74.

Johnson, Marian Ashby. 1994. Gold Jewelry of the Wolof and Tukulor of Senegal. African Arts 27(1):48–95.

Johnson, Marion. 1974. Cotton Imperialism in West Africa. African Affairs 73(291):178–87.

Kane, Abdoulaye. 2002. Senegal's Village Diaspora and the People Left Ahead. *In* The Transnational Family: New European Frontiers and Global Networks, edited by D. Bryceson and U. Vuorela, 245–64. Oxford: Berg.

Kane, Maïmouna. 1972. The Status of Married Women under Customary Law in Senegal. American Journal of Comparative Law 20(4):716–23.

Keane, Webb. 2001. Money Is No Object: Materiality, Desire, and Modernity in an Indonesian Society. *In* The Empire of Things: Regimes of Value and Material Culture, edited by F. R. Meyers, 65–90. Santa Fe, N.M.: School of American Research Press.

Kenny, Erin. 2007. Gifting Mecca: Importing Spiritual Capital to West Africa. Mobilities 2(3):363–81.

Klein, Martin A. 1998. Slavery and Colonial Rule in French West Africa. Cambridge: Cambridge University Press.

Konate, Dior. 2009. Women, Clothing, and Politics in Senegal 1940s–1950s. *In* Material Women, 1750–1950: Consuming Desires and Collecting Practices, edited by M. D. Goggin and B. F. Tobin, 2:225–246. Surrey, England: Ashgate.

Kriger, Colleen E. 2005. Mapping the History of Cotton Textile Production in Precolonial West Africa. African Economic History (33):87–116.

Lings, Martin. 1993. What Is Sufism? Cambridge: Islamic Texts Society.

Makhulu, Anne-Maria, Beth Buggenhagen, and Stephen Jackson. 2010. Hard Work, Hard Times: Global Volatility and African Subjectivities. Berkeley: University of California Press.

Malkki, Liisa H. 1995. Purity and Exile: Violence, Memory, and National Cosmology among Hutu Refugees in Tanzania. Chicago: University of Chicago Press.

Manchuelle, François. 1997. Willing Migrants: Soninke Labor Diasporas, 1848–1960. Athens: Ohio University Press.

Marty, Paul. 1917. Études sur l'Islam au Sénégal. 2 vols. Paris: Ernest Leroux.

Masquelier, Adeline. 2004. How Is a Girl to Marry without a Bed? Weddings, Wealth, and Women's Value in an Islamic Town of Niger. *In* Situating Globality: African Agency in the Appropriation of Global Culture, edited by W. van Binsbergen and R. van Dijk, 220–56. Leiden: Brill Academic.

Maurer, Bill. 2006. The Anthropology of Money. Annual Review of Anthropology 35:15–36.

Mauss, Marcel. 1990[1950]. The Gift. Translated by W. D. Halls. New York: Norton.

Mbodj, Mohamed. 1991. The Politics of Independence: 1960–86. *In* The Political Economy of Senegal under Structural Adjustment, edited by C. L. Delgado and S. Jammeh, 119–26. New York: Praeger.

———. 1993. The State of the Groundnut Economy: A 30 Year Crisis. *In* Senegal: Essays in Statecraft, edited by M. Coumba Diop, 89–125. Dakar: CODESRIA.

Mbow, Marie-Amy. 1998. African Textile Design. *In* The Art of African Fashion, edited by E. van der Plas and Marlous Willemsen, 133–68. Trenton, N.J.: Africa World Press.

Mbow, Penda. 2008. Senegal: The Return of Personalism. Journal of Democracy 19(1):156–69.

Meillassoux, Claude. 1972. From Reproduction to Production. Economy and Society 1(1):93–105.

———. 1975. Maidens, Meal, and Money: Capitalism and the Domestic Community. Cambridge: Cambridge University Press.

Melly, Caroline. 2010. Inside-Out Houses: Urban Belonging and Imagined Futures in Dakar, Senegal. Comparative Studies in Society and History 52(1):37–65.

Miller, Daniel. 1994. Modernity, an Ethnographic Approach: Dualism and Mass Consumption in Trinidad. Oxford: Berg.

Monteil, Vincent. 1969. Marabouts. *In* Islam in Africa, edited by J. Kritzeck and W. H. Lewis. New York: Van Nostrand Reinhold.

Mottin-Sylla, Marie-Helene. 1987. L'argent et l'intérêt: Tontines et autres pratiques féminines de mobilisation de moyens a Dakar. Dakar: ENDA Graf.

Munn, Nancy D. 1992. The Fame of Gawa: A Symbolic Study of Value Transformation in a Massim (Papua New Guinea) Society. Durham, N.C.: Duke University Press.

Mustafa, Huda Nura. 1998. Practicing Beauty: Crisis, Value, and the Challenge of Self-Mastery in Dakar 1970–1994. Ph.D. diss., Harvard University.

———. 2002. Portraits of Modernity: Fashioning Selves in Dakarois Popular Photography. *In* Images and Empires: Visuality in Colonial and Postcolonial Africa, edited by D. D. K. Paul Stuart Landau. Berkeley: University of California Press.

———. 2006. La Mode Dakaroise: Elegance, Transnationalism, and an African Fashion Capital. *In* Fashion's World Cities, edited by C. Breward and D. Gilbert, 177–200. Oxford: Berg.

Ndiaye, Malick. 1998. Les Móodou Móodu; ou, L'éthos du développement au Sénégal. Dakar: Presses Universitaires de Dakar.

Ndione, Emmanuel Seyni. 1989. Leçons d'une animation au Sénégal. IFDA 74(Nov.–Dec.):3–14.

———. 1994. L'économie urbaine en Afrique: Le don et le recours. Paris: Karthala.

Ndione, Emmanuel Seyni, and Mohamed Soumaré. 1983. Growth and Evolution of Dakar Suburbs: The Case of Grand Yoff. *In* Reading the Contemporary African City, edited by B. B. Taylor, 113–17. Singapore: Concept Media/Aga Khan Award for Architecture.

O'Bannon, Brett. 2006. Receiving an "Empty Envelope": Governance Reforms and the Management of Farmer-Herder Conflicts in Senegal. Canadian Journal of African Studies 40(1):76–100.

Ong, Aihwa. 1999. Flexible Citizenship: The Cultural Logics of Transnationality. Durham, N.C.: Duke University Press.

Ousmane, Sembene. 1972[1965]. The Money-Order. Translated by C. Wake. Portsmouth, N.H.: Heinemann.

Parry, Jonathan P. 1989. On the Moral Perils of Exchange. *In* Money and the Morality of Exchange, edited by J. P. Parry and M. Bloch. Cambridge: Cambridge University Press.

Patterson, Amy S. 1999. The Dynamic Nature of Citizenship and Participation: Lessons from Three Rural Senegalese Case Studies. Africa Today 46(1):3–27.

———. 2002. The Impact of Senegal's Decentralization on Women in Local Governance. Canadian Journal of African Studies 29(3):490–530.

Perani, Judith, and Norma Hackleman Wolff. 1999. Cloth, Dress, and Art Patronage in Africa. Oxford: Berg.

Perry, Donna. 1997. Rural Ideologies and Urban Imaginings: Wolof Immigrants in New York City. Africa Today 44(2):229–60.

———. 2002. Microcredit and Women Moneylenders: The Shifting Terrain of Credit in Rural Senegal. Human Organization 61(1):30–40.

———. 2005. Wolof Women, Economic Liberalization, and the Crisis of Masculinity in Rural Senegal. Ethnology 44(3):207–226.

———. 2009. Fathers, Sons, and the State: Discipline and Punishment in a Wolof Hinterland. Cultural Anthropology 24(1):33–67.

Picton, John. 1992. Tradition, Technology, and Lurex: Some Comments on Textile History and Design in West Africa. *In* History, Design, and Craft in West African Strip-Woven Cloth, edited by R. Sieber, 13–52. Washington, D.C.: Smithsonian Institution Press.

Picton, John, and John Mack. 1979. The Art of African Textiles: Looms, Weaving, and Design. London: British Museum Publications for the Trustees of the British Museum.

Piot, Charles. 1991. Of Persons and Things: Some Reflections on African Spheres of Exchange. Man 26:405–424.

———. 1999. Remotely Global: Village Modernity in West Africa. Chicago: University of Chicago Press.

Rabine, Leslie. 2002. The Global Circulation of African Fashion. Oxford: Berg.

Renne, Elisha. 1996. Cloth That Does Not Die: The Meaning of Cloth in Bunu Social Life. Seattle: University of Washington Press.

Reynolds, Rachel R. 2006. Professional Nigerian Women, Household Economy, and Immigration Decisions. International Migration 44(5):167–88.

Roberts, Allen F. 1996. The Ironies of System D. *In* Recycled, Re-seen: Folk Art from the Global Scrap Heap, edited by C. Cerny and S. Seriff. New York: Harry Abrams for the Museum of International Folk Art, Santa Fe.

Roberts, Richard. 1992. Guinée Cloth: Linked Transformations in Production within France's Empire in the Nineteenth Century. Cahiers d'études africaines 32(128):597–627.

Robin, J. 1947. L'évolution du mariage coutumier chez les Musulmans du Sénégal. Africa 18:192–201.

Robinson, David. 1991. Beyond Resistance and Collaboration: Amadu Bamba and the Murids of Senegal. Journal of Religion in Africa 21(2):149–69.

Rocheteau, G. 1975. Société wolof et mobilité. Cahiers des ORSTROM, ser. Sciences Humaines 12(1):3–18.

Roitman, Janet L. 2005. Fiscal Disobedience: An Anthropology of Economic Regulation in Central Africa. Princeton, N.J.: Princeton University Press.

Rosander, Eva Evers. 1998. Women and Mouridism in Senegal: The Case of the Mam Diarra Bousso Daira in Mbacke. *In* Women and Islamization: Contemporary Dimensions of Discourse on Gender Relations, edited by K. Ask and M. Tjomsland. New York: Berg.

———. 2004. Going and Not Going to Porokhane: Mouride Women and Pilgrimage in Senegal and Spain. *In* Reframing Pilgrimage: Cultures in Motion, edited by S. Coleman and J. Eade, 69–90. London: Routledge.

Ross, Eric. 1995. Tuba: A Spiritual Metropolis in the Modern World. Canadian Journal of African Studies 29(2):222–59.

Ruthven, Malise. 1984. Islam in the World. New York: Oxford University Press.

Salem, Gerard. 1981. De la brousse sénégalaise au Boul' Mich: Le système commercial mouride en France. Cahiers d'études africaines 21:81–93.

Salzbrunn, Monika. 2004. The Occupation of Public Space through Religious and Political Events: How Senegalese Migrants Became a Part of Harlem, New York. Journal of Religion in Africa 34(4):468–92.

Scheld, Suzanne. 2003. The City in a Shoe: Redefining Urban Africa through Sebago Footwear Consumption. City and Society 15(1):109–130.

———. 2007. Youth Cosmopolitanism: Clothing, the City, and Globalization in Dakar, Senegal. City and Society 19(2):232–53.

Schulz, Dorothea E. 2003. Political Factions, Ideological Fictions: The Controversy over Family Law Reform in Democratic Mali. Islamic Law and Society 10(1):132–64.

———. 2007. Competing Sartorial Assertions of Femininity and Muslim Identity in Mali. Fashion Theory 11(2–3):253–80.

Searing, James F. 1988. Aristocrats, Slaves, and Peasants: Power and Dependency in the Wolof States, 1700–1850. International Journal of African Historical Studies 21(3):475–503.

———. 2002. "God Alone Is King": Islam and Emancipation in Senegal. Portsmouth, N.H.: Heinemann.

Shipton, Parker. 1989. Bitter Money: Cultural Economy and Some African Meanings of Forbidden Commodities. Washington, D.C.: American Anthropological Association.

Simone, AbdouMaliq. 2004. For the City Yet to Come: Changing African Life in Four Cities. Durham, N.C.: Duke University Press.

———. 2006. Intersecting Geographies? ICTs and Other Virtualities in Urban Africa. *In* Frontiers of Capital: Ethnographic Reflections on the New Economy, edited by M. S. Fisher and G. Downey, 133–62. Durham, N.C.: Duke University Press.

Soares, Benjamin F. 2000. Notes on the Anthropological Study of Islam and Muslim Societies in Africa. Culture and Religion 1(2):277–85.

———. 2005. Islam in Mali in the Neoliberal Era. African Affairs 105(418):77–95.

———. 2007. Rethinking Islam and Muslim Societies in Africa. African Affairs 106(423):319–26.

Sow, Fatou. 1981. Migration to Dakar. *In* The Uprooted of the Western Sahel: Migrants' Quest for Cash in the Senegambia, edited by L. Gallistel Colvin. New York: Praeger.

———. 1983. Pikine, Senegal: A Reading of a Contemporary African City. *In* Reading the Contemporary African City, edited by B. B. Taylor, 45–60. Singapore: Concept Media/Aga Khan Award for Architecture.

———. 2003. Fundamentalisms, Globalisation, and Women's Rights in Senegal. Gender and Development 11(1):69–76.

Stiansen, Endre, and Jane Guyer. 1999. Introduction. *In* Credit, Currencies, and Culture: African Financial Institutions in Historical Perspective, edited by E. Stiansen and J. Guyer, 1–14. Stockholm: Nordiska Afrikainstitutet.

Stoller, Paul. 2002. Money Has No Smell: The Africanization of New York City. Chicago: University of Chicago Press.

Strathern, Marilyn. 2000. Introduction: New Accountabilities. *In* Audit Cultures: Anthropological Studies in Accountability, Ethics, and the Academy, edited by M. Strathern. London: Routledge.

Tall, Serigne Mansour. 1994. Les investissements immobiliers d'émigrants sénégalais à Dakar. Revue Européen des Migrations Internationales 10(3):137–51.

———. 1996. Kara International Exchange: Un nouvel instrument financier pour les courtiers mourides de l'axe Dakar–New York. Paper presented at Colloque International de l'APAD, June 5–8, University of Hohenheim, Stuttgart.

———. 2002. Mouride Migration and Financing. ISIM Newsletter (Sept. 9):36.

Tamari, Tal. 1991. The Development of Caste Systems in West Africa. Journal of African History 32(2):221–50.

Tang, Patricia. 2007. Masters of the Sabar: Wolof Griot Percussionists of Senegal. Philadelphia: Temple University Press.

Thioub, Ibrahima, Momar Coumba Diop, and Catherine Boone. 1998. Economic Liberalization in Senegal: Shifting Politics of Indigenous Business Interests. African Studies Review 41(2):63–89.

Tostensen, Arne, Inge Tvedten, and Mariken Vaa. 2001. The Urban Crisis, Governance, and Associational Life. *In* Associational Life in African Cities: Popular Responses to the Urban Crisis, edited by A. Tostensen, I. Tvedten, and M. Vaa. Stockholm: Nordiska Afrikainstitutet.

Trimingham, J. Spencer. 1961. Islam in West Africa. Oxford: Oxford University Press.

Turner, Terry. 1980. The Social Skin. *In* Not Work Alone, edited by J. A. R. L. Cherfas, 112–40. London: Temple Smith.

———. 1984. Value, Production, and Exploitation in Non-Capitalist Societies. Paper presented at American Anthropological Association Eighty-Third Annual Meeting, Nov. 14–18, Denver, Colorado.

Underwood, Tamara. 1988. Femmes Wolof: Pouvoirs et savoir-faire. Dakar: Enda Tiers Monde.

Venema, Bernhard, and Jelka van Eijk. 2004. Livelihood Strategies Compared: Private Initiatives and Collective Efforts of Wolof Women in Senegal. African Studies 63(1):52–71.

Villalón, Leonardo A. 2004. Senegal: Islamism in Focus. African Studies Review 47(2):61–71.

Weiner, Annette B. 1976. Women of Value, Men of Renown: New Perspectives in Trobriand Exchange. Austin: University of Texas Press.

———. 1980. Reproduction: A Replacement for Reciprocity. American Ethnologist 7(1):71–85.

———. 1985. Inalienable Wealth. American Ethnologist 12(2):210–27.

———. 1989. Why Cloth? Wealth, Gender, and Power in Oceania. *In* Cloth and Human Experience, edited by A. B. Weiner and J. Schneider, 33–72. Washington, D.C.: Smithsonian Institution Press.

———. 1992. Inalienable Possessions: The Paradox of Keeping-while-Giving. Berkeley: University of California Press.

Weiss, Brad. 1996. The Making of the Haya Lived World. Durham, N.C.: Duke University Press.

Werbner, Pnina. 2003. Pilgrims of Love: The Anthropology of a Global Sufi Cult. Bloomington: Indiana University Press.

Yang, Mayfair Mei-hui. 1994. Gifts, Favors, and Banquets: The Art of Social Relationships in China. Ithaca, N.Y.: Cornell University Press.

Zelizer, Vivian A. 1989. The Social Meaning of Money: Special Monies. American Journal of Sociology 95(2):342–77.

———. 1994. The Social Meaning of Money: Pin Money, Paychecks, Poor Relief, and Other Currencies. Princeton, N.J.: Princeton University Press.

INDEX

Page numbers in italics refer to illustrations.

BETH BUGGENHAGEN is Assistant Professor of Anthropology at Indiana University, Bloomington. She completed her Ph.D. in sociocultural anthropology in 2003 at the University of Chicago. She has conducted fieldwork in Dakar and Tuba, Senegal, and in Chicago and New York City. She is editor (with Anne-Maria Makhulu and Stephen Jackson) of *Hard Work, Hard Times: Global Volatility and African Subjectivities.* Her current research interests include the politics of social production and value, material culture, visuality, gender, Islam, and globalization.